Friends and Lovers

Robert Brain

Basic Books, Inc., Publishers

NEW YORK

Granada Publishing Limited
First Published in Great Britain by
Hart-Davis, MacGibbon Ltd

Library of Congress Catalog Card Number: 76–7680
ISBN: 0–465–02571–4
Printed in the United States of America
76 77 78 79 80   10 9 8 7 6 5 4 3 2

Contents

Friends
and Lovers

Introduction – Love and Friendship

In our cold-comfort culture the emotional demonstration of love, particularly between members of the same sex, may be restricted to the occasional handshake, a furtive Valentine card, or an annual Christmas present. Even the formal kiss on the cheek which an Italian gives his friend is looked upon by the Anglo-Saxon as a betrayal of virility. Yet when Jonathan 'fell in love' with David, one of his first actions was to strip himself of the robe that he was wearing, his sword, his bow, and his girdle and give them to his friend – the gift of his personal belongings symbolizing, according to oriental ideas, the gift of his personality. And in his funeral oration over the bodies of Jonathan and his father, Saul, David unselfconsciously admitted to a love for his friend which was 'wonderful, passing the love of women'. Achilles, on the death of Patroclus, gathered black mould from the ground, smeared his 'lovely face' in it, rent his clothes, and tore out his 'gracious curls'. Even in Europe two men who loved one another expressed it more fulsomely in the past – pledging undying friendship and even exchanging blood in the sacred precincts of a church, with a priest officiating. Why have we learnt to restrict ritual, passionate declaration, and open mourning to the association of spouses in marriage or romantic lovers? Why has friendship lost both emotional expression and ceremonial patterning in our culture?

Western culture, as in so many other things, is unique in its attitudes to love. We talk confidently, for example, of the heart as the seat of love and have convinced ourselves that this really is so. Yet the Trobrianders place it in the intestines or on the surface of the stomach. Some West Africans feel it in the nose, while Australian Aborigines use the subincised penis as an organic symbol of friendship. Among the Busama of New

Guinea love's metaphor is a phrase meaning 'internal organs excrement to be with'; but as the ethnographer writes, a Busama who speaks of love, no more has his bowels in mind than an Englishman who talks of having 'lost his heart' conjures up a piece of bleeding tissue.[1]

I mention these facts so that we can forget at the outset our own Western preconceptions of love and friendship, particularly at a time when our ideas are becoming so fluid and changing. One of the aims of this book is to investigate, cross-culturally, manifestations of friendship in exotic (past and primitive) societies in order to illuminate our own special attitudes. Weird customs, placed in context and explained, cease to be weird and may even give us a chance of reassessing our own.

In Mali best friends throw excrement at each other and comment loudly on the genitals of their respective parents – this, to us, unnatural and obscene behaviour is a proof of the love of friends. In many other parts of Africa twins are the best of friends, and best friends become twins. In Tanzania, if a man meets a woman who is his special friend, he may insult her, throw her to the ground, and pummel her like a boxing bag. In New Guinea, when a man acquires a trading partner he 'falls in love' with him as part of the deal. Also in New Guinea, the men of one tribe say that they marry women, not to have a wife, but to have their brothers as 'best friends'. In southern Ghana, friends who love each other marry, the 'husband' paying bridewealth to his friend's parents. In Latin America, a friendly tie between two men may be enhanced by performing a Christian rite of baptism over a tree – both men in this way become devoted godsibs (co-godparents or gossips) of the christened tree. In the Andaman Islands a man studiously avoids a certain category of persons all his life – because 'they are his friends'.

'Fascinating!' I can hear the sophisticate say. 'But what have these facts to do with us? Haven't you forgotten that this mirror-to-man style of anthropology is unfashionable, even tedious in its listing of the more or less cranky ways exotic cultures treat their friends and lovers?' Yet what appears at first sight a freaky catalogue of way-out customs illustrates several themes in interpersonal relations which constitute the universal institution of friendship. Despite the exotica, this book is not intended as an ethnographical Cook's tour of the world – 'one hundred styles of loving in ten easy chapters'. Nor is it a casual survey of sexual *mores* in ancient and primitive society or a Gay Guide to special friendships in darkest, deepest, or furthest Africa or Polynesia. I am simply attempting a comparative analysis of the rites, the obligations, and the sentiments of friendship.

The first task – the explanation or the function of an odd custom – is easily accomplished. The merging of twins and friends in Africa, for example, expresses the unity, even the androgyny of twins – St Augustine called his friend 'thou half of my soul'; St Thomas Aquinas said a friend is an *alter ego* – 'friendship results from a perception of the oneness of the beloved with the lover'. 'Marrying' your friend, as some Ghanaians did, sacralizes a deeply felt bond, the wedding ceremony serving to bind the couple together until 'death do them part'. Falling in love with a trading partner strengthens the interrelatedness of two men engaged in business and stresses the important element of reciprocity in friendship. By marrying his best friend's sister a Melanesian is expressing the role of women as a form of cultural communication between men. A rowdy display of horseplay or absolute avoidance between 'friends' are two very different ways of expressing the same thing – the element of strain and fragility in all friendships; both 'avoidance' and 'joking' allow love to persist without shame and may also betray a latent sentiment of aggression which is not always absent from loving relationships.

Throughout this book I shall not only be asking why exotic cultures do exotic things, but more importantly why we don't. We don't go through childish ceremonies over trees or drink our mates' blood in order to confirm our mutual obligations and loyalty. We don't 'marry' our best friends. And if we do not marry our best friends' sisters in order to have our brothers-in-law around all the time, call them 'twin', duck behind cover when we see them coming along the High Street, or knock over all the beer at their funeral wake – why don't we? We do not throw shit at our friends when we meet them at the theatre or begin to go through a violent form of pugilistic ritual; but then, again, consider the rowdy back-slapping, the jolly verbal abuse, and the exchange of filth, the dirty jokes, which are not absent from some close friendships.

Friendship, everywhere, makes the world go round – not love in its romantic, sexual sense. The oft-quoted Mary Wollstonecraft saw this when she wrote: 'Love [and she means sexually involved passion] from its very nature must be transitory. To seek for a secret that would render it constant would be a wild search for the philosopher's stone or the grand panacea: and the discovery would be equally useless, or rather, pernicious to mankind. *The most holy bond of society is friendship.*'² Similar ideas have been expressed as a commonplace from ancient times – Plato, Aristotle, Ovid, Cicero, St Francis, Bacon, Montaigne, Thomas More, Descartes, Pascal, Jeremy Taylor, and Adam Smith have all written their treatises on friendship, discussing with more or less fervour the role of love and sympathy between friends in keeping society rolling. Most of these literary attempts to portray, explain, or analyse friendship, however, are necessarily ethnocentric, restricted to the writer's own culture. Apart from titillating surveys of love-making in the South Seas and other erotica, no one has attempted a cross-cultural, comparative study of friendship and love. We have studies by Freud and Malinowski, Havelock Ellis and Kinsey on sex, a host of volumes on kinship and marriage, several scientific and not so scientific studies of aggression, refined analyses of romantic passion, and the delicately wrought accounts of amity in the androgynous Bloomsbury set. But we have no modern theorist of love and friendship. Ortega y Gasset and Santayana have tackled the problem through the eyes of civilized Europeans; while the interpretations of a philosopher like Bertrand Russell or a social psychologist such as Fromm begin with a sincere humanistic approach which becomes an impractical idealism – and sometimes mawkish sentimentalism.³

In times of swift social change when old patterns of the family and marriage, love and love-making, friendship and affection are being questioned and new forms adopted, a square look at how other cultures cope with interpersonal relations may be salutary. The need for such a study has long been recognized by anthropologists, but on the whole the vague nature of love and friendship has proved too elusive a theme for comparative study. Text-books decry the lack of any detailed treatment of 'bonding' and 'amity' as elements in social organization, but most anthropologists, having made a ritual obeisance to the importance of emotional ties outside structured kin groups, have apparently despaired of describing them in detail[4] – most probably due to their delicate and non-articulate nature. Totemism, witch-craft, and cross-cousin marriage are subjects to get your teeth into.

'Sentiment', the foremost element in friendship relations (the jargon word in sociology is 'affect') has therefore been a more or less taboo theme in anthropological monographs. Structural situations alone provided grist for the fieldworker's mill; the individual native and his personal emotions may have crept into letters home, but were not allowed to interfere with academic theories. A few years ago the combined scorn of all Anglo-Saxon structuralists and functionalists was poured on to the unbowed heads of two American sociologists[5] when they seriously, and interestingly, suggested that the important relationship between a nephew and his uncle might have a sentimental basis. The avunculate – the relationship between a sister's son and a mother's brother in a patrilineal society (see p. 104) – is well known to students of medieval literature (Charlemagne and Roland, King Mark and Tristram, King Arthur and Gawain were uncle and nephew) and is a hoary theme in anthropological literature. Most anthropologists argue that the bond depends on a structural link between a man and his mother's lineage, rather than a friendly relationship between close maternal relatives.

Recently there has been a reorientation towards an increased emphasis on psychological variables and this book is an attempt to make a study of personal relationships based on love and friendship by combining psychological, structural, and functional points of view. While friendship, by definition, involves sentiment, this does not mean that the relationship need not be institutionalized, even obligatory. Friendship is not only a loving relationship between two men, two women, or a man and a woman, each choosing their partner through a combination of moral characteristics, physical attractiveness, and self-interest; it may also be a formal bond between two persons who occupy specific niches in a social structure and whose duties to each other involve reciprocal obligations based on legal and super-natural sanctions. What we consider as the basic ingredients of loving friendship – loyalty, trust, emotional satisfaction, a psychological validation of each other's identity, equality, com-plementarity, reciprocity – are not to be separated from the role played by formal attachments in the wider society.

While this book is about friendship I have made no attempt to define friendship or to distinguish between love and friendship – it is often possible to use the two terms interchangeably. In ordinary conversation we use the word 'love' for a large number of social situations. You may 'love' your mother and she may also be your best friend – but of course she is not your lover. We do not 'fall in love' with our mates on the same factory bench. A woman means different things, perhaps, when she says, 'I am in love with that cocktail dress' and 'I love that cocktail dress'. The meaning of 'That's his friend, you know' may hint at a homo-sexual relationship if the correct nuance is given to the last word. Two Lesbians living in a semi-detached in the suburbs are called 'friends' by their neighbours, when sociologically speaking they are best described as lovers or, better still, as *de facto* hus-band and wife. The words 'love' and 'friendship', therefore, encompass a multitude of meanings – we learn that we can adore banana ice-cream, but not be friends with it or make love to it. The word 'love', in particular, may refer to a sexual or visceral appetite, romantic passion, or brotherly affection; we 'love' God and we also 'love' our mistress.

This is what European Christians forgot when they proudly and blindly descended on African and South Sea island pagans and wrote home, horrified, that the local word for love was the same as the word for sexual desire. How could they teach the natives to sing 'Jesus Loves Me' in a translation which also meant 'Jesus lusts after me'? Benighted missionaries – not for a moment did they stop to think that our word for 'love' has the same multifaceted meaning, covering sentiments from the love of the godhead to copulation, and that the natives themselves might be capable of making the distinction too. Unfortunately this is just another example of Europeans in their cultural pride denying the so-called primitive cultures the same semantic flexibility which we have ourselves. Pagans were restricted to rigid (primitive) categories of thought – 'pre-logical thinking' – for the sake of blind Christian dogmatism. Yet the Old Testament Hebrew word for 'love' was equally comprehensive; and so is the Greek word *eros*. Moreover, our own notions of the love of God, demanding union with the divinity, have always been based on a flagrantly sexual symbolism, not because this union is meant to be a fornicatory one but because sex provided the most convenient metaphors.

What about friendship? Surely friendship is more appropriately used outside the sexual and family spheres? Even the Shorter Oxford Dictionary roundly declares that friendship is different from the love we feel for a kinsman or a lover: a friend is 'one joined to another in intimacy and mutual benevolence independent of sexual or family love'. Sometimes friendship is seen as something less than kinship; blood, as everyone knows, is thicker than water. Sometimes it is more than kinship. Sir Thomas Browne (*Religio Medici*) defined the 'normal order' of loving – first parents, followed by brothers, wives, children, and friends. He, like many of us, admitted that 'I do not find in myself such a necessary and indissoluble sympathy to all those of my blood. I hope I do not break the fifth commandment if I conceive I may love my friend before the nearest of my blood, even those to whom I owe the principles of life.'

In contemporary Western society the boundaries of friendship, kinship, and loving are disintegrating, if they ever really existed. Roles which were much more exclusive in other societies have broken down. A wife is her husband's 'best friend' and fathers and sons call themselves by Christian names – like friends. When kin become friends it often means that they remove themselves from a strictly kinship sphere where roles are prescribed and determined by age and birth. Once a kinsman becomes a bond-friend or a blood-brother, or even a brother-in-law in certain societies, the amity between the two friends prohibits the suppressed jealousy and competition which seem inherent in relations between brothers and other close kinsmen. 'Between relatives,' wrote Montaigne, praising friendship above kinship, 'the expectation of the one depends on the ruin of the other.'

Friendship, therefore, is often kept outside the family. It may serve a specific purpose of providing links between structures based on kinship, marriage, and descent; this is the meaning behind the phrase, often found in ethnography, that 'brothers-in-law are the best friends'. In open societies like our own, where brothers are often more friendly than they are brotherly, there is no opposition between the values of kinship and friendship since the family has ceased to lay an exclusive claim to the loyalties of individuals, and questions concerning property are becoming increasingly matters beyond kinship. We can bequeath our house and car to friends: in most societies inheritance and succession are restricted to sons, brothers, cousins, and sisters' sons.

This situation where friendship is not automatically 'extra-kinship' has already been emphasized by Firth and Djamour: 'The prime characteristic of the South Borough [London] kinship system is this aspect of selectivity on a basis of emotional attachments rather than on a basis of close relationship; to relegate others to a social limbo, to summon up or play down the values of kinship as an instrument of social expression is personally important in the South Borough system.'[6] In America, too, there seems to be little difference between the love felt between kin and that between friends; sentiments found in the family are based almost completely on ties of love felt between unrelated friends.[7] In open societies such as our own, where kinship is organized multilaterally (not just down the male or female line), the number of possible kin is immense, and choice, outside the elementary family, determines the persons one treats as kin. There would even be a case for maintaining that all kin relations within our kinship group are based on friendship and personal choice. One chooses this or that uncle, this or that cousin, even this or that brother and sister to be friendly with. Unlike most other societies even kinship is achieved, rather than ascribed: kin do not interact because they are kin but through liking and common interests. Therefore kinship, for us, is like friendship in so far as it is a personal and private contract between individuals. The same situation occurred among the Bangwa, a people I studied; they chose from a large network of kin ties those persons who provided practical and emotional satisfactions and shed the rest. They found kin to be friendly with.

Friendly lovers and loving friends, friends who are brothers and friendly fathers. What about *real* love? The only kind of loving which has its special terminology in this book is a kind of 'romantic love' which is specifically associated with Western culture and exported to other countries along with our capitalist economy and religion. Romantic love, the sublime combination of love and sexuality, exalted by Ancient Greek and Medieval European and given an insane intensification by modern poets, film-makers, churchmen, and advertising agents, is a Western concept, with its added notion of unrequited sex. Passion, of course, is universal as the oft-quoted descriptions of Polynesian love-making and the exuberantly sexy myths of the South American Indian have shown. The theme is taken up in Chapter Ten where we shall find that men and women throughout the world act romantically, 'fall in love', enjoy the frenzy of passion, but that it is far from being considered a normal state of affairs, rarely involves the idea of unrequited love, and is never deemed a necessary prelude to marriage.

This particularly Western concept of romantic love is the only kind of love we ourselves distinguish clearly from friendship. When Oliver Goldsmith writes, 'Friendship is a disinterested commerce between equals, love, an abject intercourse between tyrants and slaves,' we immediately acknowledge the truth of it because he is stressing our own concepts of brotherly love – friendship – and the sexual aspects of romantic love. When Byron says that 'friendship is love without its wings'; and Goldsmith, again, remarks that a couple had 'more of love than matrimony in them'; and Erich Segal writes that 'love means you don't have to say you're sorry', we know what they mean because we are all members of one particular Western Christian capitalist culture. I doubt if they would translate well into Khoisan.

One of our firm convictions about friendship is that it needs no laws, no ceremonies, no material expectations. Yet in most societies love between friends is not allowed to depend on the vague bonds of moral sentiment alone, since elevated sentiments are notoriously poorly adapted to keeping two persons together in a permanent union. In our society, if a friend dies we *ought* to attend his funeral, but there is no obligation. In West Africa when a man dies his best friend *must* put on filthy rags and rush into the staid atmosphere of his funeral, jeer at the weeping mourners, and tip over jars of ritual beer which have been prepared for the guests. Friendships are considered of such importance to both the individual and society that everything is done to prevent their foundering. They need not even depend on personal choice and initial liking but may be arranged by parents, like a Hindu marriage. But are these diverse relationships really comparable? Is the loving of a David and a Jonathan comparable to that of two men who are life-long friends because they were born on the same day and united in friendship by their parents?

The point to stress is that, despite the origin of the friendship and its external trappings of pacts and ceremonial, no culture fails to emphasize the essential loyalty and love between friends. While we stress affection and trust (and do not make formal exchanges or perform ritual antics when we meet our friends) this does not mean that blood-brothers and bond-friends do not. Affection and loyalty are implicit in all friendships and in all societies. Early observers of primitive society were of the contrary opinion and went to some lengths to persuade their friends and relations at home that the native had not yet received the blessing of altruistic love. Primitive man, from the nineteenth-century viewpoint, saw love as sex and friendship as greed: he only reacted to taboos, witchcraft fears; he respected only his kinsfolk and ravished his wife. The twentieth century has seen a change, and research has shown that no culture fails to laud the undivided loyalty and selfless love of friends.

Why should we insist that love stand on its own two feet in the case of friends, when two romantic lovers who also love each other with all their heart and soul, until death do them part, hedge in their passion with a wedding ceremony, oaths, and legal contracts? In denying friendship formal bonds our society seems to undervalue love, not value it. Even David and Jonathan made a pact. In medieval times friends made blood-brotherhoods or, like Roland and Oliver, had a friendship on formal bonds based on *cortesia*. Gossipry, the relations between the parents of a baptized child and the godparents, was as much a ritual confirmation of the friendship of the adults as a spiritual relationship between godparents and child. In all societies but our own, ceremonial trappings *add* to the meaning of friendship, they do not demonstrate its weakness – it is considered too valuable an affair to remain unprotected by ceremony or contract. The present state of friendship in our society, watered down by Christianity to a kind of brotherly 'agapeism', gives us no prerogative to mock other people who love their brothers-in-law or trading partners and publicly advertise their love by drinking each other's blood or undergoing some kind of marriage ceremony.

In cases of 'arranged friendship' as well as 'arranged marriage' loyalty and affection grow with the development of the relationship. I suggest that we have overrated the necessity of choosing our friends and wives. We decry arranged marriages. Lovers *fall* in love; it is like a bolt from the blue; our wives were 'the only girls in the world'. Choice is the thing! However, this freedom of choice often means that it is never made – hence the frustrated spinsters, the friendless and the lonely, the flotsam and jetsam of an entrepreneurial society where the best man always wins and leaves the others without. We have been taught that individual freedom is the jewel of civilization, but perhaps now is the time to question this. In the Cameroon, among the Bangwa, as soon as a child is born it will find itself saddled with a lifelong friend and a wife – and nobody kicked against this form of security provided by their family until colonialists and missionaries brought in ideas of free choice, market labour, and the dubious splendours of romantic loving.

What is important in friendship is the loving itself, not the object – the friend or the lover.[8] I believe we are beginning to realize this truth when we consider the alacrity with which timid people are attending friendship clubs, visiting marriage bureaux, and showing a strange dependence on astrological predictions. The importance of a wide-open choice of friend or wife is losing its meaning to the vast subculture composed of the lonely people of a large city. There is something rather restful about the idea of

a patterned existence where friends and lovers are brought together by an unseen hand. Even sexuality may be arranged to
suit a social situation. We have banned official brothels and street
prostitutes in the interests of morality – and free choice? Other
societies satisfy even sexual needs in a formal way. Among the
Nambikwara of Brazil, homosexual relations were regulated by
restricting them to certain categories of persons: adolescent boys
who were cross-cousins could also be lovers. This relationship
meant that in the normal course of events one of them would
marry the other's sister. Here the choice of a sexual partner is
based on the same principle as the New Guinea situation where
a boy marries his friend's sister in order to have a beloved
brother-in-law. These Nambikwara youths – in-laws who made
love – continued their formally structured sexual affairs even
after they married, with the result that men who were husbands
and fathers, as well as brothers-in-law to each other, walked
lovingly arm-in-arm in the evening, and their sexual games gave
rise to much greater publicity than heterosexual affairs. Brothers-
in-law, who were also permitted lovers, did not retire into the
bushes like their cousins of the opposite sex, but abandoned
themselves to their pleasure by the campfire, before the amused
gaze of their friends and neighbours.[9]

If friendship is a universal characteristic of human society, what
are its basic elements apart from affection, if free choice is not
one of them and it even permits the trappings of ceremonial and
law? Equality – the idea of dual souls, *alter egos* – is part and
parcel of friendship. In Africa twins symbolize the two-in-
oneness and equality of friends. Even in lopsided relations between a patron and a client the use of the term 'friend' at least
implies an attempt to equalize the relationship, drawing persons
of different status towards each other. Akin to equality are the
ideas of complementarity and reciprocity. Friends exchange
goods and ideas. In some societies friendship is implicitly
associated with commerce, due to the concept of exchange inherent in both trade and friendship. Trobriand Islanders 'fell in
love' because they traded. There is an example of an Eskimo
whose wife had been abducted: when the husband was given
compensation by the abductor, the two men, through this

exchange which was only peripherally commercial, became best friends because they had conceptually effected a trade.[10] We exchange Christmas presents and buy our friends a drink; other people give cotton mats, armshells, their sisters, and balance the gift in the correct manner. In Chapter Eight I try to show that reciprocity, the communication between friends, in-laws, and traders is a greater imperative in human society than greed and aggression.

In fact aggression theorists have perpetuated a widespread myth about friendship and love. According to Konrad Lorenz, love is not found among peaceable creatures who live in herds – their association is entirely anonymous. 'A personal bond, an individual friendship, is found only in animals with a highly developed intra-specific aggression . . .'[11] From this it has become a commonplace to accept love as a by-product of aggression. Without being qualified in physical anthropology, one of my aims in this book is to show that friendship, bonding, or amity, call it what you will, is as basic a human trait as aggression, whether it is learned or instinctual. It is a sad fact that to many people the imaginary primitive is envisaged as a naked, ape-like predator, whose life is nasty, brutish, and short, and whose hopes of survival – like those of the coral fish and the grey-lag goose – depend on an efficient manipulation of their aggressive instincts. This is, of course, hardly a new theory. 'It was not peace which was natural and primitive and old, but rather war,' wrote Henry Maine, and recently the enormously popular books of amateur ethnologists such as Robert Ardrey have convinced many of us that primitive societies live in a state of permanent hostility and that the only reciprocal relations which they enjoy are warlike ones: they defend their territory against people of their own kind, for the instinctual reasons that animals protect their territory. We ourselves intruded and must go on intruding on our neighbour's property because, like animals, we are 'predatory by nature'.[12] This kind of argument condones wars and aggressive private enterprise since greed and hate are explained away as animal instincts. I shall discuss later the scientific basis of the argument that man, by his inherited and unalterable nature, is a predator against his own kind whose natural instinct is to kill with a weapon. Here it is sufficient to point out that more qualified scientists[13] have shown that both aggression and amity are basic to human nature and that both tendencies are programmed into each individual. Even Lorenz spoke of a 'parliament of instincts', aggression being only one of them. We must consider the social potential of human beings, not their destructive capacity. The work of Tiger[14] suggests that the roots of sociability are more deeply seated than aggression. There are an astonishing number of ways of 'making friends', from the instinctual smile, through gestures, invitations, winking, kissing, shaking hands, gifts. And there are norms for ethical behaviour which show that we are extremely sociable and friendly beings.

According to some scientists we even come into the world programmed to love.[15] Small children seek personal bonds with particular human beings and their need for love, which begins with the strong mother–child bond in most cases, becomes transferred to other individuals as the life cycle progresses. In our society the artificial suppression of these strong personal bonds creates experiences of deprivation among both children and adults. Our whole problem of loneliness should be seen in these terms. Children make friends easily – and their need for emotional satisfaction is expressed in the way babies make friends with people around them, through smiling, gestures, and the offering of food. Unfortunately a child's urge to make personalized friendships is often stifled before he reaches adolescence. We teach our children to stop making these outgoing gestures of friendship to the extent that to most children over eight every stranger is suspect, even if he is not a potential kidnapper or rapist.

What appear to be innate bonding urges are still played out in the school playground and in children's games.[16] Many of us have played 'friendship games' and sung the rhymes of childish love:

> I'll be your friend for ever,
> His or hers never

and used the slang words buddies, buds, butty, chum, croney, mate, my monkey, my pal. As young children we take friendship very seriously, playing intense games, exchanging stamps and marbles, walking home together. Girls give each other presents, birthday cards, lend each other things, share sweets. They like each other, frankly, for their looks, their character, the way they wear their clothes. At the same time children make and break close friendships with an amazing rapidity. Two girls will swear eternal friendship, two boys will cut their wrists and sip each other's blood; then suddenly they have a fight or are mysteriously not on speaking terms. The girls have quarrelled about a bracelet; one of the boys has found another 'best friend'.

Children, like adults in Africa, ritualize their friendships. In England a symbol of close friendship are the interlocked little fingers; in formalizing a relationship between two friends, the fingers are linked, shaken up and down and the friends declare:

> Make friends, make friends,
> Never, never break friends.

And then if they quarrel, the ritual connection must be broken with the formula:

> Break friends, break friends,
> Never, never make friends.

If they make up again, they moisten the little fingers and chant:

> We've broken before,
> We break now.

And they separate the little fingers.

> Make up, make up,
> Never row again,
> If we do we'll get the cane.

Then they intertwine their moistened fingers, squeezing tightly: or slap hands, or smack each other.

These childish rites of friendship, especially the use of the little finger and spittle, recall many primitive ceremonies which we shall discuss in Chapter Three. In Dublin, if a girl wants to make up after a quarrel she chooses a go-between who walks up to the former friend and asks:

> Are you spin, spout, or blackout,
> Falling in or falling out?

If she replies 'blackout' it means rejection and the other girl's response is 'Ahem to the dirt', but if they make up they swear friendship again: 'You're the lock and I've the key.' Customarily as a token of their restored friendship they go out shopping together.

From late childhood onwards the frank friendships of the playground are not encouraged and are even replaced by a feeling of shame and guilt towards very close friendship which seem to derive from our puritanical attitudes to homosexuality. We are nervous throughout our lives of admitting to a deep love of a person of the same sex even when it quite obviously exists and takes precedence over feelings for husband or wife. Few of us would be demonstrative enough to speak of our love for a friend in the words of Montaigne, as he dwells on La Boëtie's character twenty years after his death: 'Our spirits, his and mine, were so closely yoked together, considering one another with an ardent affection . . . which lay so bare the very entrails of being, that not only did I know his soul as I knew mine, but I would certainly have trusted myself more willingly to his hands than mine.'

My aims, as an anthropologist, are modest. I am not proposing to crack any universal code of thought, or even offer up to my colleagues a new or clever theory of interpersonal relations. I want to look at our own condition through the study of exotic societies. The Tahitians gave Diderot the chance to mock eighteenth-century society and its hypocritical morality. Rousseau used the Caribs when he wanted to read us a lesson on the evils of inequality in eighteenth-century Europe. Durkheim and Mauss studied the Australian Aborigines in order to have a clearer picture of the interrelationship of religion and society in Europe. The anthropologist today is in an advantageous position – by holding up a mirror to our modern selves he can try and persuade us to question our attitudes. If, for example, we find that love and friendship meant different things to Ancient Greeks, African nomads or Spanish peasants, we shall have an opportunity of assessing these attitudes and perhaps even try to change them.

While anthropologists have the advantage of a thousand cultures to draw on for material, there are also difficulties. A writer who discourses, in English, on love can refer casually to well-known names in European and American literature and history – Tristram and Isolde, Walt Whitman and D. H. Lawrence, Dante and Beatrice – and evoke at least a minimal response in his readers. If he becomes more abstruse they can go to their encyclopaedia or ask a friend. I, however, will only cause dismayed confusion if I scatter references to the Yakö, the Donga-duighj, and the Mbo, or such famous personages as Ogotemmeli, or the matrilateral cross-cousin. In order to avoid tribe-trotting and name-dropping I have attempted to restrict my examples to better known societies such as the Trobriand Islanders and the Azande. I have also brought in material from exotic cultures which will strike a chord in the non-anthropologist – medieval Europe, Ancient Greece, the Australian outback and suburb, the contemporary Mediterranean. My own fieldwork, among the Bangwa of the Cameroon mountains, will be used throughout the book as a first-hand check on second-hand information.

What exactly is an exotic society? 'The Savage', 'the Ancient Greek', 'the Hindu Peasant' are all exotic to inhabitants of the modern industrial world. We should, however, forget our ideas of 'primitive' and 'civilized'. For a long time now people have used the limitless data on primitive tribes in order to theorize about kinship, marriage, politics, and myth – we have become preoccupied with the primitive, a word which invokes emotions of paternalism, nostalgia, disdain, admiration, even guilt. A 'primitive' has been variously defined as a man who could not read, who lacked advanced techniques of production, or who lived in small groups. Primarily, of course, he is different and it would be idle for any anthropologist to deny that he dissects and judges primitive society through the bias of his own cultural background and personal beliefs. Always in the back of his mind and that of his readers there is the implicit 'them–us' contrast – 'civilized and primitive' or 'pagan and christian', 'black and white', 'the small-brained and the big-brained', 'the good and the bad' or 'the bad and the good' were all dual terms used by old-style anthropologists. Today we talk about 'small-scale and large-scale', 'underdeveloped and developed', 'industrial and pre-industrial'.

I should like to make my own attitudes clear at the start. I have used information from societies and cultures from every corner of the globe, from all periods of history, and at all stages of economic development. Nevertheless there is still the dichotomy, in my attitudes, between 'them' and 'us'. 'Us' are all those people, dead and alive, who exist and existed within the net of modern industrial capitalism, who shared and share the same cultural models of an individualistically-oriented society based on the open market, Christianity, and Western values. 'We' are found all over the world today – in urban Africa, changing Polynesia, most of Europe and America. 'They' include everyone else: Ancient Greeks, Australian aborigines still living their traditional way of life, Tacitus' Teutons, West African kings and their subjects, Pacific Islanders, Kalahari hunters. While it is clear that there are enormous differences between members of this latter cluster of peoples and these differences must be taken into account, it is essential to remember that when I write 'I' or 'we' I am referring to the inheritors of a Western industrial capitalist culture. Any attempt to ignore this difference when we write about the Gogo or the Ute will result in anthropological fantasy. My own personal background should also be taken into account – let it suffice, however, to say that I am an Australian, forty years old, with several years' intimate experience of England, Africa, and the Mediterranean. I belong to no party, no church, and no university. I have had no wives, but many friends and lovers of both sexes to whom I dedicate this book with as much ceremony, feeling, and self-interest as such relations demand.

1 David and Jonathan

We pay quite a lot of lip-service to love and friendship. David and Jonathan, Achilles and Patroclus, Pylades and Orestes, Roland and Oliver are all in the grand tradition of 'civilized friendship'. Platonic love is almost a British invention – it certainly was not Greek; and we confidently believe that Christianity has brought us to a unique level through our faith in the fellowship of man. Why, we not only love our neighbour, but our dogs, our gardens, and our homes!

Our gift of loving friendship became almost a prerogative of the European. One of several self-confirming prejudices of early travellers and missionaries, still repeated *ad nauseam* at colonial tea parties, is that the native could not be expected to understand the joys of disinterested brotherly love. The heathen, they wrote in their tracts and travel books, have no word for 'thank you', much less the common Christian sentiments of gratitude. Savages might give you presents and call you 'friend' – until your back was turned – but only in the expectation of material reward. The missionary, that glowing example of self-sacrificial love, taught pure friendship in the mission school and complained in his sermons that the native did not love his wife as he should – he bought her in the market place like a chattel – and that sexual rather than conjugal love was the only possible relation between spouses. Men who were not kinsmen and linked by blood could commit the most heinous crimes against each other with equanimity because they were unrelated. There was no concept of a 'brotherhood of man' before Christ or any other god, in these savage societies.

This attitude dies hard. Love makes our Christian world go round all right, but only greed and formal institutions such as the exchange of women and commercial goods keep the primitives functioning. Small-scale societies function mechanically, with the aid of kinship solidarity and taboos. The fascinating discovery of complex descent systems based on lineages confirmed this idea of a grand series of groups fitting together like neat Chinese boxes, and the possibility of altruistic friendship playing any part in the organization of these perfect snow-crystal structures was not necessary nor seriously entertained. In the indexes of early ethnographic monographs 'polygyny', 'cannibalism', 'sorcery', and 'war' warranted more space than 'love' or 'friendship'.

Our own special myth which epitomizes friendship as emotional and disinterested love is the biblical story of David and Jonathan, a beautiful tale of passionate friendship between two men, which has parallels in European literature and in ethnography from all parts of the world. While not without certain external actions of friendship – the exchange of gifts, the sanctions of a pact – the love of David and Jonathan stresses the importance of inner attitudes, of the loyalty and trust of two men untouched by sexuality. As a piece of mythical history, however, the relationship has been invested with a specially sentimental aura and a false homosexuality has been attributed to it by furtive pederasts who have taken the two biblical friends to their own lonely hearts.

David–Jonathan situations are not uncommon even in primitive societies where it is considered natural to love others, help your friends, and elicit emotional responses from individuals outside family groups.

The love of Jonathan and David was equal and harmonious. It was also passionate; Jonathan 'fell in love' with David at first sight and his love never abated. He even placed his friend's interests over those of the king, his father. After David had miraculously and heroically killed the giant, he was presented to Saul, the king, and his son Jonathan who had himself a reputation as a great warrior. While Saul was addressing him, David stole a look at the prince and saw that Jonathan's eye was fixed upon him with great admiration – David at the time was a young man 'ruddy of a fair countenance' and 'withal of a beautiful countenance and goodly to look at'. From that moment, 'the soul of Jonathan was knit with the soul of David and Jonathan loved him as his own soul'. David returned his love, based on a complete mutual understanding and limitless admiration, 'unsoiled by any selfish motive or sexual impulse', and the love remained unchanged until their death. Jonathan went so far as to strip himself of the robe he was wearing and give it to David as a symbol of his love 'even to his sword, and to his bow, and to his girdle'. Their friendship overrode political loyalties; Jonathan made a covenant with David, even accepting the idea that David might become king instead of him. Between the two friends there could be no secrets – when Saul proposed to suppress David he could not tell his eldest son since he knew he would divulge it to his friend. The pact between the two even involved David in the undertaking to look after Jonathan's children if he were to die.

The intense friendship of the two Israelites, lasting till death, depended on the complete willingness of each man to give for that which is received, to forgo self-interest, to convert separate identities into togetherness. As is frequently the case between friends the most splendid occasion for the demonstration of love was the death of one of them. When Jonathan perished on Mount Gilboa at the hands of the Philistines together with his father Saul, David rent his clothes, performed all the customary and conventional acts of mourning, and retired into privacy to ponder the situation. Then he lamented the death of the king and his best friend in a moving funeral oration:

> Saul and Jonathan were lovely and pleasant in their lives,
> And in their death they were not divided.
> They were swifter than eagles,
> They were stronger than lions . . .
> Ye daughters of Israel, weep over Saul,
> Who clothed you in scarlet, with other delights,
> Who put on ornaments of gold upon your apparel . . .
> How are the mighty fallen in the midst of battle!
> O Jonathan, thou wast slain in thine high place . . .
> I am distressed for thee my brother Jonathan;
> Very pleasant hast thou been unto me:
> Thy love was wonderful passing the love of women . . .
> How are the mighty fallen
> And the weapons of war perished.

*

These elements of friendship – loyalty, union, even passion – are found in other well-known myths of friendship.[1] In the *Chanson de Roland*, for example, Oliver joins Roland on the battlefield. 'For love of thee, here will I take my stand; together we endure things good and bad. I leave thee not for all incarnate man.'

In feudal times there were special ties binding a man and his 'companion'. It was the custom to send a boy to be 'fostered' in the household of one's overlord, where he learnt manners and was trained in arms, horsemanship, and sports. Two young men thus growing up side by side from early youth and competing together in games would become special friends or 'companions' and this intimacy and rivalry continued throughout their lives as warriors. The affection between companions was very strong indeed, frequently overshadowing those ties binding blood relatives. In medieval epics, as in Homer, the relationship found most moving was that between a man and his companion in arms. As far as these medieval friendships went, one of their most striking aspects was their formal courtesy: in grief or in fondness, in fighting and in dying, the mode of address is always 'Fair sir, companion . . .'[2]

These friendships in medieval epics were given all the glamour of a real love bond, with all its passion and devotion. It is only in our present times that we have managed to cheapen the friendship between two men – two women for that matter – so that if it is represented in a frank manner it provokes a knowing smirk or is dismissed as sentimental. The medieval classic of romantic friendship was *Amis and Amiloun*, popular from the thirteenth to the fifteenth century; like the friendship of Roland and Oliver it was imbued with the ideals of courtesy – personal integrity, the love of God, an insistence on benevolent actions and speech, the praise of beauty, self-control, bravery, and purity. In this song of love and loyalty, two young men, both physically beautiful, are in love, a mutual love which like that of David and Jonathan was held dearer than the love of a woman.

In *Amis and Amiloun* the poet stresses the unity of the two friends and the plot consists primarily in the testing of their mutual love. Amiloun chooses leprosy and poverty rather than desert Amis in an unjust quarrel, while Amis kills his two small sons in order to heal Amiloun. This bond is well expressed in the couplet:

> Hold together in every need,
> In word, in work, in will, in deed.

The loves of Jonathan and David, Amis and Amiloun, and Roland and Oliver are peaks in our cultural history of friendship. Yet in ethnography we find tales of friendship to the death between warriors and heroes, offering many similarities with these legends. Unfortunately, while the relationships are not rare, it would seem that the art of a poet rather than the science of an anthropologist is needed to describe them. Friendship and love are notoriously difficult to present in sociological terms. Perhaps a description of what I found during my own fieldwork might help.

I spent two years among the Bangwa of the Cameroon; they are a people who had acquired a reputation for sculpture, war, and an elegant way of life among those British colonial officers who had climbed the mountain passes to visit them in their picturesque compounds scattered over a broken terrain up to two thousand metres above sea level. The Bangwa have kings and princes and princesses who rule over miniature states of a few thousand subjects. They grew rich by controlling the slave trade from the plateaux to the forest and had sunk their wealth in wives. The chiefs were the focal point of the whole culture: they distributed land and women to their subjects, they were the high priests of the ancestor cult and made sacrifice to long lines of skulls, and they ruled the country through innumerable secret societies staffed with their retainers and henchmen.

I was lucky to have made my way to Bangwa. First of all I was made welcome and was allowed to attend the constant round of ceremonies, rituals, dances, and meetings. Every other day there was a market to visit; or I could sit in the 'palace' – a vast domed structure embellished with sculpture and much too grand to be called a hut – and listen to endless court cases. I watched the doctors, the herbalists, the priests at their work; I learned their divining techniques; I puzzled over the innumerable anti-witchcraft rituals. I watched the men carve stools and masks and grow coffee and oil, and the women as they hoed and weeded in their precipitous farms or vociferously sold their wares in the markets.

The Bangwa, on my unexpected arrival, showed *their* friendly intentions by cleaning out a house for me and visiting me formally on the first day with ceremonial gifts of kola nuts, splendid cocks, and firewood. As time went by I made special friends. Some men, bolder than the rest, visited me with small gifts and received gifts in return. I moved around, acquired an interpreter, and began to make my visits and ask my interminable questions. Things settled down to a fairly regular routine and I began to acquire the kind of information we anthropologists were seeking at that time.

Although I made no special study of friendship I soon found that the Bangwa liked to stress the values of friendship between persons not related by kinship or sexual attachment. To have a friend was as important as having a wife or a brother; in any case the poorest orphan could have a 'best friend', while he might have to wait until his mid-thirties to have a wife. I was even a little surprised at their fervent and demonstrative attitudes to friends, being used to modern coolness in these matters. None the less I remembered my own condition as a child without a 'best friend' and marvelled at the Bangwa insistence that everyone should have one. I also made friends myself – I doubt if life would have gone on so smoothly if I had not and in any case there was very little choice.

I watched how Bangwa 'best friends' behaved, continually verbalizing their affection, giving each other gifts, accompanying each other on journeys, being demonstrative almost to the point of 'petting'. It soon became clear that friendship was endowed with a greater intensity of meaning than in our own society, even to someone like myself imbued with the traditions and sentiment of Australian mateship. Certainly the behaviour of Jonathan and David would be normal and comprehensible to them and the words of Roland and Oliver not at all romantic. Moreover, they would not be in the least tempted to presuppose or imagine any homosexual overtones in these classical European friendships since as far as I could make out, and I certainly made enquiries, these practices were unknown between adult men.

I was brought face to face with the strong parallels between Bangwa friendship and the biblical story of David and Jonathan when I attended my first funeral. It was early on in my fieldwork and I watched the goings-on in great confusion; it took me months to sort out the comings and goings of all the categories of kith and kin and put some kind of order into the natural chaos of a Bangwa ritual, so on this day I desperately noted down simply what people were wearing or doing. Some women had on men's clothes, others were naked to the waist; some had a long cloth tied around the waist; others had red mud on their foreheads, or white clay on their cheeks. I sat nervously beside the corpse inside the hut with all the important men who talked and sipped palm wine. Outside, the women danced and wailed and swayed close to the ground in an ecstasy of flamboyant grief for their husband or their kinsman or their in-law. I decided to record one of the songs which a particular man every half-hour or so sang outside the door of the hut. He was a youngish man, wearing a loin-cloth, waistcoat, and cap, and he sang a heartrending funeral lament, tears pouring down his already tear-stained face, mud on his brow, the waistcoat torn. He sang his pathetic song while holding out the dead man's cap to the wailing women and as he sang some of them swayed towards him and theatrically wiped away his tears. When I had filled my tape with this song, I was glad enough to blame a splitting headache for wanting to get out of the hut and the nearness of the dead man and went back to the relative quiet of my own house. The next day, during my daily Bangwa lesson I asked my teacher to translate this dirge and found that it was sung by the dead man's best friend, who sang his praises in the most extravagant and emotional terms, recording details of his life, his brave deeds during the hunt, his generous and kindly nature to his friends and kin.

This was a step ahead in my knowledge of Bangwa friendship. I learnt that at a 'cry-die' – the local English term for the funeral – a man's best friend is one of the chief mourners; he not only sings a lament and recites the events of the dead man's life, but he organizes a good deal of the entertainment by providing food, drink, and musicians, and sees to the post mortem on the corpse if witchcraft has been suspected. A best friend is expected to make a public display of his grief like the widows and children.

I later recorded many of these songs, some of them sung by women for their friends; they are songs of praise for the great warrior whose friend stupidly thought he could never die, of the wonderful father, of the brilliant judge. The friend sings of the days they spent hunting together, visiting markets, gossiping over palm wine and kola nuts in their private huts. He sings of his friend's humility, his love of birds and flowers; of his special gifts as a climber of palm trees or a carver of wood; most of all he sings of their friendship.

I believe that in a mundane way – mundane because I am no Homer – this is the context in which we should try and understand the few details we have of the famous loves of David and Jonathan and Achilles and Patroclus. I read the eighteenth book of the *Iliad* with different eyes when I came back from Bangwa:

With both hands he rent the black mould from the forced earth and
     pour'd it on his head,
Smeared all his lovely face, his weeds (divinely fashioned)
All filde and mangl'd, himself he threw upon the shore,
Lay as laid out for funerall, then tumbl'd round, and tore
His gracious curles.[3]

The Bangwa path of friendship runs fairly smoothly. Best friends are made in childhood, usually among age-mates. The emphasis on age equality is brought out by the fact that the best of friends are twins or two children born on the same day. If a boy or girl is not given a best friend by his or her parents he will associate with several acquaintances, gradually selecting from them a friend of the same sex whom he feels he can trust absolutely. The importance of having a friend is impressed on children by their elders, by example, through folk tales, and by dire warnings of what happens to a man who is without friends. Youths who become friends exchange confidences, discuss their secret ambitions, hunt together or plan, endlessly, their amorous adventures.

Curiously enough a similar method of training young warriors and princes is used in Bangwa as it was in feudal times in Europe. The chief's palace was a large complex of meeting-houses, reception huts, and individual huts inhabited by the chief, his wives, his servants, and his pages. Most of the work was done by slaves or the descendants of slaves but formal duties were reserved for children of sub-chiefs and notables who were sent to live and learn in the palace when they were about ten or eleven. They served for a period in the palace as pages, under the care of a special retainer, and at the same time learned dances, games, hunting, and fighting. Friendships grew up between these youths which lasted a lifetime and, as in feudal times, were often strengthened by being sent out on a head-hunting expedition or on a *razzia* against the neighbouring Mbo.

The Bangwa spoke of ideal friendship as one of equality and complete reciprocity, backed by moral, rather than supernatural and legal, sanctions. He is my friend 'because he is beautiful', 'because he is good'. Although there is in fact a good deal of ceremonial courtesy and gift exchange it is seen as a relationship of disinterested affection. Youths who are friends spend long hours in each other's company, holding hands when they walk together in the market. As they grow older friendships become increasingly valued – elders have little else to do but sit around with their friends, chatting about local politics, disputes over land boundaries, trouble with an obstreperous young wife. The most bitter complaint of one old Bangwa man to me was that he had grown so old that he had not a single friend to gossip with.

Friendship is valued far above kinship; between kin there are niggling debts and witchcraft fears. Friendship lasts till death; kinship is brittle and involves inequalities of age and wealth and status. Friendship alone can cancel these out. A chief born on the same day as a slave automatically becomes his 'best friend' and is bound to treat him in a friendly manner, at least in some contexts. The son who succeeds to a chief's position depends on the friends he made as a child – not his kin – in the crooked corridors of palace politics.

Most important, friends are not dangerous as far as witchcraft is concerned. Close kin – half-brothers, uncles, even fathers – are constantly being accused of the most heinous supernatural attacks. A friend, on the other hand, is outside the category of persons who can 'eat' you. If your best friend's child is ill, you would be the appropriate person to ask advice from the diviner and seek out the witch. A best friend may be asked to perform the autopsy on a child's corpse in order to divine, through a close inspection of the viscera, the supernatural causes of death. When a man is dying he calls his friends, not his relatives: the latter are the ones whose witchcraft he fears and, moreover, they are interested in his death since the property a Bangwa notable leaves behind for his kin may be considerable – land, wives, oil palms, money. A friend has no rights to this property, in fact he may often have to fight off greedy relatives and ambitious mothers in the general scramble for property which can occur in a Bangwa compound even before the corpse is cold in its grave.

Bangwa men live in continual fear of supernatural attack. Their sleeping-houses are down in the darkest recesses of the compound, surrounded by fetishes and medicines, a place where few people are allowed, not even wives. A man's best friend, however, has complete freedom of this apartment and of his compound – he is trusted to the extent of sharing the same bench as his wives, which is tantamount to flagrant adultery if done by anyone else. At European-style dances a best friend is one of the few categories of persons allowed to partner a man's wife during a 'ball dance' – most women have to be content with their husband or a small boy, under ten and sexually 'harmless'. If the impossible happened and a best friend seduced his friend's wife, the mystical dangers which resulted, in the form of some hideous skin disease, would automatically descend on the head of the wronged husband and not the adulterer.

The list of obligations and duties of a best friend is endless. One of these obligations is to act as middleman if his friend decides to 'marry' a baby girl recently born in the village – he joins in the rush to get to the compound first and place the ceremonial log on the fire which symbolizes an intention to marry. If the parents accept the middleman's offer they begin the long and tedious discussion of bridewealth which does not end for another thirteen years. Young men who have left Bangwa to work in the towns and in the plantations send their friends back to the villages to find them a bride; nowadays this almost always involves the tricky business of arranging for the divorce of a young girl from the husband to whom she has been betrothed since infancy and repaying him every piece of meat, jug of wine, or roll of cloth he has handed over to her kin since then.

I have dealt in some detail with the relationship between Bangwa friends, which could be repeated for many African societies.[4] Bond friendship is well-nigh ubiquitous – traders form friendships, chiefs make friendly alliances, friends farm together or fight together, friends marry their friends' sisters or cousins. The Bangwa situation in its general outline is not unique, only in its details – perhaps in the association of friendship and twins in their cosmological beliefs (see p. 131) and in the role it plays in providing an outlet from the claustrophobic restrictions of kinship ties.

The Bangwa and other African societies have not had their friendship laments recorded by their poets. Nevertheless, the values of friendship have been expressed in their oral literature, in tales which are well known from Liberia to Tanzania.[5] They are usually trickster tales of the Brer Fox kind and most of them are about the friendly pranks of two animals. Almost invariably the structure of the story involves a movement from close friendship to enmity, beginning: 'The tortoise and the hare were the best of friends . . .', and the making and breaking of the friendship through the wicked tricks of the hare (the trickster) serve as a frame. The story usually involves a contract between two friends which is broken by the trickster, who deceives the dupe by convincing him that it was really he who broke the pact. The story ends with the statement that the original friendship has been dissolved through the breaking of an agreement, sometimes a blood pact. This pattern (of friendship, agreement, violation, and discovery) is one which is familiar throughout Africa.[6] A most common example is the killing of the dupe's mother in a time of famine in order to provide food for the two friends, after the contract had explicitly arranged for the killing of both mothers.

In these stories, which are rather like biblical parables stood on their heads, we have a kind of joke in which the values of friendship are upheld, not by direct moralizing on how things should be, but by a hilarious account of how they should never be. The stories all suggest that friendship is closely related to contractual agreement and reciprocal behaviour. The strange structure of the story – the breaking of the contract, the eating of the mother and the ending of the friendship – also seems to offer an outlet from the binding nature of friendship relations. In these trickster tales there is the paradox that, although friendships are ideal norms, the narrator and the audience identify with the trickster who ignores these norms – rather like the adulterous tales of romantic love which were the reading matter of the devoted Victorian wife.

In Africa, therefore, we can find behaviour among close friends which approximates to the David and Jonathan ideal. The Bangwa sing loud and clear in praise of their friends. During annual ceremonies at the palace it is a wonderful sight to see two friends, in full warrior gear, greeting each other on the dancing floor, striking each other's swords high in the air with a splendid clash, as a public demonstration of their friendship. And at funerals – like Achilles and David – they vent their grief in ostentatious poetry, in fainting, in tearing at their clothes, in a lament for the lost friend. Fainting, weeping, and lamenting is considered the behaviour such a situation calls for. As Dorothy Sayers pointed out,[7] open displays of grief and other emotional demonstrations for the sake of friends are – and were – more common than the monstrous ideal of our society, where the strong man reacts to great personal loss 'by a slight compression of the lips and by throwing his cigarette into the fireplace'.

In fact it would appear that our society is the exception in a world where friendship is a social and psychological need cemented by formal behaviour and ceremony. In Polynesia and Melanesia, the evidence for the universality of bond friendship is as strong as it is in Africa. Malinowski[8] describes the close ties of Trobriand adolescents, who become best friends, embrace in public, sleep together, and walk around the village arm in arm. Some of these friendships survive into adult life, becoming permanent relationships based on affection and mutual assistance. The same word is used for a friend as for heterosexual lovers, as well as for a man's partner in the local gift exchange system, the *kula* (see p. 159 ff). Margaret Mead[9] has described relations between Samoan youths who become inseparable companions after undergoing circumcision rites together. Bond friendship among the Polynesian Tikopia of the Pacific islands[10] is an institutionalized and lifelong bond, cemented by reciprocal obligations and the exchange of gifts. In Tikopia, young men who go about in groups, fishing and farming and dancing, choose special friends from among their group; one of a pair of men will propose a bond friendship and if it is accepted it is ratified by an exchange of food.

The Trobriand Islanders, mentioned above, are one of the five or six peoples I have selected for continual reference in this book. They include another African society apart from the Bangwa – the Dogon of Mali; two contemporary Mediterranean people – Spanish peasants of an Andalusian pueblo and a Greek shepherd community; and a Latin-American community, the Chinautleco of Guatemala.

The Chinautleco are Indians of Mayan descent, who have constituted a distinctive group for hundreds of years and live a few miles from Guatemala City. In the early sixteenth century the indigenous Indians were defeated by the Spaniards whom they accepted as conquerors; they brought blankets, feathers, and gold as tribute and since then contact between Spaniard and Indian has been continuous, the Spaniard coming as priest, administrator, teacher, and landowner. In Chinautleco today Indians live alongside Ladinos (Latins), who are people of the pueblo who transmit the Spanish heritage. The relationship between these two groups pervades Chinautleco life – Indians are proud of their descent from an ancient Mayan race, while Ladinos consider the Spanish conquerors as their ancestors. Ladinos are 'civilized'; Indians are 'natives'.

Ruben Reina[11] describes the interaction of Indian and Ladino with sympathetic insight. The Indian community maintains a suspicious attitude, not only to the small Spanish population, but to the whole outside world, and envy and mistrust also mark the attitude of different Indian groups within the community. It is in the Catholic church and bonds of friendship that individuals seek emotional fulfilment and an escape from the press of a hard life – marriage does not provide this release, since husband-and-wife relations are conducted on a businesslike and formal basis.

Apparently Chinautleco friendship – called *camaradia* – reaches its highest intensity at that transitional stage in life in which young men achieve adult status without acquiring its emotional rewards. Most adolescents and young men have 'best friends' with whom they share secrets and ambitions and plan love affairs. The relationship is institutionalized in so far as the particular friendship between two men is publicly known and talked about – 'Yes, Miguel is Antonio's friend' – and it is implicitly inclusive. Friendships are made and broken almost with the ceremony and formality of a betrothal between a youth and his fiancée.

Once a friend has been acquired Indians treat the friendship with grave seriousness and jealous passion. They expect complete *confianza* from their friends, which in itself means that the relationship is explosive and hence fragile; it involves affection of an extreme kind which more often than not is short-lived and resembles more the passion of heterosexual lovers than the calm friendship of equals I have described in the case of the Bangwa. *Camaradas* are so jealous of each other that the frustrations engendered by possessiveness and love often end in an equally passionate state of enmity. And once a friend becomes an enemy the situation is dangerous since the confidences between the two men have been total and the secrets shared give each a power over the other long after the end of the affair.

I believe that an element of homosexuality allowed in the relationship – always covert – provokes the excessively passionate and turbulent nature of Chinautleco friendship. Reina describes the course of one such friendship. Juan and Pedro had become firm friends in their teens, and at twenty and twenty-two they were still the greatest of friends. The death of Pedro's mother caused the relationship to increase in passionate intensity. The two youths met every evening, went to local feasts and celebrations where they danced with each other all night, and usually returned to sleep together at Juan's house, although they sometimes went to Pedro's in another part of the village. The frequent visits by Pedro to Juan's house caused some hostility in Pedro's section of the village, especially when Pedro began to court Juan's cousin. Pedro said to Reina afterwards that on various occasions, during the festivities which everyone enjoyed so exuberantly, he had protected his *camarada* from being beaten up by youths of his quarter. Everyone knew of their relationship and it was of the kind which was considered normal between two unmarried men of their age. After marriage it would become less emotional, less absorbing. Juan and Pedro continued to go to parties together. They held hands and chatted endlessly, they danced and drank, and the one who was less drunk helped the other home to bed. They spoke up for and defended each other. They embraced, they joked, they kissed in a teasing fashion; they said they would love to marry if one of them were a woman. These were all manifestations of friendship and love between men in Chinautleco. Everyone in the village had such a friend, then or in former times, and did the same kind of thing.

Suddenly this friendship was broken off. Pedro had got so drunk at a fiesta that he was no longer able to dance with Juan; consequently Juan danced with another man from his own part of the village, who had already been seeking him out as a friend. Pedro, seeing them dancing, took it as an act of infidelity and went out angrily to find himself another partner. Dancing, they pushed and shoved each other and jealous Pedro even hit Juan in the face. The relationship grew suddenly precarious and day after day there were frequent scenes of jealousy and mistrust. They fought, they drank, and they insulted each other in public.

Chinautleco friendship is not allowed to end in this manner, apparently. Pedro and his father went to the mayor of the village, and Juan was called to his office to give an account of his behaviour. The two men did not want to continue as friends and were to be officially separated as if they had been partners to a legal contract like betrothal or marriage. Juan said he would never force anyone to be his friend and told Pedro he was free to find another *camarada*. That was the end. They ceased even to greet each other in the street, although they avoided as far as possible talking derogatorily of each other, and everyone said that they sadly missed each other for the first months. Pedro even sent some messages to Juan but the latter had already begun to work out a new relationship with another boy in order to forget his ex-*camarada*.

In Chinautleco the emotional aspects of friendship are possibly overvalued, since they make the relationship as explosive as a love affair; not infrequently, as in the case of Pedro and Juan, it ends in jealous bickering and violent trauma. They are friendships undertaken with great earnestness, preceded by several months of passive companionship, during which time a formal friendship prevails. Although there is no bond pact initially as, in Tikopia and the case of David and Jonathan, the public termination of the separation indicates its formal nature.

Similar homoerotic friendships find their counterparts all over the world. In Mediterranean countries, extremely high value is placed on intense, sentimental relations between youths and men. Outsiders, especially Anglo-Saxons, confronted with these passionate friendships between men which receive some degree of public physical expression, feel at first that they have entered a world of wild homosexual licence, which is far from being the case. A frank and open acceptance of friendship and a delight in the company of members of the same sex are possible in societies other than our own, where a man's panicky fear of being thought homosexual may cause him to repress expressions of amity and affection with other men. Schoolgirl crushes and adolescent love affairs between schoolboys are presented in a ridiculous light by their elders and ruthlessly mocked by their peers. It would be wiser to allow such friendships, along with their physical expression, and permit them to develop into mature, adult friendships. Today no one would write about youthful love as simply as Disraeli did in *Coningsby*:

> At school friendship is a passion. It enhances the being, it tears the soul. All the loves of after life can never bring its rapture, or its wretchedness; no bliss so absorbing, no pangs of jealousy or despair so crushing or so keen . . . What tenderness and what devotion; what illimitable confidence, infinite revelation of inmost thought; what ecstatic present and romantic future; what bitter estrangements and what melting reconciliations; what scenes of wild recrimination, agitating explanations, passionate correspondence; what insane sensitiveness, what earthquakes of the heart and whirlwinds of the soul are confined in that simple phrase, a 'schoolboy's friendship'.

It is sad that these passionate affairs should often be condemned by the phlegmatic English as the frenzy of an illicit and romantic passion rather than the stirring of a normal loving friendship. The need for emotional experience of the Pedro–Juan and David–Jonathan type is openly recognized in many cultures, and not relegated to the ignominy of *la vice anglaise*. In a Thailand village emotional friendships are recognized, openly encouraged, and even institutionalized. Villagers live in an atmosphere of open mistrust and suspicion, almost as oppressive as in Chinautleco, an atmosphere which is relieved by a bond between men known as 'friendship to the death'. A man chooses a friend from whom he can expect complete trust and emotional security, in which case blood is exchanged between the two men – a failure to observe the most complete commitment to a friend leads to the extinction of the defaulter's family and his precious herd of buffalo, the blood acting as a supernatural agent for the curse. Friendship is formal in one sense but also very passionate, it is an admission of the dangers of personal isolation in a society which offers little trust. Friends verbalize their sentimental attachments in romantic terms which are normally only used between members of the opposite sex in our own society. The anthropologist tells us that these emotional friendships make possible a degree of vicarious gratification of a desire for love which is strongly felt but often frustrated in the selfish, back-biting world of everyday life – although it hardly needs the adjective 'vicarious'. As far as a later discussion of romantic love is concerned, it is of interest to remark here that these passionate relations between best friends survive most strongly when the geographical distance between them is great.

In the West, friendship seems to have been discouraged in favour of close intimacy between husband and wife and the strength of the notorious 'team spirit'. In Mediterranean countries friendship not only provides individual emotional satisfaction but also helps to oil the wheels of the wider social structure. The villagers of Alcalá in Andalusia[12] are bound together by ties of friendship as important as those of kinship. Alcalá, with a population of just over two thousand, is an agricultural pueblo of whitewashed and red-tiled houses in a landscape of swelling hills and sharp escarpments, where the peasants raise cattle and sheep, make charcoal and grow grain. They are known as the 'lard-eaters' because of their attachment to raising pigs. Love of the pueblo is strong and there is a corresponding hostility to neighbouring peoples, particularly those living in richer villages or shepherd communities. Membership of the pueblo is acquired through birth, and identification with it is symbolized by nicknames given by other townspeople. On the whole, the inhabitants form a typical Andalusian community with their own special accent and customs. Although proud of their pueblo the people constantly complain of the town's poverty and its deadness – 'nothing ever happens here'; all admit that they long to leave and, in fact, if they get a chance they do so.

In Alcalá, friendship between two persons is a sacred relationship, emotionally more meaningful than relations between members of the kin group, except perhaps that of parent and child. Friendship here, according to Pitt-Rivers, is a disinterested sentiment endowed with *simpatía*, yet at the same time the governmental and mercantile institutions of the village could not function without it. Friendship is also the only mechanism for maintaining economic cooperation between different pueblos. It is a sentiment which is diffused between neighbours and members of the local community and is expressed as a mutual respect for the personality and social status of each individual villager. In this way friendship can be seen to be basic to the system of values of Andalusian society, underlying all social behaviour and recognizable in all social contexts. The worst plight for a man is to be without friends, a situation which is symbolized to the people of Alcalá by a dead man's coffin being carried to the grave by *paid* pall-bearers – a sure sign that a man lived and died unloved, without even a couple of friends to carry him to the grave.

Friendship is thus prosaic and romantic. In fact in most of the examples of this book we shall find that friendship is both interested (directly relating to social function and social structure) and disinterested (satisfying the purely personal needs of an individual). Friends in Alcalá and Bangwa, and probably in ancient Israel, not only provide each other with emotional satisfaction but cooperate in specific tasks.

With the Saraktsani shepherds of continental Greece, however, we seem to have an exception. These close-knit families who guard their flocks and live suspicious and apart from sedentary villagers, rarely speak in praise of friendship. Friendship, they say, is a betrayal of the small corporate groups which struggle to maintain a subsistence living from their flocks of sheep and goats.[13] The Saraktsani live in a tight-knit world of kinship, inward-looking and mistrustful even of kin outside the limited extended family. If a man should form an intimate, sympathetic relation with a person who is not a member of the family it would represent a kind of treason. The shepherds believe that the interests of unrelated families are opposed and mutually destructive and local groups only have cohesion in their enmity to outsiders, particularly the villagers.

The Saraktsani – who, with the people of Alcalá and Chinautleco, will keep cropping up in this book – are well known to tourists in mainland Greece who travel north of Corinth, the men in their rough black suits and immense goat-hair capes, guarding their flocks, and the women sitting outside their circular domed huts of wood and thatch. The Saraktsani have a simple social organization, the family being the basic unit; the family by itself, however, cannot manage the flock and two or three families come together to form a 'company' of four adult males and from fifteen to fifty other members. They exploit the grassland belonging to a single village in the mountains of Xagori, but in winter they are forced to disperse, moving to the coastal plains and valleys over a large area from Albania as far south as the towns of Arta and Preveza. Winter weather and lambing-time isolate the shepherds and their personal flock, but in the summer they visit kinsmen who live at a distance and attend weddings and festivals.

I have chosen to use data on these shepherds to illustrate several themes of friendship, since amity outside the family is explicitly said – by the anthropologist and the people themselves – to be alien to their way of life. The shepherd believes that his world is a closed universe, and that there is only enmity and competition in a world where there is never enough wealth, particularly in grazing land. A disaster for one shepherd, even, can only be seen as a benefit to the others, to such an extent are their interests inimical. The shepherd is also convinced that the administration, the local villagers, the merchants, are all antagonistic to him and his way of life.

It is true that the shepherds of Greece deny the existence of friendship between unrelated persons. Emotional needs almost seem to be supplied by enmity; enmity rather than amity is the mainspring of relations between men who have common economic interests. Nevertheless it will suffice here to state that friendships – close emotional ties between men of the same age – do occur; but they are restricted to first cousins. These men enjoy an association based on mutual sympathy, sociability, and the sheer delight of one another's company. These close friendships are permitted between relatives who never cooperate in daily work, since work and friendship are considered incompatible. Men who herd sheep together are partners and, as I mentioned above, business partnerships have elements which conflict with the free and unrestrained attitudes of personal friendship. Between cousins, however, there is an outlet and friendship is allowed to flourish, since the demands fall into the category of free favours.

Among the Saraktsani, therefore, attitudes to members of their community who are not close kin are unrelentingly hostile. Aggression theorists, such as Robert Ardrey, who have neatly but unscientifically transferred instinctual intra-specific aggression from fish and birds to human beings, might be pleased indeed to find a situation where a man's loving-kindness is reserved to close kin and bonding with unrelated persons is considered impossible, a betrayal of the interests of the in-group. Cousins are even expected to sacrifice their friendship if there is friction between two families over grazing rights or the ownership of stock. However, despite the ethnographer and the statements of the shepherds, the reality is not so bleak and friendless as it appears. While the shepherd may be convinced that the administration, the local villagers, and the merchants are all his enemies, he needs to get on with them, even gain their protection, and the way to do this is not through hostility and aggression but friendship. The Saraktsani make friends – as clients – with officials and village notables, thus relating their isolated pastoral communities to the wider society. And interpersonal relationships involving sympathy and friendly interest, such as the co-godparent link between shepherd and villager, help the smooth functioning of intercommunity relations and are always endowed with a certain amount of affect.

*

What about the women? As usual in ethnography, fifty per cent of the population in our exotic societies get hardly any attention. Do women have friends, allies, among the men and other women? Apart from my experience of the Bangwa I am afraid I have to answer, through paucity of evidence, that I don't know. There are not even any myths of devoted women friends comparable with those of Achilles and Patroclus, Roland and Oliver. And Sappho and her friends have been relegated to the dark limbo of lesbianism – on the shaky grounds of a few lines of verse.

Women in our society have not been encouraged to rejoice in their own kind and in their femininity. Women do not go to the local and rarely play football on Sundays. The most important fact, of course, is that men do not believe women capable of friendship. From earliest records to recent diatribes we have this sneaky, half-humorous attitude to women who make friends or form groups. 'Men are thoroughly at home with one another, but a curious discomfort often pervades a meeting of women.' 'There is a lack of conviviality in women, and their friendships for one another, genuine as they may be, are bounded by a kind of primness, a kind of watchfulness which entirely precludes that hail-fellow-well-met feeling that brings out the latent boyishness in man.'[14]

Women have even been blamed, having reached their modern semi-emancipated state, for carrying out ceaseless and often successful campaigns against male friendships, isolating their husbands and lovers from male companionship in the interests of their marriage or their affair. Charles Lamb expresses this *égoisme à deux* imposed by the wife in an essay called 'The Bachelor's Complaint'[15]:

If the husband be a man with whom you have lived on a friendly footing before marriage, – if you did not come in on the wife's side, – if you did not sneak into the house in her train, but were an old friend in fast habits of intimacy before their courtship was as much as thought on, – look about you – your tenure is precarious – before a twelve-month shall roll over your head, you shall find your old friend gradually grow cool and altered towards you, and at last seek opportunities of breaking with you.

While this situation is not uncommon, it is no justification for the denial of women's capacity for friendship with other women. More serious is a scientific, or pseudo-scientific, contribution from Lionel Tiger[16] which asserts that women are simply not genetically programmed to bond like Jonathan and David. I shall discuss this in a later chapter; let it suffice for now to suggest that the natural attraction of people of the female sex has been culturally obstructed to a greater degree than that between males. We all know of instances of passionate friendships between women, both with and without homoerotic elements. Germaine Greer writes that

> It is dangerous to admit that inseparable girls are often fascinated by each other, deeply altruistic and cooperative, and often genuinely spiritual, as well as utterly sexual if not literally genital . . . Learning to dissemble these feelings, among the strongest and the most elevated that she will ever feel, is a squalid but inevitable business.[17]

Men, who exclude the possibility of bonding between women, must have lived with their eyes tight shut. The data are more limited since literature and ethnography have been written from the male point of view – even if the writer or anthropologist is female – but few of us would have trouble in recalling examples of friendships between young girls, wives, older women, which are as binding and loyal as the most glamorous male friendship. Ethnography, as well as any complete account of a woman's life cycle, reveals instances of important emotional and institutionalized bonds between girls, women, and old ladies.

Women in Bangwa at first give the impression of the usual oppressed class of African peasant woman, at the beck and call of their menfolk, existing to bear children, suffering the ignominy of farm labour and polygyny. They are politically, religiously, economically, and socially *un*emancipated. Men marry them off, pray on their behalf, send them out to work in the fields and to trade in the markets, and restrict them to certain spheres of life. Bangwa women were forbidden until recently to wear even a stitch of clothing. They approach men bent double and shielding their female breath from contact with their lords and masters.

While deprecating the condition of the general run of Bangwa women, one is obliged to state that they have managed to preserve more individuality and positive personality – as *women* – than the unsexed creatures of contemporary English and American society. There is a specifically woman's world which is not despised and where men do not belong. Bowed down with childbearing and farming, as well as from the necessity of etiquette in the presence of a man, they retain an integrity and pride associated with a downright femininity (and by that word I do not mean the softness, the 'unmaleness' of the European 'feminine' woman) which is their salvation. Women in Bangwa are not 'man made'; they are not less or more than men – they are just women.

One of the props of this female world is close friendship between two women – women born at the same time (similar to the ascribed friendships of men); women who like each other; women of the same status (a princess, a priestess, a fortune-teller); or women who simply have a hut next to each other in the compound of a polygynous chief. These women friends offer each other trust, loyalty, and companionship. They belong to the same dancing clubs, attend the same markets to earn pin-money and the fees for their children's education. They make regular visits to each other's compounds, carrying gifts of food and special delicacies such as honey or smoked meat. They attend their best friend's funeral, sing dirges in her praise, and dance in her honour.

A wealthy chief often marries several girls in a 'mass wedding' and special friendships may be made during the fattening and ritual seclusion periods that precede consummation of this multi-union. If not, a woman will seek out an intimate friend in the same compound – sometimes it will be her 'mother', the woman who guides her through the early days of marriage and keeps her in her hut until she has her first child. If a man has only two wives, and this is the norm, they become almost by prescription 'best friends', sharing domestic chores as well as their husband's bed. Friendships of this kind lighten the peculiar burdens of life in an African harem. Certainly the emotional satisfactions from a husband may be as meagre as the sexual ones if a man has to share his duties among fifty women. Many a wife counteracts this kind of deprivation by strong attachment to a friendly co-wife, along with a passionate devotion to each other's children. Women friends in the same compound support each other in the case of minor domestic tragedies, in quarrels they may have with their husband, and in the constant crushing fatigue of providing for their children with only the minimum of support from harassed fathers.

In the compound of a chief there may be a number of former widows, and even young wives, who have no children. It is not uncommon for a girl of fourteen or fifteen to marry and grow to young middle-age as the wife of a doddering old chief and on his death be inherited by a young man in his early teens who will not willingly do his sexual duty by a long-neglected and ageing widow. Such women, without children, obviously need compensation in a society which values nothing and nobody if it is not motherhood and the large family. Childless, a woman may care for the children of her co-wives or become indispensable in the compound for her accomplishments as a bone-setter, a potter, or a fine cook. More than other women she needs friends, particularly as she grows older; widows in a compound of ailing children are a prey to accusations of witchcraft from young mothers and in these situations they need fortitude and support. As a result women do establish lifelong friendships. Widows, growing old, share one hut and one farm. Almost all their satisfactions, without the blessings of children and grandchildren, may be concentrated in each other. The death of one is a bitter blow, and the ritual mourning of the survivor may be as moving and pathetic as that described for men friends. With her friend gone an old widow is friendless and alone; old age, an enviable state for most Bangwa, has nothing to offer her but the nagging fear that she is occupying a hut in the compound of her husband's successor, which he probably has his eye on for a new wife.

As for friendships between men and women, the myth dies hard that sexuality, often in the form of romantic passion, utterly forbids the achievement of platonic devotion unless it be between a homosexual and a devoted woman friend, or a woman and an impotent man. Montaigne, the arch-propagandist of male friendship, is emphatic about the impossibility of friendship between men and women:

As for comparing [this friendship] unto the love of women, this cannot be attempted. That fire, well I know it, it is more restless, more scorching, more arid. But it is forked fire and changeful ... As soon as it entereth upon terms of friendship ... it languisheth and fainteth. Contrariwise, friendship ... increaseth only when it is enjoyed, for that it is of the spirit, and that by use the soul is sharpened.

George Santayana, in his *Little Essays*,[18] stresses elegantly the permanent element of *eros* which male writers believe is an indestructible obstacle to understanding between a man and a woman:

Friends are generally of the same sex, for when men and women agree, it is only in their conclusions; their reasons are always different. So that while intellectual harmony between men and women is easily possible, its delightful magical quality lies precisely in the fact that it does not arise from mutual understanding, but is a conspiracy of alien essences and a kissing, as it were, in the dark ... Friendship with a woman is therefore apt to be more or less than friendship: less, because there is no intellectual parity; more, because (even when the relation remains wholly dispassionate, as in respect to old ladies) there is something mysterious and oracular about a woman's mind which inspires a certain instinctive deference and puts it out of the question to judge what she says by masculine standards. She has a kind of sibylline intuition and the right to the irrational *à propos*. There is a gallantry of the mind which pervades all conversations with a lady, as there is a natural courtesy towards children and mystics; but such a habit of respectful concession, marking as it does an intellectual alienation as profound, though not complete, as that which separates us from the dumb animals, is radically incompatible with friendship.

My own limited experience of other cultures, first- and second-hand, does not support this racist and sexist view of women as friends. In Bangwa I was formally pronounced the friend of many different kinds of people and for many different reasons. Most Bangwa who asked me to be their friend were of roughly my own age – age equality in itself implying friendship. I acquired both men and women friends in this way – I happened to have been born in the year that an adventurous English district officer drove, or had had carried, the first motor-car into the

Bangwa mountains, an incredible feat in a country where the paths are six inches wide and the rivers as many feet deep and fast flowing; so that age-parity with Bangwa was easily determined by this yardstick. I also made friends with much older men and women, the friendship implying equality of status; when I received a Bangwa title, men and women who bore the same title and had the same right to attend clubs and dances and eat the same amount of meat, began to call me 'friend'. I also had friends who were in no sense my equals, sentimental ties replacing those ascribed through birth or position. Thus one woman, a high-ranking princess – or 'queen mother' – took a great interest in my activities and personal life and became known as my 'good friend'. She sent me food, showed me how the women used to make pots, prepared me simple medicines. Other women were friendly towards me, sending gifts of food and talking of local affairs; quite clearly in these relationships sexual affinity was not part of the deal and imposed no obstacle to the feeling of companionship experienced between men and women. In Bangwa there are no unmarried women, since they are betrothed at birth and widows are inherited by their husband's successor. Nevertheless a woman whose husband is too young to cohabit with her – he may even be a babe in arms – is allowed to take lovers. 'They are our prostitutes,' a Bangwa man pointed out proudly to me; and in these cases their sexual availability was made abundantly clear and their 'friendly' advances strongly differentiated from those of other women.

Bangwa boys and girls also form friendships in early childhood and these friendships are never confused with love affairs. They continue throughout the couple's lifetime and do not differ much from informal relations of companionship between men. When a man is with his woman bond-friend their friendship is immediately apparent since the woman relaxes her usual demeanour of almost theatrical deference before any man, and they are permitted to joke, talk frankly, and even eat together – a practice normally taboo'd between men and women, particularly husband and wife.

Equality of friendship cuts across the basic inequalities and allows communication between men and women, without sex in any way disturbing it. In Bangwa, my own understanding of strange customs was often clouded by ingrained prejudices and I also doubted the platonic nature of these friendships. Old men, who talked endlessly about the golden, olden days, told me about similar friendships. In the good old times, they said, there was no adultery and no divorce; their wives were not attracted to wealthy young men who seduced them from their rightful husbands by promises of a life of permanent ease, European clothing, and streets paved with gold in the towns and plantations in the south. In the past, young men waited their turn to marry, patiently, content with the platonic friendships they were permitted with the old men's fiancées. These friends spent the day together, talking, playing games, even sharing the same bed. If the girl came to her husband with her virginity intact her friend was rewarded; if not, the friend paid an adultery fine. In the beginning I preferred to disbelieve the platonic nature of these friendships – how could young women and virile men spend all day and night together, half-naked, petting even, in a relationship of pure friendship? Like Santayana I found it hard to accept that sex can be banished from friendship. We have been brought up as 'dirty old men', assuming the worst when two men are constantly and devotedly together or when a boy and girl travel together as friends – if they share the same bedroom or tent, they *must* be lovers. We have imbued friendly relations with a smear of sexuality, so that a frank platonic enjoyment of a friend for his or her own sake is becoming well-nigh impossible.

The fact is that sex can be switched on or off as a situation demands – between brother and sister for example – and frequently this favours a more lasting friendship. We all know that sexual appetites once aroused are destructive of friendship, but they can and often do remain dormant. For this reason I now believe the Bangwa historians who maintained that young men and women shared a straightforward companionship, while admitting that it may have offered compensations of a covert kind. Moreover, I have since come across other examples in Africa. Among the Nzema of Southern Ghana,[19] where friendship is highly valued, formal friendships are instituted between men and women which last their lifetime. Men set up amicable relations with women before they marry, 'in order to have the pleasure of their companionship and without feeling any amorous feelings towards them'. These friends 'become like brother and sister'. The two may even sleep together and banish every desire, without any member of the community finding it laughable. If sexual desire does make itself felt it must be rigorously fought. In any case the families of the two friends would never give their permission to the marriage of a man and a woman who were already bound in this platonic relationship. Even after the marriage of the girl (and the choice of her husband even concerns her friend) the friendship continues. A woman's friend may intervene in quarrels between the married couple and should protect her from any brutality on her husband's part.

These examples may suggest a less cynical attitude towards platonic friendships and even to the pure love advocated by Avicenna and twelfth-century troubadours, or towards the chaste and spiritual marriages between early Christians or to those priests in the centuries immediately following the birth of Christ who kept *agapetae* or 'spiritual sisters'. Nobody would deny sex as a source of power behind love, but it is not inevitably nor overtly expressed. More important than carnal urges or 'sublimated homoeroticism' are affection, friendship, companionship, and the need to care and be cared for.

2 Female Husbands and Male Wives

Perhaps my own best woman friend in Bangwa was Mafwa, the chief's titled sister who took an interest in me and my work in between her chores as a councillor, the head of local women's clubs, and general supervisor of the fifty-odd wives in her brother's palace. After the chief she was the most powerful person in the palace neighbourhood and often stood in for him on ceremonial occasions. I have seen her grandly organizing a bevy of women as they dammed a stream to net tadpoles and frogs; holding forth to women on their rights in the independent Cameroon state; settling a dispute between two old men in the court-house as a representative of the central government; cooking a delicacy of ground melon seeds and termites for my supper; and singing a lullaby to a fractious child. I liked Mafwa very much and fortunately for me and my work she liked me as well. We spent happy hours drinking and talking together, usually in the local colourful pidjin which she spoke 'like a man'. If there were a funeral or rite to attend I tried to go with her since I knew she would be diverting and instructive on the long trek across the mountain paths. If I needed an introduction to a hide-away priest or some woman's mystery, Mafwa was the best person to approach.

Mafwa, of course, contrasted strongly with the general run of Bangwa women: her bearing and her elegant clothes set her – and other titled princesses – apart from the humble, tattered appearance of most local wives. Mafwa smoked, walked, talked, and sometimes dressed like a man. She had the right to attend all the men's clubs, secret societies, and rituals; in public gatherings she sat on a raised dais with the chiefs, while the women and children (children being the general classification for untitled men!) found places where best they might.

To me Mafwa was very impressive. She, along with all women of her rank, had the reputation of being rather fast. Princesses were certainly free and easy in their ways and were allowed the kind of freedom not permitted their sisters: they dressed up to the nines, flirted with men, even strangers, stared their equals and betters straight in the face, and lived more or less independent lives. Mafwa had had a husband, one of her father's servants – princesses married only men of low rank, even slaves, to preserve their liberty – but had divorced him not long after their marriage.

On ceremonial occasions Mafwa put on the splendid clothes of royalty, dancing before the crowd in the thickly pleated loin-cloth reserved for chiefs, wearing a man's embroidered waistcoat and elaborately sprouting cap, and waving in her two hands carved ivory horse-tail whisks. This vital, smiling, and shouting figure – lean and boyish despite her fairly advanced years – contrasted strongly with the woman who had drunk beer with me on my balcony the day before in her print dress, white sandals, beaded handbag, and colourful head-scarf.

It was not until some months after I first knew Mafwa that I found out that my rather androgynous princess had her own wife. Not that she had kept it back from me on purpose, but she was simply not the kind of person to volunteer personal information; in any case she was hardly to know that this was the kind of dramatic personal situation which warmed an anthropologist's heart. She had always answered my persistent questions on kinship or magic or history with a precise answer or a straightforward 'I don't know'. And the fact was that I had never thought to ask her – once I knew she had divorced her husband – whether she had a wife! Her compound was a romantic, old-fashioned huddle of three huts, cut off from the rest of the palace behind the patch of forest in the market where important rituals were performed and where royal babies were buried. She had her 'great' house or meeting-house like all Bangwa nobles and a sleeping-house behind it, surrounded by banana trees. I had noticed a woman of her own age who lived in the other house and imagined she was one of the chief's cast-off widows who 'helped her around the house'. As I began to understand some of the language, I heard this woman greeting her with the exaggerated formality of a slave or a wife, calling her 'my master' and sometimes 'my husband' when she brought her food in a carved bowl, and politely leaving the house as she ate it. I considered this an example of 'respect'. The woman had one child and it was only when I heard this small girl call Mafwa 'father' that I knew I was confronted with an example of what anthropologists call by the blunt term 'woman–woman marriage'. I now learned that when the old chief, Mafwa's father, had died his widows had been distributed among his sons and Mafwa had received two – altogether the chief left over a hundred women. Mafwa married these women off to new husbands and pocketed the bridewealth. After a while, good business woman as she was, she decided to invest her capital by marrying her own wife. At least she could now be the father of the children she had and claim the bulk of the bridewealth when her daughters married.

Woman–woman marriage, when it occurs in Africa, serves the same prosaic functions of enabling a wealthy and titled woman to found her own lineage, as 'father' instead of mother. It also allows her to have her own compound, with a wife to cook for her and her own children around, without the overbearing or annoying presence of a husband. Mafwa's wife took a lover (or lovers, this aspect of the business was always kept secret), whether chosen by herself or her 'husband' I don't know.

This kind of marriage is by no means an exceptional case, to be explained by extraordinary mental abnormalities. The marriage of two women presents no problems in cultural anthropology. There are many peoples for whom the *kind* of spouse – his or her status – is much more important than the match they will make together. For this reason they are ready to accept unions which to us would seem not only incredible but in direct contradiction to the aims and purposes of setting up a family. A woman marries another woman. A Bangwa man marries a child, nurses her as a baby, gives her presents as she grows up, and finally cohabits with her sexually after she reaches puberty. A young man may marry an old widow in order to have a wife who farms and cooks for him. I have observed a polygynous group of widows who are married to a child of a few months – while they wait for their husband to grow up they take authorized lovers, their children belonging to their 'legal' husband.

'Husband and wife' are joined in marriage for many purposes – not merely to enjoy sexual intercourse, companionship, or even have children. Marriage is a 'bundle of rights'. The youth who marries a widow marries her for economic services. The small boy married to a woman who takes lovers still has rights in their children. In woman–woman marriage even the normal duality of the sexes is not respected. In Bangwa and other parts of Africa women of high rank are allowed to marry other women and have them bear children through the service of authorized but un-acknowledged lovers, the high-ranking woman becoming the 'father' and transmitting to them her name, status, and wealth. She is just as much a 'husband' as the child of a few months and his harem of wives, or even a senile old man who permits his wives to take lovers and bear children for him. Rights of sexual access and domestic companionship are only some of the aspects involved in marriage. When a Bangwa woman marries another woman, the bridewealth exchanged and the legal provisions of the union make it a correct and real marriage. Technically there is also no reason why two men should not 'marry': the only specific rights not transferred would be those in the 'wife's' biological children, since 'he' would not be able to have them. We shall also discuss some examples of man–man marriage in Africa in the light of single-sex marriages recently publicized in Europe and America.

In this marriage between two women, therefore, I had not stumbled on a unique example of institutionalized friendship between women or a form of sanctioned lesbianism, but a form of union between two women which has already been reported from East Africa, Dahomey, and the Ivory Coast. Nevertheless, behind the façade of etiquette imposed by their formal roles as husband and wife, Mafwa and her spouse were great friends. The mere fact of their long intimacy and their obvious satisfaction in each other's company are evidence of a perfect alliance between two mature women who felt no need of the presence of a male husband.

Writing this I was compelled for some reason to compare Mafwa's life with that of Victoria Sackville-West, whose love affair with Violet Trefusis and marriage with Harold Nicolson had been the subject of a voguish book.¹ Such a comparison is traditionally outside the scope of anthropology but does not seem to me infelicitous. Both Mafwa and Sackville-West were extremely independent women, proud of their rank and lineage and the traditions of the aristocracy to which they belonged. Both were beautiful and conscious of the effect they had on both men and women. One lorded it in a palace of thatched huts and the other in one of the most splendid private houses of England. Mafwa was courted by chiefs, entertained embassies in her father's grand meeting-house and paraded in her finery at the annual dances. Sackville-West won the hearts of dukes' sons, was the debutante of the season, and received her father's peers at Knole. Mafwa judged disputes between her brother's subjects and administered the complex accounts of a large African court. Sackville-West, when still a young girl, acquitted herself notably in two much publicized court cases. The African princess was an accomplished potter, married her own wife, and sought lovers outside the calm domesticity of her own compound. The English woman wrote novels, married a homosexual, and fell in love with members of her own sex.

Two oddly assorted households – one composed of two women, husband and wife, and their children; the other, two English homosexuals and their two children. Both the African and the English women could have been said to have 'made out of a non-marriage a marriage which succeeded beyond their dreams'. Both had the satisfaction of children, the delight of outside lovers, and the permanent security of married life and a family. Both couples had injected a formal relationship with a quiet love which provided warmth and psychological satisfaction. In the African marriage, however, two women found their psychological satisfactions in themselves as women. In the English situation, part of the reason for the calm loyalty and loving complementarity of Sackville-West and Nicolson lay in the fact that each sought lovers – of the same sex, as it happened – outside their almost totally asexual marriage.

We know very little about the secret lovers of Mafwa and her wife, apart from the fact that they would have been chosen from the myriad of eligible bachelors living in the neighbourhood of the Bangwa palace. Victoria Sackville-West has revealed in her autobiography her romantic passion for Violet Trefusis during the early years of her marriage and her son has disclosed the existence of many others. Had these two women, in their different ways, found an answer to the problems inherent in sexual and romantic love? By excluding sexuality and jealousy from the domestic scene, a friendship grew up between husband and wife which kept the relationship on an even keel – no storms of jealousy, no calms of boredom, no threat of divorce. Both couples believed, in their different ways, that people of the same sex can love and that a marriage deeply rooted in mutual affection need not suffer as the result of 'infidelity' – if that is the right word in the Bangwa situation! – but can be enriched by it.

A perfect arrangement or a peculiar one?

If nothing else, Sackville-West has placed women fairly and squarely on the map of love. She had no idea of any moral distinction between homosexual and heterosexual love and when she discovered the Lesbian side of her nature Mrs Victoria Nicolson accepted it wholeheartedly. In her account of the affair she confesses to a conscious feeling of androgyny, a dual personality in which the feminine and the masculine elements alternately preponderated. Differently, but interestingly, the African princess saw no difficulty in marrying a man or marrying a woman. Both women indulged male and female leanings equally, although Mafwa was never a Lesbian. Sackville-West even proposed a 'reconstruction of the system' of marriage – did she propose marriage between persons of the same sex, if they are heterosexuals, with physical love enjoyed outside matrimony (as in woman–woman marriage); and marriage between persons of different sex – if they are homosexuals – with sex again satisfied outside marriage? The idea of separating marriage and sex may seem an outrageous prospect, but not an impossible one in a world where the disruptive effects of passion may be unwanted and unnecessary in marriage which aims at companionship rather than the procreation of children.

Once we begin talking in this way, you may object, all kinds of marriages become possible – between two women, between two men, why not between a man and his dog? The Reverend Troy Perry who began a church for homosexuals in California celebrates marriage between men and between women. Californian law recognizes all marriages between partners who can show a certificate from an ordained minister proving that their marriage has been solemnized in a church ceremony. The law does not stipulate that the partners should be a man and a woman, only a 'husband and wife'; and in the wedding ceremony the word spouse is substituted for the usual terms. The marriage of homosexuals who are in love, however, hardly fits into the schema demonstrated by Mafwa and her wife and the Nicolsons, since there it is modelled on heterosexual married love and there is still the possibility of sexual strife, jealousy, the waning of passion, divorce, a new affair and remarriage.

Similar marriages between men, in which at least one of the partners is homosexual, have been reported among the American Indians and some African peoples. In North America, effeminate youths who did not wish to enter the lists as daring and warlike braves assumed the dress, the role, and the attitudes of women and cohabited with normal heterosexual males. Among the Nuba,[2] marriages between older men and youths were apparently fairly common although these homosexual marriages were for a limited time. Here it was the older man who was the passive partner, dressed as a woman, and performing all the functions of a good Nuban wife. After a period of homosexuality the youth normally married a woman. In one case a man was married to two wives, one man and one woman, but was forced to get rid of the former due to their furiously jealous quarrels. Among the Nuba, as among married Californian homosexuals, marriage was frankly sexual, although the companionship between husband and wife, who were both men, was emphasized. An important factor in Nuban marriage – as far as the heterosexual partners are concerned – is that the men are convinced that continuous sex with women is debilitating and detracts from their prized virility and general strength as farmers and warriors. Homosexual relations lack these disadvantages!

Homosexual marriages of this kind are not examples of companionship marriage of the sort I would place side by side with the Sackville-West–Nicolson union, since their prime motive is obviously sexual and they suffer the same ups and downs as normal marriage or Californian unisex marriage. Fortunately I have one good example of marriage between men in which the motive is asexual love.

It was precisely during an intensive investigation into the – ultimately non-proven – homosexuality of the Nzema of Southern Ghana, that an Italian anthropologist[3] 'unearthed' this apparently unique form of marriage between men. Reacting to his persistent enquiries about sodomy the Nzema stoutly denied it – 'Not even two men who are married to each other and sleep in the same bed would do such a thing!' From this beginning the investigator ceased to work on the homosexual theme and began his more fruitful enquiries into Nzema friendship. Nzema men 'fall in love', form bond friendships, share their beds, and even marry, but they do not have sex.

Apparently bond friendship is common among the Nzema. Once two men become friends they make a pact which is accompanied by libations to the ancestors; from then on their love is reinforced by formal and informal rights and obligations. They help with money in times of debt, they play a special role at the funeral of the bond friend. If they have wives, they keep an eye on them when one of the friends is on a journey. Apparently adultery with the wife of a bond friend is 'impossible', even though she may be called 'my wife'.

The Nzema are frank about the attraction of members of the same sex towards each other. 'I loved him because he was beautiful', or because the friend is kind-hearted or 'speaks well'. Here is a circumstantial account of two men who became best friends.

Steven Enda was fifteen years old and had a friend called Sando, who was thirty-five and a latrine attendant. They had met for the first time when Sando first arrived to take up his job and asked Steven the way to his lodging. Sando was apparently very impressed by the youth's beautiful hands. After a long chat the older man asked the boy to draw some water for him and told him to come back in the morning. Steven came back and cleaned his house. Sando wanted to make friends with Steven properly and they went to the compound of Steven's mother where Sando was formally presented as his friend. The mother expressed her contentment with the arrangement and advised her son to behave well towards Sando, who seemed to her to have a 'good mind'.

Steven then moved into Sando's compound and slept with him every night.

This story of two friends is a prosaic illustration of how a friendship is formed in Nzema. In our own society the suspicion of homosexuality would be immediately cast on this relationship – Sando loved the boy's hands, asked to be his friend, and shared a bed with him. In most African situations the idea of sex between two men involved in friendship would simply not occur. I mentioned earlier the Nzema case of friendships between men and women in which, again, sexuality did not arise.

Sando did not make Steven his wife. In other cases marriage may result from initial ties of bond friendship, a man asking his friend's parents for his hand in marriage. If accepted, bride-wealth is paid to the parents of the 'bride' and a marriage ceremony takes place. Ideally everything happens as it does in a normal union between a man and woman – apart from sex. The male wife calls his husband's other wives by the usual Nzema term meaning 'my rival'. If the 'wife' has his own wife or wives, the husband will also call them his 'rivals'. The laws of exogamy which apply to spouses also apply here – no man may marry his male wife's sister, mother, or daughter.

Both formally and psychologically Nzema man–man marriage is a real marriage even if it is not consummated. Even divorce is envisaged. A man marries another man because of his character or his physical beauty or because he wants to gain prestige by the presence of a male wife in his compound. According to the ethnographer the physical attraction between the two men is important despite the asexual nature of the union. In many ways, of course, despite the odd nature of the ceremony binding the two men, their love is no different from that of a Jonathan and a David, an Amis and an Amiloun. Like these bond friendships, Nzema love is reinforced by a ritual pact. Two men, not in the least homosexual, fall in love with members of their own sex and enjoy a relationship which provides as much aesthetic and psychological pleasure as the love of a man and a woman.

Here are two cases of man–man marriage among the Nzema:

Noba of Bonyere was thirty when he met twenty-year-old Ambrose and was struck by his attractive physical appearance and his powers of oratory. He asked the man to marry him, was accepted, and received the blessing of both the mother and father. Noba gave a gun and £1.10 as bridewealth and then went with his 'wife' to Bonyere, where they remained together with Noba's first wife – a woman – who was quite happy about the arrangement. Later Ambrose went home, returning to visit his husband once a week. Later still, when Ambrose found a suitable girl and wanted to marry her, he told Noba who gave his approval only after he had met the girl and she had made a good impression on him. Noba contributed to the bridewealth and explained to the girl the nature of the ties between himself and Ambrose so that she should not be jealous. The girl expressed no objections and the two of them continued to visit Noba. About ten years before this story was being told, Noba became a leading member of the Apostolic Church and moved to Kumasi where he followed his profession as priest-healer. Since then Ambrose has been to visit his husband only twice, on each occasion sleeping in the same bed with him, the wife moving out to a makeshift bed in the porch.

In another case, an elderly man named Aboagya married a youth named Bile Kaku, paid £2 to the father and gave cloth, soap, mirrors, talcum powder, and a comb to his bride. The presents were brought by two messengers, a woman and a man, in the customary way. The husband also gave the youth's husband a bottle of gin, since he would have to make a libation to the ancestors. After the wedding banquet Bile Kaku was led to his husband's compound and slept with him in his bed. During the early days of the marriage the husband provided his 'wife' with a woman for his enjoyment. According to the narrator the man married the youth in order 'to have a beautiful person near him' and to publicly demonstrate he was worth the large expense of the wedding.

This book has turned out *not* to be about the erotic nature of friendship, mainly due to the nature of the material. Very few of the examples of friendship and love between members of the same sex have any overt homoerotic element and in some instances it is actually taboo. Our own culture has thought fit to overlay historical and mythical friendships with a supposed homosexuality. Even D. H. Lawrence's tortured attitudes to the possibility of male love caused him to misread the friendship of David and Jonathan. In ancient Israel close relations between warriors and youths, expressed in florid terms, were the rule and even if they were given a degree of physical expression they in no way interfered with the normal uxoriousness of the two men. David was passionately in love with Jonathan's sister Michal and when he was sent into exile without her he was distraught at the thought of her being in the arms of another. There is not a hint of any physical passion between Jonathan and David apart from a bad-tempered but scarcely credited imputation made by Saul to Jonathan when the latter was protecting his friend against the king. Between Amis and Amiloun there is no hint of a homosexual element in their love, despite the fact that sodomy was a familiar fourteenth-century vice. Sodomy in medieval times was considered the very antithesis of romantic friendship.

It is maligning friendship always to associate it with sex, and silly to assume that physical contact is in itself evidence of homosexuality. Hrothgar embraces Beowulf, Dr Johnson was always kissing Boswell, Roman soldiers in Tacitus fell on each other's necks when their legions were dispersed. To imagine homosexuality in these situations is a sad comment on our modern fear of physical contact.

What about the Greeks, then? – Achilles and Patroclus, Orestes and Pylades? Homer is surely only depicting normal friendship between heterosexual males. Achilles' exuberant grief at Patroclus' death was the usual behaviour of the times in those circumstances. He wept in his tent for a bond-friend, not a lover; and his sentiments towards Patroclus are more profitably compared with those of Roland and Oliver, or two Bangwa or Nzema friends, than with the homosexual love supposedly felt by Plato for Dion. Plato and his friends, overt homosexuals without a doubt, read a sexual element into Homer's friendships, transferring their own subjective sentiments to a quite different situation.

Greek homosexual love of the fourth century was passionate and genital, pederasty gilded by philosophy and the morals of friendship. As far as Plato himself was concerned, romantic passion – a mad, God-sent affliction – was only possible between men and boys. Plato loved his Dion romantically. In poems attributed to Plato we feel the sense of suffocation produced by the appearance of this young man, his wonderful beauty and stature, his train of adorers, the children who could not help staring at him, and, above all, his own agitation as Dion casts his eyes in Plato's direction. Dion was beautiful in both body and soul, and Plato's love for him survived the test of time and his passion for other men. Even Dion's twenty years' absence in Sicily did not allay his love.

Plato's love for Dion remained a model for many ideas about romantic love until the medieval period – a romantic love not, of course, restricted to pederasts. The whole homosexual situation was cast in the same mould as our modern romantic love for women, the love for boys causing frenzy and divine favour. For Plato this passionate love enabled him to see, through the medium of terrestrial beauty, the beauty that was eternal. He later came to sublimate the sexual aspects and in so doing prepared the way for Christian love – *agape* – the dissociation between soul and body which added its own flavour to European ideas of romantic love and provided the basis for popular notions of platonic love.

Platonic friendships in ancient Athens were hardly chaste. Sexual experiences, even orgies, were supposed to bring about catharsis and purgation to both body and soul – the embrace of a male prostitute and a pretty boy led to salvation! – an inconceivable notion if applied to the opposite sex, at least according to the pederasts.

However, it would be a mistake to consider homosexual loving in Greece as the rule. It was certainly never condoned by the man in the street or by the city laws and it was mercilessly mocked in Aristophanes' plays. The explanation we have more or less accepted for this element of pederasty is that women were not fit companions for Athenian intellectuals. A woman lived a life of obscurity, illiteracy, and devotion to the household if she were poor, or dress and cosmetics if she were the wife of a rich man. According to received ideas the Greeks, like the Moslems in a later epoch, did not even expect the refinements of romantic loving from women. They defended their passionate attachment to boys on the plea that the company of youths was so much more entertaining than that of women, with their total lack of education and sensitivity. In praising the mind and the soul as well as the body of a boy, the Greeks gave their genital perversities a complex, romantic justification.

I wonder if we have not misread history again in the interests of the modern situation encouraged by members of monastic colleges and effeminate intellectuals in nineteenth- and twentieth-century England. I do not see how homosexuality can be gilded merely by pointing out that women are cloistered, untutored, and uninteresting. Moreover, sophisticated women were available, as Demosthenes made clear: 'Courtesans we keep for pleasure, concubines for daily [sexual] attendance on our persons and wives to bear us legitimate children and to be our housekeepers.' The housewife was a respected slave – but then she almost always is. In Bangwa, Mafwa with her accomplishments and fine clothes was hardly the same creature as the naked wife, slaving in her *cocoyam* farm any more than Vita Sackville-West was in any way comparable with the 'dreary slut of a housemaid' who got in her way on a London doorstep when she was visiting her lover. Athenians, English, and Bangwa appreciated the value of a highly civilized woman. 'They [the Greeks of fourth-century Athens] knew that without an admixture of the feminine point of view and the feminine reaction, without feminine taste, perception, intuition, wit, subtlety, devotion, perversity, and scepticism, a civilization must be lopsided and incomplete.' Clive Bell (in *Civilization*)[4] shows quite clearly that Athenians not only had their pretty boys, but they also had their courtesans or *hetairae* – a word which derives from the Greek for friend or companion. Their role was not to be sexually attractive but to be 'exquisitely civilized demi-mondaines'. If Greek civilization had been studied more by clear-sighted women than by cloistered bachelors we might have had greater emphasis on the values of friendship between Greek intellectuals and these women. We know that *hetairae* were girls of exceptional intelligence with a liking for independence who were respected, even adored, by heterosexual Athenians, but were distinguished more by their wit and intellectual powers of fascination than by their beauty. These women certainly counted for something appreciable in

Athenian civilization and exerted an influence over their age – they even sat at the feet of Plato.

My own country, Australia, has a tradition of friendship which lacks its Plato, but has instead the misogynist Henry Lawson, who is perhaps the most widely known of Australian 'folk-poets'. He was of Norwegian descent and was born in a tent on the New South Wales goldfields in 1867. A bushworker in boyhood, he moved from job to job across the continent in the nomadic Australian bush tradition, using his experiences to write short stories such as 'While the Billy Boils', 'On the Track', and 'Over the Sliprails', successfully interpreting the humorous and tragic events of the outback and the city. His style is natural and direct, although sometimes flawed by excessive sentimentality. Again we have the theme of a masculine society without women of the companionable kind, which led to the development of intense male friendships – in this case, however, open homosexuality did *not* flourish as a result. Mateship has its roots in the early colonial period and was a functional friendship between lonely men in the bush: later it was portrayed by writers as a sentimental passion and provided the theme for countless novels, stories, and songs extolling the companionship of stock-riders, tramps, and goldminers. Today it is slowly being de-bunked – particularly by writers like Patrick White – although in the Australian armed forces and particularly between members of the Returned Soldiers League (Australia's powerful and conservative clubs of former soldiers) the 'china plate' – the mate – is still a living force.

As an honourable institution, mateship began with the mutual regard and trust between men working together in the lonely bush, men whose isolation and need for cooperation called for mutual helpfulness. Cooperation was the first essential of survival, but the eternal search for gold and fresh frontiers in the outback obviously carried overtones which went beyond mere materialism and affected the once straightforward relation between mates. There grew up the idea of a kind of holy grail, the 'bonanza', which helped bind men together in a mystical friendship: Lawrence exploits it well in his novel *Kangaroo*. The chief article of faith was that mates should 'stick together'. This was and still is the one law which the good Australian should never break and has even, in a strange way, become bred into the way of thinking and behaving of the large majority of Australians who live in the towns and cities of Melbourne, Sydney, Adelaide, and Brisbane. At their best, many Australian values were based on the miner's and the stockrider's ideal of friendship, the co-operation between men bound to a common life of hard toil and often futile hopes.

Mateship has been explained by the absence of women in the outback and in the mines. More so than in the Greek case, there seems to be some justification since Australian women hardly existed as sexual, domestic, or intellectual partners. Mates provided fellowship, protection in times of trouble, and sanity during extreme loneliness – they were also cooks, launderers, but not, apparently, sexual objects. True mateship was confined usually to two men and only exceptionally extended to three or four. Their intimacy depended to a great extent on the complete loyalty exacted from each other which was naturally expected to override loyalty to kin or wife. In 'That Pretty Girl in the Army', Henry Lawson writes:

> A bushman always has a mate to comfort him and argue with him, and work and tramp and drink with him and lend him quids when he's hard up, and call him a b— fool and fight him sometimes, to abuse him to his face and defend his name behind his back, to bear false witness for him . . .; to secure a 'pen' for him at a [shearing] shed when he isn't on the spot . . . And each would take the word of the other against the world and each believes that the other is the straightest chap that ever lived, a White man.

It was a relationship as highly charged and emotional as that between Pedro and Juan in Guatemala and jealous scenes were not infrequent. Mateship, however, lasted. It was a complete union between two men which was as close if not closer than marriage, based on complete understanding and sympathy between two persons living and working together in daily partnership. It continued, ideally, until death.

Nineteenth-century Australian life has many parallels with the traditionally accepted view of Plato's Athens. The few women were relegated to 'womanly' – that is, domestic – roles, and cultural values were and still are based on masculine ethics which are relics of pioneering days in the bush and goldmine. Even today conversation between an Australian man and woman is an embarrassing and often empty experience since they usually have nothing to say to each other. Go to an Australian country dance, watch groups of Australian mates bumbling around the door with their beer cans comfortingly stored in the boots of their cars, and then watch the girls hopelessly herded to one side of the dance hall. Talk to groups of bored Australians on unisex groups as they do their tour of Europe – more intent on covering the distances than anything else. Analyse Barry MacKenzie cartoons and the strange male obsession with other males, toilets, beer cans, penises, peeing, and vomiting. The emptiness of much Australian culture, evident in the conversation of most individual Australians, may be due to their traditional and vociferous flight from women. Australian men even drink alone. When I was in Australia, women who were bold enough to enter the sacred precincts of the men's 'hotel' were relegated to a dark, smelly hole called the 'Ladies' Lounge', usually down the passage to the men's toilet. There they sat with their port and lemon or cherry brandy fluffed up with advocaat and dry ginger ale and waited patiently while their men celebrated male togetherness and mateship, downing gallons of frothy beer.

It will be clear that modern Australian mateship is a far cry from the friendships forged in loneliness and converted by eulogists of the outback way of life into a myth for the consumption of frustrated stockmen living in their bungalows in the great Australian urban sprawl. As an Australian writing about mateship, a strange flavour of mixed mawkish and decent sentiments comes back to me over the years. At school we read the sentimental tales of Henry Lawson, of the bush mates who died for each other, the tramp and his faithful 'mate' – his dog. As an adolescent I remember those black months of failure when I was without a mate. Without his own special 'cobber', an Australian child, youth, or adult – male, of course – is scarcely integrated into local or national life. Mateship may be reality for a bushworker or for soldiers fighting in foul tropical weather, supporting each other in spite of wounds or the danger of imminent capture. There comes, however, an inevitable sentimentalization, played out in the beery friendships of ex-soldiers of the R.S.L. clubs.

Even mateship has been subjected to the slur of homosexuality. Australians, of course, are loud in their denials, without of course knowing anything about the real situation of goldminers and stockriders who did not see a woman from one month, even from one year, to the next. Australians have a panicky fear of homosexuality and only a foreigner who happened to be a professor of obstetrics at Sydney University would dare to brave Australian men's furious reaction by a statement like this: 'I have no real grounds for this but I've always suspected the Australian male is undersexed, if anything. Many countries seem to have their obsessions – France with the liver, Britain with constipation, America with a combination of psychiatry and male – yes male – penis envy. Australia's is with the mateship thing.'⁵ We may wonder for ever whether the mate who tramped the outback and his friend were not more than platonic companions. Henry Lawson's stories are told by a character who is a yarnspinner with a pathological hatred of women. And while it is certainly true that the male–male bond is much more highly valued than any male–female tie it would be wrong to give the love of a man for his mate, a relationship which provides many touching and curious stories, any openly homosexual imperative.

Another writer, an outsider, D. H. Lawrence, was fascinated by mateship but I think struck the wrong note by injecting a high degree of physical attraction into friendships between Australian men. Lawrence's belief in his own bisexual nature made him attribute a life-enhancing, nourishing homosexual love to affection between working-class mates. He takes mateship, spiritualizes it, glorifies it, and sexualizes it. Simple colliers and mechanics talk of the beauties of friendship and love between males like members of Plato's *Symposium*. 'Mate love,' says the Australian hero. 'He is my mate. A depth of unfathomed, unrealized love can go into that phrase: My mate is waiting for me, a man says, and turns away from wife and children, mother and all. The love of a man for his mate.' Again: 'You can't make bricks without straw. That is, you can't hold together the friable mixture of a modern mankind without a new cohesive principle.

And this will be the new passion of man's absolute trust in his mate, his love for his mate.' Along with a very real physical expression Lawrence injects a nightmare note of hard sadism into the personality of these diggers, which is again sexual in effect. 'Cripes, there is *nothing* bucks you up sometimes like killing a man – *nothing*. You can feel a perfect *angel* after it.' 'Having a woman's something isn't it? But it's a fleabite, nothing compared to killing your man when your blood comes up.' The same character expresses another Lawrence bogey: 'You won't give in to women, Mr Somer, will you? You won't give in.' The passion of mateship comes out again: ' "If we was mates, I'd stick to you through hell fire and back . . ." As he spoke he was pale and tense with emotion, and his eyes were like black holes, almost wounds in the pallor of his face.'

Lawrence brought a great writer's art to the difficult job of putting into words the often unexpressed love of friends, and succeeded in an extraordinary way in recording some aspects of mateship, as well as Australian urban life and landscape. Unfortunately the novel's emphasis on the physical nature of friendship has made Australians suspect even more the purity of the love of mates. Australians regard homosexuality with an out-and-out dread, rather than mockery, distaste, or disgust; and it is seen as an immediate and personal threat to each individual and even the whole Australian way of life. Swaggering about sexual exploits, dirty jokes, manly manners – all become an attempt to prove you and your mates are as straight as apple pie. Even the physical expression of friendship has been reduced to a strangely ritualistic feinting – as between sparring partners. Australian friends do not hold hands in the street like Trobrianders, caress each other like Bangwa friends, kiss when they meet like Italians, or sleep together like the Nzema, but greet each other with the flamboyant punches and hearty backslapping of professional boxers!

To end this chapter I should like to include a light-hearted parallel of male friendship from the animal world, where friendly, even passionate, relationships between male ganders, remarkably similar to the mateship situation, have been reported by Konrad Lorenz.[6] When a stalwart young gander makes a triumph-rite proposal to another male, instead of a female, the two males each find a better dancing-partner and friendly companion than they would have done if they had chosen the normal way – at least in so far as this all-important triumph ceremony is concerned. Two gander mates, in performing triumph ceremonies, stimulate each other to acts of courage and attain high places in the ranking order of the colony. Like Australian friends they keep together for life, just as faithfully as a pair of heterosexual individuals:

> When we separated our oldest gander pair, Max and Kopschlitz, and sent Max to our branch colony on the Ampersee near Fürstenfeld-bruck, after a year of mourning both ganders paired with female geese and bred successfully, but when we fetched Max back – without his wife and children whom we could not catch – Kopschlitz immediately deserted his family and returned to him. Kopschlitz's wife and sons seemed to understand the situation and they made furious but un-successful attempts to drive Max away.

This series of events almost directly parallels a Henry Lawson story, 'Meeting Old Mates', in which two mates effect a senti-mental reconciliation after the marriage of one had separated them after long years in the bush.

Unlike human homosexuals, but like Australian mates, Lorenz's ganders seldom copulated or performed substitute actions, although in the spring they could be seen celebrating, with graceful neck-dipping, the ceremony of pre-copulatory display together. In a case like this a goose learns to follow the two ganders at a respectful distance if she happens to fall in love with one of them – like the patient Australian wife, perhaps? When the ganders make unsuccessful efforts to copulate she cunningly learns to push herself between them and remain in an attitude of readiness when the male of her choice is trying to mount the other. After they have mated, her gander returns to his friend and addresses the ceremony of post-copulatory display to *him*. In some cases a goose would wait in a certain area of the pond for her gander, who immediately after mating flew straight back across the pond to his friend. 'She never seems to take offence.' And in the gander such a loveless copulatory relation-ship with a female becomes a habit.

Australian mateship and the relationship between the sexes

are paralleled rather comically in this situation between friendly ganders, with the goose left out in the cold – in the Ladies' Lounge. I must stress here that any use made of animal behaviour in this book is done in a light-hearted, unscientific way, since the present state of knowledge does not allow us to make direct comparisons between human antics and those of animals.

I should not like to leave this discussion of Australian friendship without stressing its importance as an institution which provided Australians with a continuing tradition of disinterested devotion to friends, often existing throughout the lifetime of two mates without ceremony or ritual, formal gift exchange or legal sanction. Mateship also played a role in the development of social equality and the strong Australian democratic tradition. Socialists extended the idea of this intense personal relationship between mates in a bush environment and elevated it into an inspiring political ideal – it became the basis of a concept of a communistic Utopia in the form of a fraternal socialist society.

3   Friends in Blood

Few writers have treated friendship between men with the seriousness of D. H. Lawrence and the theme of several of his novels is the hero's search for a satisfying relationship with a man, paralleled by a mutually destructive conflict between a man and a woman. Lawrence's friendships are explicitly modelled on the biblical friendship of David and Jonathan but he adds erotic undertones to their spiritual, asexual union.

In his play *David*,[1] Lawrence has the heroes say:

JONATHAN: We have sworn a covenant, is it not, between us? Wilt thou not swear with me, that our souls shall be as brothers, closer even than the blood? O David, my heart has no peace save all be well between thy soul and mine, and thy blood and mine.

DAVID: As the Lord liveth, the soul of Jonathan is dearer to me than a brother's. O brother, if I were but come out of this pass, and we might live before the Lord, together.

Jonathan and David represent a model of loving friendship and a perfect reciprocity of feeling: they wanted to be one soul, one blood, and live together for ever. The mere expression of these sentiments, however, was not enough and the two men swore a covenant. In our own society equal and harmonious love is not considered to need the backing of a ceremonial pact. Friendship should be 'free', 'pure', and based on moral obligations alone. Unlike most societies, we have no means of embellishing friendship with ritual or pact, and except in the children's playground it is not even allowed an exchange of vows.

In *Women in Love*,[2] Lawrence attacks the theme again, putting the idea of a blood pact into Birkin's head:

'You know how the old German knights used to swear a Blütbruderschaft,' he said to Gerald, with quite a new happy activity in his eyes.

75

'Make a little wound in their arms, and rub each other's blood into the cut?' said Gerald.

'Yes – and swear to be true to each other, of one blood, all their lives. That is what we ought to do. No wounds, that is obsolete. But we ought to love each other, you and I, implicitly, and perfectly, finally, without any possibility of going back on it.'

Many societies consider friendship to be as important as marriage and hedge it in with oaths, ceremony, and ritual. Blood brotherhood has been a well-nigh universal means of both formally and magically cementing close friendships and alliances between two or more men. Instances are common in both history and ethnography: Herodotus mentions it for the Scythians and also for the Medes and Persians. It seems to have been widely known as a pre-Christian rite in Europe as well, since we hear of it in the Norse Sagas and the Irish Sagas. It was apparently common in the Welsh highlands up to the seventeenth century. In the Old English version of the *Gesta Romanorum* we read: 'If so be that thou wold do after my consaile, I pray the let me drinke thi blood and thou shalt drink myne in tokening that neither of us shall forsake other in wele ne in woo.' Descriptions of the practice among the Russians, the Slavs, and the Turks are given in a comprehensive study devoted to the subject.[3]

Blood pacts usually achieve more or less the same ends: two persons who are friends or who wish to become allies for a specific purpose, enter into a dyadic relationship which is sanctified by the ritual of the exchange of blood. The rite endows a purely sentimental relationship with important supernatural sanctions – having shared each other's blood the couple are considered to have part of each other's essence or being. Blood is universally considered a highly suitable vehicle for such abstract concepts, although in some societies saliva may be exchanged to make similar kinds of bonds, or beer or milk may be sprayed into the friend's mouth. In English playgrounds, as we have seen, saliva was an important ingredient in friendship rites. The sticky substance – the red blood, the spittle – forms a *quasi* material or organic bond between the two persons whose complicity and trust is further strengthened by the threat of a curse if one of them should betray the other's trusting love. I doubt whether Lawrence was aware of the nature of the blood symbolism – the blood is not merely an emotional expression of reciprocal love, but acts as a magical sanction against the failure of the bonds of friendship. Perhaps our understanding of the magical elements in Christian communion would be enhanced if we considered the wine – the transformed blood of Christ – as a kind of earnest not to sin against his name. We have a little bit inside us of the 'friend we have in Jesus' which keeps us to the straight and narrow track of Christian morality, at least until the next communion.

Blood pacts, therefore, add a magical dimension to friendship. Blood brothers are friends in the last resort not only because they are motivated by sentiment but because if they fail to abide by the contract, if they fail to help each other 'in wele and in woo', the blood will cause illness or death by virtue of its supernatural power. However, it would be wrong to make the magical nature of the contract the primary one, either in friendship or Holy Communion; the exchange of blood, like the exchange of vows between a bride and groom, usually reinforce already existing bonds of affection. And even in political alliances celebrated by blood pacts, affection and sentiment between the allies is always enjoined.

Details of blood friendships were first described in detail by European travellers and missionaries in Africa and the South Seas. Curiously enough, even the proudest and most dogmatically Christian of them seemed quite pleased to undergo these exchanges and accepted the pagan rite with equanimity. In many cases journeys and longer sojourns among some peoples would have been impossible without the friendship of the local authorities and self-interest probably dictated their compliance. The procedure was usually much the same: having mixed his blood with that of a native chief, sometimes added to wine or gin or food, an imprecatory formula was pronounced and the travellers were assured of the complete protection of their blood brother throughout the territory under his control. Sometimes it was sufficient to make an incision in the forearm and rub the bleeding wounds together so that the blood of both partners was mixed. A particularly queasy traveller sometimes persuaded his future blood brother to accept a servant as proxy. Stanley was forced to go through the operation every time he had to buy or beg for food in the Congo villages he passed through. In Unyamwezi he made a blood pact with a chief called Mirambo, who had a fearful reputation in the region, and the imprecation made went like this: 'If either of you break the brotherhood vow established between you, may the lion devour him, the serpent poison him, his gun burst in his hands and wound him and everything bad do wrong to him until his death.'

The Bangwa and neighbouring tribes of the Cameroon were no strangers to these political blood pacts. Chiefs made temporary alliances with visiting German colonial agents and traders looking for wild rubber and ivory. In the 1890s one of these, Conrau, made his way from the forest up the Bangwa escarpment in a search for labourers for the new German plantations in the south. He was forced to stay a long time, persuading the chief to round up some unwilling men. During this time he collected Bangwa sculpture and became, according to his own admission, great friends with the hospitable and generous chief, Assunganyi. Assunganyi at this time was about thirty years of age, very attractive, and a great dancer. He entertained Conrau with performances of jujus and made him gifts of local ivory and brassware; he also showed a great interest in German goods and ideas. According to Bangwa folklore, the German agent became the lover of Assunganyi's sister – Mafwa's aunt and the titled princess of the time. Conrau and Assunganyi became blood brothers in order to celebrate their friendship, the two men drinking from a bottle of trade gin mixed with their blood. On the strength of his friendship with the German, backed by the blood pact, Assunganyi persuaded his councillors to let him take away seventy of his subjects to the plantations. A year later, Conrau came back alone – most of the men had in fact died from nostalgia, forest diseases, and the general effects of plantation labour. Assunganyi considered that Conrau had broken his side of the bargain implicit in the blood pact and in the ensuing quarrel the German agent was shot and killed. Sorrowfully Assunganyi ordered Conrau's head removed from the body after the correct period of inhumation and prepared it ritually for its place in the family skull cult. Some Bangwa, less respectful of European feelings, declared that his mistress had delighted a huge crowd at a local funeral by dancing a victory march wearing the dead German's scalp.

Blood pacts were the rule between local chiefs and Germans at this time. Zintgraff, the first explorer of the central highlands of German Kamerun, has left us a vividly detailed account of two such alliances:[4]

I left Fobessong in no doubt that I suspected him of treacherous designs and that seemed to impress him so he offered me blood relationship the next day. At that time I regarded this festive ceremony as a pretence for begging and did not have much faith in its particularly binding strength, but on Muyenga's advice I agreed to it. As a matter of fact he maintained that a blood relationship would be regarded as a holy pact in this part of the world.

In the gloom of my house we sat – Fobessong and I – on round carved stools, facing each other, a jug of palm wine in front of us and our two interpreters at our feet. With a razor we made incisions in each other's forearms so that the blood oozed out. Then we squeezed the blood into my tea mug, which served as both a mixing and drinking cup. Thereupon Fobessong gave me some pepper to chew, while I split a kola nut into two parts, handing one of them to him. He took some and pepper as well. When they had been chewed up each of us had to put the mess on the freshly cut wound on his arm so that some blood was absorbed into this odd plaster. Then – and this needed something of an effort – I had to remove with my mouth, and without the help of my hands, the peculiar paste from Fobessong's extremely dirty arm and swallow it, while he did the same to me. Finally we rinsed the whole thing down with blood-tinted wine from the tea cup, but not before Fobessong had stirred it up well with his revoltingly filthy fingernail. Our two interpreters also got something to drink before the oath formula was announced. Between Fobessong and myself there should be only *one* word. For himself he would allow no evil to overcome me, at least within his village. For my own part I promised to shield Fobessong from his enemies, in the same way. If either of the partners to the pact should betray the other his belly would swell up within nine days and a horrible death would ensue. It would have been against the custom not to drink innumerable mugs of palm wine to celebrate the union . . .

My interpreter, Muyenga, informed me during the feast that with the blacks a blood relationship is the same as an oath on the Bible for a Christian. The blood relationship is altogether a solemn communion for the black man. Now there would be no danger, we could be quite certain . . .

[The next day] after Fobessong had been presented with a few rockets and an old ship's bell which I had taken from Defang as booty, we went on our way at seven o'clock. He sent his brothers, his prime minister as well as his personal slave retainer with us, he himself taking leave of us at the market place . . . First of all he repeated that he had spoken truth fully and that no danger would threaten me although he was not responsible for anything that happened to me outside his village. Afterwards he took hold of both my hands, and in order to 'blow away' all bad spirits he spat lightly on my hands and then on my face so as to make my Vai servants who stood around whisper 'bush nigger'. I quietened them, since although the farewell was a little extraordinary and certainly not the best drawing room manners, everything was well meant.

Fobessong proved a very reliable friend and ally of the expedition, which was very important to me since he and his mountain villagers entirely dominated the approaches to the Grasslands on this side.

Later Zintgraff made another blood covenant with Galega, Fon of Bali, whose words to him were:

'You came, white man, into my house like a chicken and I could easily have killed and robbed you of your treasures. But since you have been staying with me I have learnt the white man's way. Of course there are many of my people who want me to kill you. However do not fear anything. I shall cause you no harm, nor shall I permit any other man to do so. It is best to learn the ways of white men and to have them as friends and a continual benefit rather than take a shortsighted advantage by robbing them.

Zintgraff adds, à propos the blood pact:

Here in the Grasslands the blood relationship is a religious institution by which as far as it is at all possible under human conditions the holiness of the pact has an unconditional guarantee. The ceremony is not always the same . . . however the drinking of your partner's blood, the 'mixing of the two bodies', and the joining of both body and soul forms the main characteristic of the rite. That is why Galega used to say in his dramatic way 'Although we have two bellies, we have only one head.'

I have included Zintgraff's description of these blood pacts since although they are obviously superficial in their grasp of the meaning of the blood pact to Africans in day-to-day living, they are marvellously evocative and enlightening about their political function. The initial aim of the pact between the white explorer and the local chiefs was to procure mutual assistance, obligations of hospitality and unconditional help for Zintgraff when he should need it, and the benefit of the white man's friendship and goods for the chiefs. The blood was clearly seen as the organic vehicle of a tremendous curse – should one ally betray the other his belly would swell up within nine days and a horrible death would ensue. 'A horrible death' includes dropsy even today in the Cameroon; if such a death occurs the body is considered a pollutant, it is jettisoned in the bush and no funeral made. A death of this kind requires costly and complex rites over a period of forty days to purify the people and the land.

It is important to note that after the ceremony Zintgraff and the chiefs did become friendly. The pact itself seemed to encourage a community of interest, and inspired Zintgraff with a respect for the dirty-fingered chief. He received his unorthodox blessing and manifestations of friendship the next morning with more than usual good grace.

The significance of the blood in the rite is also brought out by his interpreter's insistence that the exchange of the blood between the two men was like an oath taken by Christians on the Bible and was a 'solemn communion for a black man'. It was this very exchange of blood, this pagan communion between two men rather than a communion with the Christian God, which caused the Church to attack blood brotherhood in medieval Europe and colonial Africa. In most cases it succeeded in destroying it – in Europe and Latin America blood brotherhood was replaced by a friendship pact based on the Catholic rite of co-godparenthood (see pp. 91–5), while in Africa the pact lost its significance with the penetration of missionaries. Since the exchange of blood was an essential part of medieval and African rites – solemnizing the oath and symbolizing the curse – it was seen by the Church as a form of attack on religion and a mockery of holy communion.

Sometimes blood pacts were purely opportunist and even missionaries were on occasion forced to undergo it to continue their conversions, often without realizing the full meaning of the formal friendship they had entered into. One missionary in New Guinea became the blood brother of a local chief in order to smooth the way of his work. When he died on the job his successor found that according to custom the dead man's blood brother had buried him with the appropriate rites and much mourning, and taken over all his property – inheritance from a blood brother was part of the contract.

In Australia blood exchanges ensured peaceful contacts in the land of traditional enemies or allied traders. The drinking of the blood of an enemy automatically prevented any further treachery – if a party of aborigines wished to set out on an expedition against the people of a neighbouring locality and had an enemy prisoner in their camp, they forced him to drink blood from their veins whereupon he was securely and magically obliged not to harm his new-found friends by warning his kin of their danger. Even in this situation the members of the pact stress the friendliness of the alliance. Some Australian aborigines had a veritable passion for making these blood friendships and many adults had a series of little lumps marking the course of the veins of the forearm – a symbolic map of their appreciation of the values of friendship and alliance rather than war. Blood pacts were also associated with whole groups who had fought or been on bad terms and sought a reconciliation.

Blood pacts therefore sacralize alliances and frequently convert neutral persons, even enemies, into allies and friends. These 'achieved' friendships are the result of a specific situation and the ceremony and exchange of blood helps establish the bond. In normal circumstances, particularly in Africa, blood pacts need not have any selfish aspect but join friends in a sentimental alliance. Among the Pende[5] blood pacts expressed a deeply felt emotional friendship between two men or a man and a woman which became a permanent and total union – at least ideally – due to the magical solidarity between the partners. The Pende expected that once a blood friend died, the blood would cause the death of the other soon afterwards as a matter of course. They maintained that in partaking of a beloved person's blood – either of a man or a woman – one partook of a little of his soul. The main aim of these 'unions in death' was to make the affection and love between two friends of such a strength that nobody would wish to remain alive after his friend's death. In any case, if the death was delayed the partner was expected to commit suicide; there is a recorded case of a pact between a brother and a sister in the seventeenth century in which the sister committed suicide on the death of her brother. If the partner did not take his own life, the dead partner came back to haunt him and call him to the world of the dead. Death is more than the logical conclusion of a blood exchange, however – in the after-life, blood friends become eternal friends by assuming the role of twins, the closest of all couples.

A similar situation of sentimental friendship celebrated by blood exchange is recorded for the Nepalese. In Nepal, the predominant reason for entering into ritual brotherhood is mutual affection between the participants and their desire to strengthen and formalize the ties of their relationship. Naturally the advantages of mutual aid are not overlooked but in the main the emotional reason is primary. Many informants stated simply, 'I liked him . . .'.

The Azande provide the most comprehensive material on blood friendship.[6] Among local villagers, blood brotherhood is marked by deep affection and most commonly cements already existing bonds of comradeship by giving it a concrete form and religious backing. Between two Azande men the exchange of blood attempts to achieve the kind of bonds Birkin wished to have with Gerald in *Women in Love*: between men who loved each other 'implicitly, and perfectly, finally, without any possibility of going back on it'.

Azande blood friends are mostly neighbours who are not kin or in-laws. Complete reciprocity between the two is implied, which is why it is rare to find the relationship between Azande nobles and commoners, the former keeping clear of personal involvements outside their own class since they have to remain impartial judges of disputes between all Azande; in any case they could hardly have a reciprocal, equal relationship with a commoner. This equality is emphasized in the rite. The two blood friends cut each other's chest and arms and smear their blood on pieces of wood which are exchanged, swallowed, and then 'talked to' within the stomach. Two peanuts from the same pod are used to symbolize the equality between friends, and the enumeration of obligations and sanctions underlines the reciprocal nature of the relationship.

Loyalty to a friend is placed above that to a chief as

representative of the state – an Azande blood brother seeking to avoid justice is to be supported regardless of all risk. Normally, however, blood brothers act like friends – they are always in each other's company, eating meals together and attending beer parties. They expect a share of the meat when one of them kills a large beast. The intimacy of friends is expressed in the freedom of their conversation; they may insult each other without any of the affronts causing umbrage. A favourite practical joke played on a blood brother consists in announcing the death of a friend's kinsman, the father's elder brother, for example. This news, if true, would mean a serious blow to a man and his whole lineage. However, the victim is not allowed to be upset at what would amount to a terrible insult if it had come from anyone else but his friend: he must remain unaffected by anything he says.

None the less, the Azande were not behindhand in using their friends to assist them in various ways. A blood brother might have access to powerful medicines, another may be a smith or a hunter. Outside Azande-land friendships were fairly practical affairs. Traders who travelled through enemy country, or even in unknown districts of their own tribe, sought blood friendships as a kind of passport. In the old days the most frequent use of this kind of freemasonry was to give protection to parties of Azande who travelled together to collect an important magical wood, known as *banga*, which was used for oracular consultations. This wood only grew in hostile regions occupied by foreign peoples, regions which offered dangers and risks which were lessened by setting up blood friendships with some of the local inhabitants who then ensured the Azande safe conduct through their territory. Other Azande made blood friendships with the people to the north for the purpose of obtaining vegetable oils and dried meat. A man's blood brother reserved oil and meat for him and received Azande goods as gifts in return – spears and locally made cloth. Blood friends therefore provided security; Azande knew that they had friends or allies in distant villages and foreign tribes and could count on their hosts when travelling or if they had to run away from home as the result of some misdemeanour.

Partners to a blood brotherhood are not brothers, of course, since friends who exchange blood are in no way accommodated in each other's kinship group, nor do they adopt behaviour based on relations between siblings. The social behaviour required between partners to a pact – familiarity and mutual assistance at all times – is incompatible with behaviour between kinsmen. The very intimacy and equality found between friends, the joking and bawdy insults, are an indication that among the Azande, as elsewhere, the relations are not brotherly. Friends are much more emotionally involved than brothers and the sanctions for betraying a friend are much stronger than for any default in the obligations of kinship. Among the Ganda, for example, a blood friend could refuse his friend no request of any kind, from a drink of beer or safekeeping for his cattle, to a wife, the payment of a heavy fine, or the concealment of a fugitive from justice. It was a relationship of such power that it took precedence over kinship. A murderer could count on finding refuge with a blood friend – but not his brother – even if the latter were a relative of his victim.[7] Among the Azande, as well, blood friends played completely different roles to kinsmen. They were specifically required to bury their friends or their friends' relatives, as well as perform autopsies. And in ritual exchanges at mortuary feasts, blood brothers and relatives-in-law formed a party distinct from consanguineal relatives and exchanged formal gifts with that group.

Blood brothers are friends and not kin because their relationship is one of absolute equality; between kinsmen there is always superordination and subordination. Within a lineage an elder kinsman has rights and expects quiet obedience from his juniors. Kinship terminology may ignore the division of the sexes, but elder and younger siblings are always distinguished by different terms of address. The only equals in a kinship system are twins, which possibly explains their anomalous situation and why their very parity is used to symbolize the norms of friendship (see p. 124).

The term 'brotherhood' is therefore a misnomer of long standing, based on the misconceptions of early observers of the rites. The assumption was that there was no kinship without community of blood and that there were no obligations in primitive societies except those of kinship, so that anyone wanting an alliance or friendship had to adopt the notion of artificial kinship.

Blood partners were 'brothers' and not friends to Robertson Smith[8] whose ideas were sensibly opposed by Westermarck.[9] Westermarck maintained that members of a clan did not see themselves as being literally of one blood. He criticized Robertson Smith for seeing the exchange of blood as a crude artificial transfusion of blood, imagined as a symbol of kinship.

Ethnography has proved Westermarck right. Blood is a universal symbol, but not of kinship. A brother is a brother, while blood brothers are really friends. In some societies where blood brothers give each other mutual privileges over wives and property it does look as if the relationship is based on kinship, particularly as the children of each often regard each other as 'brother' and 'sister' and are not allowed to marry. Among the Ganda,[10] a person adopted his friend's status and totem, was not allowed to marry a woman of his own clan, and was referred to by other members of the clan by the same kinship terms as his partner. However, in cases such as these it would be better to interpret them as using kinship and its prohibitions as a means of strengthening friendships which have been ritualized through blood.

Westermarck was also right when he maintained that the really important element in the blood covenant was the curse, for which the blood was merely a suitable vehicle. In Azande, in the last resort two men were blood friends not from sentimental motives, but because if you failed to help your friend in need his blood would kill you by virtue of its magical powers. The nucleus of the relationship and the rite is the blood, a substance charged with supernatural force. The Azande priest who performs the ritual tells the blood to act in certain ways and in certain contingencies. In the Cameroon, it was the blood which caused dropsy if one friend betrayed another. In Angola, friends followed each other even to death by virtue of the shared blood. Evans-Pritchard says that the Azande priest makes his address to the blood and imagines that it absorbs every clause of his speech. The object of the Azande rite is to compel the two friends to fulfil their obligations, and they confirm this in a long unformulated rambling speech, full of appropriate imagery and gestures: the blood is drunk, a cord is twisted in the hair of both men, the partners' bodies are mysteriously tapped.

Without the consumption of blood the covenant of friendship is null and void. At one time a Zande priest went through a blood friendship rite with an Egyptian official whom he hated. The priest carefully dropped the blood-soaked piece of wood on the ground and chewed, instead, one without blood on it. Since he had not eaten his enemy's blood none of the obligations of the rite was binding on him; he felt quite free to act against the interests of the official and did so. Once an Azande actually eats the blood the sanctions begin to work automatically. If you commit adultery with your blood brother's wife, the blood itself will destroy you and your kin even if your friend is unaware of the act. The blood knows exactly what to do and the Azande can quote cases in which there was no doubt that the blood had taken a terrible toll of a family for a breach of friendship obligations. The action of the blood may also be hurried along by further rites: a man who has been betrayed by his blood brother takes the piece of cord which had been twisted in their hair during the rite and mutters a spell over it, calling upon the blood to avenge the injury and exterminate his blood brother, summoning up lions, leopards, snakes, thunder, dysentery, European justice, and a host of equally horrible disasters.

Blood also sanctified relations between men and their wives. Among the Pende it could be used between spouses, not to ensure the wife's fidelity as in some cases, but to express the affection and love between a man and a woman which they wished to make permanent even after death. This union, however, has its own divorce, since there is a rite in which a sterile wife in a monogamous marriage can be made to vomit the blood so that the husband may re-marry. In the case of the Pende these passionate pacts between husband and wife were welcomed by missionaries who proselytized in the Congo in the seventeenth and eighteenth centuries, since they provided a magical sanction for monogamous marriage.

Blood was also used in ceremonies formalizing alliances between clans or villages. The Pende made political alliances between village heads, the relationship of friendship between the blood partners becoming a hereditary one and serving to link the two groups until such a time as the rite was formally revoked.

In West Africa long-standing alliances between tribes or caste groups within a society are supposedly founded on an original act of friendship, expressed through the exchange of blood. Among a Mali people, the pastoral Fulani and the blacksmiths have a reciprocal relationship based on the idea that in the beginning they made a blood pact – the blood of their ancestors was mixed together during circumcision. Because of this relationship and in order to preserve it the two groups will not mix their blood in marriage – in this way blacksmiths and Fulani form two endogamous castes. Even the relations based on ritualized joking (see p. 139) between the Dogon and the Bozo are based on an original pact whereby part of the vital force of each partner, symbolized by a piece of flesh and blood, was deposited in the other. When the relationship between Bozo and Dogon is activated, each party is supposed to act on that part of himself which is in the other and which forms a sort of foundation, in the other person, on which he can work. Among the Tallensi of Ghana,[11] there is a blood pact in their myth of origin – the ancestors of a group of immigrants, the Namoos, and the ancestors of the first occupants of the land, the Tales, mixed their blood and bound themselves and their descendants to a permanent peace.

Blood, therefore, is an efficient symbol linking friends, husbands and wives, clans and castes, allied nations, even man and God. In one case it links man and culture – since in some West African myths culture is seen to have originated through a blood pact. This is the foundation of a Dahomeyan myth[12] which attributes the revelation of the blood pact to the genie Aziza, king of the forest. A hunter who came across a doe in the act of giving birth refrained from killing the mother and the young animal. Aziza, who was secretly observing the scene, imbued the hunter with a feeling of pity for all animals in similar circumstances. The genie and the hunter performed a blood pact, the former compensating the man by showing him the secret of farming techniques. On another occasion Aziza allowed the same man to watch some people dancing in a clearing to the accompaniment of drums. When he returned home to his people he taught them dancing and drumming; and it was through these activities, performed on a village green which was extended to represent the whole universe, that they were able to forget for a moment or two their daily cares and woes and perform the 'Game of the World'. By means of a blood pact man was able to learn techniques which enabled him to escape from a hazardous dependence on animals, at the same time discovering life in society.

From personal friendship to the origin of culture: blood exchanges are the framework of a multiple series of alliances between individuals and all kinds of groups, in which friendship – a relationship of equality and reciprocity – is at work. Blood brothers may sometimes appear to be political allies or economic partners, but they are also real friends. As in marriage, which is also superficially a practical and businesslike affair, the signing of a contract and the existence of sanctions do not preclude love. Blood brotherhood offered increased social and economic opportunities outside the field of kinship, without degrading individuals into patron–client relations and at the same time acting as a voluntary contract (unlike the relationship between kin and age-mates), providing valuable emotional outlets which were freely chosen.

However, the complete trust and reciprocity between blood brothers in Africa was too complete to survive the new era introduced by European colonialists and marked by the advent of a market economy. Many of the obligations of the old friendships ceased to apply in the new conditions. People no longer needed protection as they travelled in foreign countries, or friends to help them against the depredations of local chiefs. The introduction of money and international commerce meant that most people could dispense with circuitous means of acquiring wealth; moreover, the increased possibility of getting into debt would make Africans hesitate before accepting the unlimited responsibility for a friend inherent in these blood pacts. At the same time Christianity, jealous as ever of strong emotional attachments outside its fold, maintained that these pagan institutions, involving belief in supernatural causes of misfortune and death, had to go.

Fortunately blood exchanges were only one of the many means of institutionalizing friendship in societies outside the network of a European industrial economy. We have already seen that even a marriage ceremony is not considered too extreme a step to express the emotional and practical elements involved in ties between two men, which with us are limited to sentimental declaration and frequently not even that. Other societies adapt many of their ritual and social institutions to the interests of friendship and adapt friendship to the interests of their ritual, social, and political life.

4 Gossips and Godchildren

In the early Middle Ages in Europe blood pacts fulfilled the role of formalizing and sacralizing friendships. Initially the Church itself had sanctioned this rite, the priest offering up a prayer in which he dwelt on the duties of the two comrades who wished to become blood brothers. He then witnessed the declaration of a solemn oath between the two friends, who kissed and then scratched each other's arms, mixing a few drops of blood with wine, which they drank.

Later, however, when the exchange of blood between friends was banned by the church, friendships of a similar nature continued to be sanctified by Roman Catholic ritual. This was the beginning of the institution of co-godparenthood, a relationship which developed from the rituals of christening and confirmation. This institution, still widespread today (but mostly outside Europe), is known in anthropology by the Spanish word *compadrazgo* since it primarily survives in Spanish-speaking communities of central and southern America.

Compadrazgo or co-godparenthood is the relationship between the parents and godparents of a child christened in church; through their participation in the ceremony, godfathers and godmothers, the parents of the child, and sometimes the priest who baptized the child, become ritually related. Having replaced the 'pagan' institution of blood brotherhood, compadrazgo became common all over Europe and still exists in parts of Greece, Spain, Italy, Serbia, and Russia. In England co-godparents were known as god-sibs (that is 'siblings in God'); here, however, the relationship did not endure as an institution and went through the vicissitudes of social change which the etymology of the word – from godsip to gossip – indicates.

Compadrazgo has had a long and interesting history.[1] It

flourished during the early years of feudalism when the extended family and the clan declined in importance and a greater emphasis on individual relationships developed. Compadrazgo relations between peasants also served to keep property within a group of 'ritual brothers' or co-godparents which prevented reversion to the lord's demesne if a man should die without kin. The church itself was materially involved, since the priest who baptized the child was also a co-godparent: as an independent landowner, the church used the enforcement of religious rules regarding exogamy to profit from land redistribution. Marriage within the kin group and within the community of affinal relations had heavily reinforced the weight of the old Germanic limitation on the right of individuals to dispose of their property as they wished, and the church had been in a disadvantageous position. Since co-godparents were not allowed to marry, the artificial kin group based on compadrazgo grew very large and these new exogamic laws allowed the church to be residual heir to individual property.

In an earlier period Justinian had issued an edict prohibiting marriages between 'spiritual relatives', but the full acceptance of the separation between parents and sponsors and the rule forbidding their marriage came about gradually. In the eighth century, for example, priests in France maintained that a man who married a widow, to whose child he had acted as godfather, was guilty of a very serious crime. A John Howthon of Tonbridge was whipped three times around the market place and church for having married a girl to whom his first wife had been godmother. These exogamic extensions between artificial kin did not indicate that the co-godparents were in fact kin, any more than the same situation made blood friends real kin. The Church, anxious to establish itself as an independent landowner in its own right, capitalized on the changes in the process of inheritance to press its own claims. Through the enforcement of religious rulings regarding exogamy, the Church won a struggle with feudal lords to gain control over legislation covering the making and the execution of testaments.

Despite these exogamic restrictions and the use of kin terms such as sib, brother, co-pater, and co-mater, the relation between co-godparents in Europe was no more a kinship one than that between a priest and his flock – 'father and children'. Co-godparents (gossips, *compères, comadri*) were friends and allies, patrons and clients or close neighbours who, through a Christian ritual, added an extra dimension to their friendship. With the gradual evolution from tribal to state institutions in Europe, compadrazgo reflected the increasingly impersonal structure of society in terms of person-to-person relationships.

Compadrazgo, therefore, as well as giving a child a spiritual guardian, cemented ties between individuals of the same generation. Parents of a child often sought to obtain material advantages through the choice of co-godparents among feudal lords or members of a city council. Mercenaries sought them among nobles. An abbot, for example, petitioned the Holy See for a dispensation from the ruling that monks could not be co-godparents since he wished to set up friendly alliances, through this means, with forty local lords.

Among the common people, however, compadrazgo was used to form solidary relationships between neighbours and friends in a rural setting. This is shown linguistically in the widening of the word godsib in English, and *compare* in Italian, to mean neighbour. In the Tyrol, strangely enough, *Gevatterschaft* (the co-godparent group) was actually used to draw a contrast with the group of kinsfolk known as *Freundschaft* (*Freund* being the old word for kinsman). Here we have another indication that co-godparenthood, despite the use of kin terms and the ban on intermarriage, was not a kinship institution, but one of friendship and alliance between unrelated persons. In fact compadrazgo, like blood friendship, is more than kinship. Between real brothers there is an ambivalence and hostility as well as love and mutual obligation: the friendship of co-godparents, on the contrary, should be immutable and free of this kind of ambivalence and the common jealousies of kin.

Prejudice against ritual and all things Roman meant that Protestant Europe, under the guidance of Luther, came to ban compadrazgo. Good reformer that he was, Luther was always suspicious of the extension of ritual to include this large group of co-godparents and he restricted ceremonial kin relations to the priest, the child, the parents, and the sponsors, thus putting an end to the large Catholic spiritual fraternity based on compadrazgo. 'Love needs no laws,' Luther said and swept away 'these stupid barriers due to spiritual fatherhood, motherhood, brotherhood, sisterhood and childhood. Who but superstition has created these spiritual relations . . .?' In this Luther was asserting the 'new spirituality' in both religion and friendship; he also seems to be acting as unconscious agent for the coming industrial and capitalist culture whose new ethic put a premium on the individual as an effective accumulator of capital and virtue, an ethic which certainly discountenanced the drain on individual resources and the restrictions on individual freedom implicit in the wide extension of these friendship and ritual ties.

In fact, the compadrazgo tie disappeared almost completely from areas which witnessed the widespread development of industrial capitalism, the rise of a strong middle class, and the disappearance of feudal tenures. It lost its old functions where the family did not form the primary unit of production and where friendship ties between such family units no longer were essential for survival. Alliances between individuals and kinship groups became non-functional over most of Europe and were replaced by more impersonal, contractual forms of organization than the alliances and friendships between individuals based on the dogma of Christian baptism.

Conversely, in Roman Catholic or Greek Orthodox communities where the family remained the prime unit of production and where production is for immediate consumption, the institution has flourished: in peasant Spain, Italy, and the Balkans as well as throughout South America. In all cases compadrazgo provides friendship links between households and families in village or peasant situations where mistrust is mitigated by extra-kin bonds. *Compari* and *compadres* adopt a friendly mien, trust each other and help each other in time of trouble. Like blood brothers they share a complete confidence even as far as their wives are concerned – a godfather and a godmother are usually sexually and maritally taboo so that a man can even trust his wife alone with the godfather of his child, or the father of one of her godchildren. Both co-godparents and blood brothers are persons set apart from the rest of society – they are both significant sets of persons at funerals, for example. In both institutions, if a friend betrays the other supernatural sanctions automatically begin to work – in blood brotherhood the blood wreaks its vengeance on the betrayer; in compadrazgo it is usually the child which suffers. Interestingly, when there is blood brotherhood there is no compadrazgo. In South America, Catholic since the sixteenth century, blood brotherhood left few traces and was completely replaced by compadrazgo. Moreover, like blood friendship it ceases to operate altogether or changes its function in an urban environment where an industrial situation demands complete individual responsibility in matters of work, debt, and the like.

For my own purposes I have stressed ties between co-godparents, as if the spiritual ties between godparent and godchild were and are secondary. But behind the complex relations between priest, parents, and co-godparents – with the child at the centre – there is a profound religious backing. Inherent in compadrazgo there is the logical distinction between man as a spiritual and natural being; through baptism the child escapes from nature (the taint of original sin) to spirituality (a state of grace). The sin of Adam is washed away and the human being is regenerated. The child is reborn to Christ and receives a second set of parents, his godparents. However, while this complex clearly involves spiritual rebirth for the child and spiritual paternity for the godparents, it would display a very limited sociological viewpoint to insist on the spiritual relationship between the godparents and the child as its prime aspect. In most cases it is the reciprocal relations between the parents of the child and the godparents which explain why this Christian institution flourishes in parts of Europe and South America today. The christening ritual sanctions a relationship between friends and neighbours, the child acting as a symbol – an expression and a guarantee of this friendship. How else can we explain the christening and sponsoring of a tree or a shrine by a couple of unrelated acquaintances? If co-godparenthood existed purely to seek the moral and practical welfare of a child, why should friends want a ceremonial blessing, complete with sponsors, of a marriage, a child's first haircut or the sale of a cow? Christian ritual provides the sanction for a friendship contract between adults and a purely theological account which stresses the need for a child of a spiritual protector on earth and in heaven, a supplicator before God, ignores these aspects. In both Europe and Latin America the child is primarily a hostage to the future relationship between co-godparents whose alliance is sanctioned through the ritual baptism of the child; the sacred nature of the rite corresponds to the sacred nature of the blood in blood pacts.

In Europe where compadrazgo survives it is the social effects of the institution rather than its ritual aspects which play the primary role. In southern Italy, *comparaggio* has become a secular relationship, involving generosity and friendship towards the child rather than religious obligations.[2] It promotes the stability of group relations in a peasant society not yet touched by the impersonal characteristics, social, legal, and economic, of the strong industrial state with its dense urban population. Comparaggio provides social security and emotional satisfaction rather than spiritual strength. Although *compare* relationships are established through baptism – or sometimes other passage rites such as an ear-piercing ceremony – they can also be made in Italy at the altar, at festas, or in new houses. As a practical institution it serves to help poverty stricken peasants in time of famine, war, and feuding, as well as for such prosaic purposes as getting loans, finding bail, and making up dowries. It also functions in sickness and old age, and in the care of orphans. In community projects and in commercial undertakings it generally brings about cooperation.

In Italian the co-godparent is known as *compare*, a word also used for members of gangs and bands, particularly the *mafia* and the *camporra*, and indicates close, loyal ties: a *mafia* boss is known as the *padrino* or godfather. As we shall see (p. 203), the entire male inhabitants of a village make themselves *compari* of St John on Midsummer's Day in order to make the village a more solidary unit. In other parts of Italy *compare* is used as a word for friend or colleague – in an Italian translation of *Hamlet*, when the prince speaks to his 'friends' the players, they are called his *compari*. It denotes bond friendship and comradeship and has lost any religious significance; in fact the child, fictive or otherwise, hardly enters the picture. Even in Sicily *commari* (co-godmothers or gossips) are two women who live in neighbourly and chatty harmony and the 'merry wives' of Shakespeare's play become *Le allegre commari* in Italian.

In other peasant communities, more complex ties between co-godparents have been described where individuals still act as sponsors for the children, thereby creating compadrazgo relations which may be given a collective character since the kin group of the sponsor then becomes allied to the kin group of the child. The exercise of sponsorship functions, at particular crisis rites in a child's life, depends more on the role of the godfather as a representative of his kin group and reflects his position in the group rather than a specific dyadic contract between two individuals. Here group alliances rather than personal friendships are emphasized. In parts of Serbia patrilineal descent, relations through marriage as well as compadrazgo are all techniques of social integration and allying groups.[3] In this case the original friendship role of the co-godparents becomes an inherited role, passing through the male line: members of one patriline are godparents to those of a second, who are godparents to those of a third and so on. This notion of separate social groups engaging in social intercourse and alliance between donors and recipients takes our discussion to a higher, more academic level. It is a basic factor in Lévi-Strauss's work on exchange and alliance and in a more general way is germane to my arguments concerning the relationship between group alliances and individual friendships which I discuss in Chapter Eight. In Serbia kin groups are allied through the ritual of baptism which brings about exchanges between the groups in both a reciprocal and circulating way, reminiscent of Leach's analysis of multilateral cross-cousin marriage.[4]

In Greece, we have already seen that the moral obligations of the Saraktsani shepherd are concentrated almost exclusively within the family and the close kindred at the expense of relations outside this limited circle. Friendships are not sought except between first cousins, and families associate with other families more through feelings of enmity and mistrust than alliance and friendship. This anarchy, however, seems more apparent than real since various links between shepherd and shepherd,

shepherd and village, do bring communities into a form of social, economic, and civic cooperation. Although hostility between local villagers and the nomadic shepherd is a fact, a symbiotic relationship exists and is helped along by the institution of compadrazgo.

A Greek shepherd frequently chooses a villager to become the godfather of his child and in so doing a relationship is established between the parents and the sponsor or sponsors of the child at the christening. By giving the child its name the godfather is considered responsible for the spiritual condition of the child. At the baptism, the godfather gives his godchild clothing, a gift which is later reciprocated when the family presents him with a lamb, its fleece dyed red at Easter. A similar kind of spiritual friendship is set up between a shepherd bridegroom and his wedding sponsor. Again the sponsor is usually a villager, not a shepherd, and he supports the bridegroom by his assistance and presence in the secular marriage customs during the feast and the wedding service. He stands at the right of the groom and has the privilege of exchanging three times the bride's and the groom's crown. At a wedding the villager provides the bride's dress and a gift of money; he also pays for the wedding crowns, candles, sugared almonds, and a share of the meat, bread, and wine; he tips the band and makes an offering to the priest. The bride reciprocates by giving their sponsor the choicest blanket from her dowry. On a spiritual plane, just like a godfather, he becomes responsible for the couple. In this case it is an ongoing obligation, the same man usually sponsoring all their children at baptism and confirmation.

In this way ties are formed between shepherd families and wealthy and socially superior villagers. Although unequal in many ways the relationship is still that of friendship, the godparents and sponsors achieving a mutual intimacy which allows some semblance of equality. An element of camaraderie enters into an otherwise unpleasantly lopsided relationship and the ritual sanctions involved help to convert hostile contacts into helpful ones. Baptisms and weddings provide opportunities for friendship between disparate groups who *have to be friendly to survive*.

Although godparents and parents of a child are seen to have a joint spiritual responsibility for the child, it is in the values of friendship attached to the contract between the shepherd and the villager that the strength of the relationship lies. This is made clear by the supernatural sanctions behind the alliance. If any evil, wanton, or sinful actions occur between the parents and the godparents it is the child which becomes impure and his right relationship to God is ruined. As in medieval Europe and South America the child is used as a symbol of the relations and a vehicle for a curse in the same way as the exchanged blood is the agent and symbol of blood friendship and the source of supernatural sanction.

It is clear that in a divided society like this the relationship between persons not connected by kinship and marriage must be inherently fragile: the ritual of baptism and marriage helps discipline the attitudes and feelings on both sides. Between groups who become allied in these ways – co-godparents and their sponsors and their respective families – there is a taboo on marriage and sexual relations which also plays its part in linking rather than dividing these groups. Among the Saraktsani and the local village population, two formerly unrelated persons are drawn into a friendship bond in which their mutual esteem and respect (or we might say love and friendship) are profoundly committed. On top of this the day-to-day behaviour between sponsors and a wedding pair or a godparent and the parents of a child are commonly expressed in the values of friendship: there must be mutual confidence; they must never quarrel or gossip; their behaviour is that expected of comrades and companions.

In the Andalusian pueblo of Alcalá, *compadres* are acquaintances or kin of the parents of the child who enter into a formalized friendship with them through the baptism of their children – in a very similar way to that described for the Greek shepherds and villagers. Here the godparents are usually a married couple who may be distant kinsfolk of the parents of the child. While godfathers help towards the cost of the ceremony and accept spiritual responsibility for the child, it is the relationship between the parents and the co-godparents which is the most esteemed. A *compadre* becomes an honorary member of the elementary family, but not a kinsman as such since the relationship is seen as one free of the trammels which may bring dissension among kinsfolk. If they were formerly cousins they now become friends, since the sponsoring of the child removes them from the kinship context. The seriousness of the tie is stressed by the fact that in popular conception (although not in the Spanish civil code) it creates an incest taboo: you could not have sex with a *compadre*. In Spain, strangely enough, the friendship involves a note of formal respect – even the term of address, *usted*, is adopted instead of *tu* even when an informal intimacy had existed before. Yet *compadres* become friends and respect one another; they are never stiff with each other but speak with great ease. Like friends, *compadres* are under an obligation to do anything the other may ask; compadrazgo is a tie of mutual trust which is stronger than kinship but at the same time is different from 'ordinary friendship' because it is sacralized. Because of the ritual bonds it is considered permanent, a relationship valued because it cannot be renounced.

In Latin America the historical importance of compadrazgo parallels its significance in medieval Europe. Ethnographic material shows that Indian society before the conquest was marked by much more widespread clan, lineage, and extended family organization, which meant that people were automatically aligned to a much larger group than was possible with the elementary, bilateral family which has been the basic unit of social organization since; through compadrazgo it was possible to recapture some of the security which was lost with the destruction of old forms of social organization. The assumption is that prior to the conquest Latin American Indian groups lived in patrilineal clans with individuals having no private rights to land. The conquest brought devastation, depopulation, and general havoc among these groups, particularly as regards the joint ownership of land by kin groups. People were forced to seek contacts outside kinship through a selective network of ties, with the individual himself as the central nexus of relationships. As in medieval Europe, the model for this new kind of friendship was provided by the ritual of baptism.

Compadrazgo was again used as a means of gaining new friends and allies among kin, acquaintances, equals, and superiors; or, by imposing a ritual element on established friendships, it gave them a greater degree of stability. In Chinautleco, the Guatemalan village described by Reina, parents are careful to find the right person to accept sponsorship of their child. It is believed, for example, that a *compadra* with 'good luck' can influence the course of his godchild's life. When an Indian chooses a superior Ladino as godparent of his children, however, he is consciously using the institution as a means of building up materially advantageous relations for himself as well as for the child. Ladinos and Indians who are *compadres* address each other on equal terms – they use the *tu* form of address instead of the formal *usted*, like Andalusia – and refer to each other as 'my *compadre*'. It is interesting that between villagers who are both Indian – i.e. natives – the term *compadre* is not used, possibly because the notion of equality does not need to be stressed as it does between the wealthier, Spanish-speaking Ladino and the inferior Indian.

In Chinautleco, in fact, many other institutions reinforce friendship and compadrazgo is relatively insignificant. We have seen the institutionalized friendships between young men; and in the *confradria*, the association which organizes fiestas in honour of the saints, cooperative friendships are formed between individuals of both sexes. Nevertheless, friends are bound together through the ritual sponsorship of baptism, marriage, confirmation, and even the blessing of a shrine or a saint. Relations between co-godparents are usually renewed when other children are born and it becomes an on-going relationship. When a woman becomes pregnant it is immediately known, therefore, that the godmother of her other children will become responsible for the coming child. In one case, reported by Reina, the child of a woman was born dead and the godmother – the woman's *commadre* – hurried to the house, made the sign of the cross over the face of the child, baptizing it in the name of the Father, the Son, and the Holy Ghost. And by placing a grain of salt on its lips she further ensured its future life as an angel. She then made a shroud of bright crepe paper, fired rockets at the house and the cemetery, headed the funeral procession, burning incense all the while. She brought one and a half quarts of beer, a dollar's worth of bread, a chicken, and other food. In this relationship, brought about through compadrazgo, a woman was able to depend on her friend, the godmother of her children, to help at the death of her baby, since a permanent alliance had been set up between them at the birth of her first child.

In other parts of South America even greater emphasis is placed on the relationship between *compadres* than between godparents and their godchildren and compadrazgo as often as not is institutionalized friendship, rather than spiritual kinship, and derives from the affection felt between friends. In Moche,[5] a coastal community in Peru, compadrazgo is the main means of establishing important interpersonal networks outside the family. For this purpose it is hardly important who or what is being sponsored: birth, baptism, the cutting of a child's nails for the first time, confirmation, engagement, marriage – all can serve to establish friendship relations between *padrinos* and *madrinos* and the parents of the child or other persons involved. And if there are no specific life-crises rites to sponsor, the people of Moche become co-godparents of a fiesta, a housewarming, a first-maize festival, or merely the taking down of a family altar.

The friendship aspects of compadrazgo are given special emphasis in a society where there is no form of community organization and no other means of maintaining solidary relations. Apart from confirming pre-existing affective friendships and setting up useful alliances, compadrazgo is used as an excuse to further acquaintance in general, extending one's personal network: during carnival, for example, men and women tie themselves together with strips of coloured paper while dancing, and this relationship of friendship, created so spontaneously, is extended to the friends' spouses. In this way the whole of Moche has become interlocked with *compadre* dyads of greater or lesser intensity.

Baptism is the most important single event which brings *compadres* together. The group of co-godparents usually consists of the mother and the father of the child, and the godfather and godmother: the same *compadre* terms are then extended to the godmother's husband, the godfather's wife, and the parents of the nurse who carries the child. The terms may be generalized to blood relatives of the parents and the godparents. Nevertheless the relationships are quite distinct from kinship and the ties are considered stronger in some cases. Feuding and quarrelling are common between kin and in-laws but impossible between *compadres*.

The procedure of choosing the sponsors is simple. Either kins-folk or friends are chosen and the acceptance of a *copita* of brandy seals the arrangement. There is often a preference for financially responsible people as godparents and usually the two are neither married nor related. It is their role to provide the printed announcement cards which are given to the guests at the feast following the baptism and which are either pinned or tied on their clothes with coloured ribbons. They give presents to the child and have the duty of burying it if it dies before its first year. The parents provide an elaborate party with much drinking and happy dancing, which is seen as a public recognition of the newly established ceremonial kin partners, the *compadres* and *commadres*.

The relation between them is one of mutual obligation and help when in difficulties although the heaviest obligations fall on the *compadre* who is the father of the child. Two men who are *compadres* become very special friends, a friendship manifested by camaraderie spiced with sexual joking. At funerals of each other's kin they act as pallbearers. A man may have up to sixty or seventy *compadres* and *commadres*, although of these only a small proportion are kept bright with use. Compadrazgo is seen as an institution which offers opportunities for Moche people to increase their range of intimate friends and achieve a greater security in a society where there are few organized groups with special status. Relationships are all described in terms which denote interpersonal connections and friendships between individuals.

At each compadrazgo rite, therefore, at least four people are joined in a relationship which immediately has less timidity and less shame. Any occasion in a child's life is taken to gain these valued friends. At the age of two and a half or three, for example, a new *padrino* and *madrino* are chosen to sponsor its first hair-cutting rites. The two godparents of the haircutting ceremony choose the coloured ribbons with which the child's hair is tied into small tufts. At the fiesta, the child is dressed in his or her best clothes and seated on a stool in front of another on which is placed a plate. The godfather places some money on the plate, and snips off a tuft of hair below the knot in the ribbon; the godmother does the same and the other guests all follow, leaving smaller gifts and receiving a beribboned lock of hair which they pin to their clothes. Once the ceremony is over the child has had a complete if uneven haircut and four more Moche adults have assumed a new intimacy through compadrazgo.

In England and America there is no formal 'gossipry' although it is usual for friends to be chosen as godparents of a couple's children. Sometimes the relationship between the godparents and the child is stressed, sometimes the friendship between the 'godsibs'. A godparent may be an uncle, a respectable neighbour, a wealthy bachelor friend, or someone with influence in the father's business world. The rite of baptism may be used, therefore, to achieve an alliance between two persons or to enhance an already existing friendship.

Compadrazgo as a friendly alliance has much in common with other institutions which fulfil the same functions. One example is the special relationship between a mother's brother and a sister's son (and their respective groups) in patrilineal societies (see p. 169). In Russia for example the functions of a godfather are similar to those of an uncle on the mother's side, since the mother's brother is the prototype of the godfather, while the godmother is merged with the uncle's wife. This explains the specific traits of the relationship between a child's parents and his godparents – since they should be in-laws, and as in-laws, best friends. Sexual intercourse between the godfather and the child's mother is considered a mortal sin for they are seen archaically as brothers and sisters. At the same time intimacy between godfather and godmother is permitted since they are theoretically husband and wife. This complicated network of relations will become clearer when we discuss the role of the mother's brother in certain African societies (see p. 176 ff.). In the Russian language, interestingly, the word *kumovstvo* (co-godparent) is synonymous with nepotism and denotes protection of a nephew or any other kinsman.[6]

*

These ritual relations between friends serve very practical purposes and at the same time offer a means of greater emotional fulfilment and an assurance that an individual does not stand alone. *Compadres* lend each other money; a woman will work in her friend's house when she is sick; they mourn the death of a relative. *Compadres* must be kind and friendly and a network of ties, spread widely as they are in Moche, help maintain community order, preventing upsets such as drunken brawls, and serving as a kind of multiple non-aggression pact. Throughout Latin America, for example, it is a friendly bond which may be used to forestall sexual aggressiveness; you can avoid trouble with a man who is determined to seduce your wife by making him your *compadre*! He cannot refuse the offer of friendship and once it is made the wife is henceforth sexually taboo.

Compadrazgo is ritualized friendship. Although modern values stress friendship's spontaneity and freedom of choice, I believe that in this way we are betraying our nervousness of close bonds other than those of matrimony and close kinship. Are we afraid that a formalization and ritualization of friendship roles would make them as unambiguous and permanent as those between husband and wife – and therefore inescapable? Unlike compadrazgo, blood brotherhood, bond friendship, and unisex 'marriages', the unstructured intimacy of Western friendship is a non-finite ambiguous relationship that weaves in and out of other roles. We have no *specific* obligations to each other. Friendship is not initiated with a pact. There is no legal separation as in the case of Pedro and Juan. Close kinsmen can be friends – even husbands and wives, even the employee and his boss; the Englishman's best friend is his dog, or his mother. It might even be maintained that friendship has become a residual category, degenerated into a kind of friendliness, replacing the permanent, demanding, exclusive bonds of a Roland and an Oliver or two Azande blood brothers Friendship has become a means of getting on with people – neighbours, workmates, members of the family; or a means of escaping from rigid role structures – not so much a teacher as a friend: 'my husband is my best friend'.

In societies where friendship plays a more specific role the rights and duties between partners are clear-cut. A friend drinks with you on Thursdays; is the best man at your wedding and godfather of your child, and carries your child to the grave if it dies; and gets the doctor or the diviner if you are ill. In Europe and America this kind of formalization is the antithesis of friendship – friendly roles are free-floating ones, chosen by a free man in a free society. A man can choose his dog, his wife, or his mother as his best friend if he wishes.

How far is it true that formal obligations and formal ceremony are incompatible with friendship? Ritual, for example – Protestants have always looked down on Catholics for allowing a personal commitment to God to be embellished, suffocated, with ritual and conformity. And even modern Catholics are rejecting a lot of their religion's external ceremony (such as the Latin mass and Friday abstinence) in favour of greater spirituality. Yet all communication, between a man and his gods as well as between two friends, depends on symbolic action and it is doubtful whether permanent relationships can survive without them except in very special circumstances. Christianity uses the universal symbol of blood in the eucharist; the Azande use it in friendship pacts; in Dahomey it expresses the origin of culture. Friends in our culture are left to find their own symbols and make up their own rituals – private jokes, special greetings, nicknames, regular meetings. For some people this does not seem enough and, like Lawrence, they seek promises, covenants, and formal behaviour from their friends.

We should, therefore, think twice before rejecting out of hand the external paraphernalia of ceremony and sanction: to blood friends and Catholics they may merely externalize sincere convictions. In the examples of formal friendship in this book I hope it will become clear that friendship – like the love of a man and a woman – in becoming sacralized takes on a further dimension. In some cases ritual can convert hostile contacts or at least neutral ones into helpful and often emotionally satisfying relationships. We might use formal ceremony as an excuse for making friends. As we saw in the purely political alliance between a German explorer and a Cameroon chief, the existence of the ceremonial structure made possible the beginnings of a sentimental exchange between two very different and potentially inimical men. Moreover, those people who have exchanged a formally sanctioned married life for the casual union of a man and woman who are free of the ritual bonds of the Church or the legal ones of the state have often found the second relationship more difficult to maintain – and relinquish. In such relations there are no rules and no expectations, and purely sexual or sentimental unions often dissolve in meaningless bitterness and disappointment.

I hope I will not be misunderstood. I am not in any way waving the flag of ritual and the 'old marriage', based on romantic love, frustrated sexuality, and the sanctity of procreation in wedlock. I am suggesting on the contrary that friendship – without romantic passion and sex – may prosper and expand with a dose of ceremony. At the same time I must also stress that no amount of ceremony or formal bonding can make a friendship survive without the initial element of affection; even treaties and alliances are underwritten by an element of affect.

5   Lopsided Friendships

Half-way through a book on friendship and I have left far behind the usually accepted bond of loving trust between equals freely entered upon and backed by moral rather than legal or magical sanctions. An uncle and his nephew, friends? Neighbours linked through the accident of a child's baptism? Even friendships brought about through the accident of birth?

It is not that I and the members of the societies so far considered do not see any great difference between sentimental and formal friendships. The Bangwa, great adepts at friendship of every kind, recognize a clear difference between chosen or 'achieved' friends, who are called 'friends of the heart', and obligatory or 'ascribed' friends, who are known as 'friends of the road'. A man's best friend, however, is a 'friend of the road' since he is the one born nearest in time to himself – twins are therefore the best of best friends. Brothers-in-law are also automatically friends. Or a Bangwa may find that he or she suddenly has a 'best friend' in a neighbouring village because the diviner has told him that they had travelled together in the spirit world before birth. A man after whom a child is named becomes his friend and also a friend of the parents; a man's name is given to a boy or a girl since there is no sexual divide in Bangwa nomenclature – either a boy or a girl could be called Nkenglefak. My name was frequently given to Bangwa children although out of consideration for European ways the female namesakes were called after my mother. There are quite a considerable number of little Dorothy Brains and Robert Brains in Bangwa although they all have a Bangwa name as well for decency's sake. The giving of a name in this way was a means of making new friendships, consolidating old ones, or showing respect to a superior who is rendered more friendly through his participation in the naming rite.

Bangwa friends are sought and found by many different means and to them the obligation to be friendly in a situation chosen by another or by the divining spider does not seem contradictory. I myself, however, found it difficult always to summon up friendly feelings towards persons who gave my name to their babies or roundly declared that we were born on the same day. It seemed, at first, false to have a friend simply because his child had the same name as myself. It seemed false to establish friendship through 'empty' ritual in the same way that it seems wrong to us for two persons to marry who have never set eyes on each other before the wedding day It also seemed false for relationships to be set up between a poor man and a rich man in the name of friendship, when it was obviously more like clientage.

However, not all friendships are the perfect unions of twin souls we read about in myth and story. Countless couples do not find the perfect balance and reciprocity of a Roland and an Oliver. Moreover, it would be wise for us to accept the notion of self-interest in most friendships. Most of us use our friends in some way or another, seek friendly alliances with people in superior social groups, for the most material or snobbish reasons. Friendship is ideally a sharing and a reciprocity between equals but it can quite as well be used to smooth out the ugly discrepancies between classes, the rich and the poor, the rulers and the ruled – and nowadays between men and women.

In many societies, the lopsided, utilitarian bond between patron and client is quite happily called 'friendship'. Here amity, liking, or love – call it what you will – oils the wheels of hierarchical societies where some kind of confrontation between the haves and have-nots is essential. While equality, a basic element in most friendships, is subordinated to the notion of help and complementarity, there is always some attempt to level out or at least gloss over glaring discrepancies of social and economic status. These friendships between members of different groups, classes, or castes serve as a kind of escape from anonymity by seeking out satisfying personal relationships between persons of heterogeneous interests as valuable in themselves. While a patron and client who call themselves friends may be master and slave, the give and take in their partnership – of goods, political influence, moral support – certainly endows it with another tremendously important aspect of friendship, complementarity.

In Alcalá, friendships are of many kinds, equal and unequal, instrumental and expressive. They are both highly charged relationships which function primarily through *simpatia* and a complete assurance that friends will be loyal and loving at all times; and they are alliances based on mutual interest. People have friends and townspeople talk about them as if they were lovers, spending hours gossiping about how one man spoke to his friend or how another looked when his friend's name was mentioned. However, they know that friendship does not and cannot survive simply on love and according to Pitt-Rivers considerations of interest more often than not dictate the expression of esteem. In Alcalá it was a commonplace that no one could get anywhere without friends and the more friends you had the greater your sphere of influence. So that even friendship, an ideal relation of equals, merges into a relationship of economic inequality which is the foundation of patronage systems. In Alcalá a rich man employs, assists, and protects his poor friends and in return the latter work for him, give him esteem and protect their patron's interests by seeing that he is not robbed, by warning him of the intentions of others, and taking his part in disputes. A man's friend or patron is valued as a connection with the powers outside the pueblo. A friend who is rich signs the application for an old age pension, testifying that the applicant had once worked for him: many such applications are signed by people who never employed the applicant. Without a patron to lie for him a man would never get a pension.

In Andalusia economic dealings are usually carried out between friends – that is, without the aid of a middleman or broker – the values of friendship providing the obligations which exist between buyer and seller. However, these friendships cannot be dubbed purely instrumental — self-interested – since affection even between business partners or a rich merchant and a peasant client is considered part and parcel of the deal of friendship. Some farmers complain that friendship obligations force them to sell at a loss, or part with an object they would otherwise not have sold.

Friendship therefore becomes a model for equality and free exchange which is transformed in a situation of inequality into a patronage structure. Pitt-Rivers coined the term 'lopsided friendship' for this system,[1] insisting that *simpatia*, the sentimental expression of friendship, is never excluded between friendly patrons and clients. Friendship also serves to cloak purely practical arrangements; it is used to link the authority of the state and the power of wealthy men to the general network of pueblo neighbourly relations.

In Guatemala friendships between Ladinos and Indians would be best described as patron–client relations. The interplay between these two very different sections of the population of Chinautleco pervades their way of life. An Indian owns a piece of land, makes charcoal, and has a wife who dresses in local costume and is a potter; he lives in a Mayan-style hut without beds or Western furniture. Ladinos are 'guests' of the Indians and form only four per cent of the pueblo population. They are entrepreneurs and administrators, bus drivers and shopkeepers – they never till the fields. Ladinos feel superior and part of the Guatemalan nation rather than part of the Chinautleco pueblo. There is also a difference in language, Indians speaking Pokoman as their native tongue and Spanish as a second language, while the Ladinos speak only Spanish.

Indians are more religious, Ladinos more secular. Cultural norms for the Indians are associated with beliefs expressed in church festivals and the worshipping of saints, which provide a basis for their local laws. Ladinos, on the other hand, acknowledge only national norms and attend to their religious duties perfunctorily. The important factor here, however, is that these two groups do get on; and they do it through a form of friendship. 'While within the social structure the principles of social discrimination are at war, the people are not.' The social game is workable.

Friendships are not equal. Even compadrazgo is structured vertically between patrons and clients. While friendships between Ladinos and Indians are more selfish than mutually satisfying from an emotional point of view, patrons and clients were proud of the relationship between them and stressed the affection it inspired. *Cuello*, however, is the operative word; it means 'pull' or influence and this is what the Indians require from their influential friends. With *cuello* legal matters can be accelerated or a job secured. Ladinos have access to economic and political power through their roles as urban traders or bureaucrats and Indians secure them as patrons to help them.

On the whole Ladino–Indian ties approximate the personal friendship of equals, even if the initial bond is not made for sentimental reasons. *Compadres* are expected to like each other, for example, and as well as do business they have fun together. Through the patron–client relation two groups could overlook social distance for a while, entering into a weak form of friendship which allows a degree of confidence and cooperation.

The Saraktsani shepherds also use compadrazgo to protect themselves from threats to their security and livelihood by setting up friendly links with wealthy and powerful villagers. Inevitably the relations between shepherd and villager are seen in terms of superiority and subordination and the ties of friendship which allow cooperation amount to a clear system of patronage. If a shepherd talks of his 'friendship' with a villager, he means a relationship of mutual advantage with a person outside his community who is in a more powerful position. Even between co-godparents, or a man and his wedding sponsor, the word is rarely encumbered by any grand theories of equality and disinterest. Lawyers and village presidents are the most sought after patrons, but merchants, cheese-dealers, shopkeepers, lorry-owners, and teachers are also valuable friends. Between patron and client material gifts are exchanged, credit is extended by the patron, or contacts are made with important bureaucrats on behalf of the shepherds. There is also some degree of increased sociability between a patron and his client which adds to the prestige and sense of well-being of both men. A poor shepherd meeting his patron in the local coffee shop has the 'right' to sit down and chat to him without the usual formal and humiliating ceremony.

For the shepherd these friendships are extremely important. Personal bonds must be established with merchants, for example; they sell their wool and cheese and usually carry a dead weight of debt which is never called in from a friendly client. Patrons with political power cannot ignore pressure from shepherds who claim their friendship, since ignoring it would endanger the important network of relations on which the influence and prestige of such men largely depend. Shepherds make gifts of cheese or money to state servants and lawyers, who then become their friendly protectors; the shepherds as good clients must show esteem and respect and give the patron the political support on which much of his power depends.

Campbell, in discussing these unequal friendships among the Saraktsani and villagers, suggests that in this society there is an absence of universally applicable values and the system of village friendships and patronage achieves for the shepherds a share of various facilities. Although the exchange is never equitable, at least the shepherd families are protected from complete exclusion. This system of friendship, of clientage, achieves this – not by upholding the rights of a man as an equal member of the community, but through an appeal to individuals, to friends in a superior group. We shall find the situation repeated in caste-type societies where the frontiers between well-nigh exclusive categories are breached by the same type of institution.

Lopsided friendships serve political functions, therefore, working in societies where authoritarianism and hierarchy are the rule; relations between the wielders of power and the powerless are based on informal relations, approximating friendship, between individuals. Sometimes it is the only way a conquering race can rule. The Lombards, for example, who conquered the Italians in the sixth century, imposed on the local people a tribute of one-third of their crops and did so in such a fashion that every single individual among the conquerors depended upon the tribute paid him by particular individuals among the local community. In this situation of conquered and conqueror, overlords and peasants, the hatred of the Italians for their oppressors could not continue unabated since the relationship set up between individuals, the personal interdependence of tribute-payer and lord, led to an element of friendship and a community of interest. The very circumstances which cause the animosity, the enforced participation of the Lombards in the enterprises of the natives – made for a convergence of interest. Divergences and harmony became inextricably involved and animosity actually developed into the germs of future amity.

Friendship also played an important part in the Bangwa system of government. A Bangwa chief may have a few hundred or a few thousand subjects organized into a political system of quite extraordinary complexity. A chief ruled a segmentary system of subchiefs, sub-subchiefs, and sub-sub-subchiefs and each of these minor chiefs had his own segmentary system of minor nobility, derived from lineages descended from sons of chiefs, commoners, and retainers. The geographical centre of each of these groups within the segmentary system was the palace where the chief or notable lived with his wives, his retainers, his pages, and, formerly, his slaves, linked in an intricate system of protocol and precedence, rank and status. A palace slave, for example, was differentiated by dress and ornament according to his exact status as a bought slave, the son of a male slave, the son of a female slave, or a local man reduced to slavery in punishment for witchcraft or adultery. Retainers were also ranked, some of them occupying the highest posts in the administration, others acting as pipebearers or nursemaids. Royals were of different classes according to their genealogical proximity to the reigning chief. Princes and princesses were either politically powerful or more insignificant than a commoner according to whether they succeeded to special titles or were born before or after their father became chief – in or out of the purple. In such a rank-conscious society, special status was claimed through mothers as well as fathers and on top of all this the whole country was divided between the original inhabitants and their conquerors.

The complexity of the hierarchy was backed by fantastic protocol and etiquette between the higher and lower echelons. There were, for example, special hats for special ranks and refined rules for putting them on and taking them off. Certain chiefs could put iron anklets on both legs of their wives; others had them on one leg or not at all; still others were only allowed wristlets. According to a man's rank he had one, two, or three doors in his house. In the largest palace meeting-house the kings and queens, princesses and princes, lords and ladies, chamberlains and marshals all had their allotted place and a special kind of stool which went with their rank.

But it was not only a chocolate-soldier world. Each status had its backing of wealth and its political function. From the lowliest widow to the sacred chief there was an interconnection based on patronage and lopsided friendships. For a society like this to function the poor need friends among the rich and the high-born: every commoner had his alliance with a rich royal or a titled retainer; bachelors sought the friendship of chiefs who had daughters or marriage wards to bestow on their clients.

Between a Bangwa patron and his client the terms used are usually 'father' and 'child'. Bangwa's highest ranking woman, Mafwa, was always addressed as 'father' when one of her clients sought a favour from her. The term 'friend' is possible if the relation between a patron and client becomes an on-going one, and is bolstered by the exchange of small gifts. Clients give their patrons esteem and verbal praise in return for support in legal disputes or in any situation where the help of a powerful or wealthy person is useful.

In Bangwa, personal ties (even between a great chief and his subject) are always based on a respect for individuals as persons; this fact smooths the path of government and lessens feelings of envy between rich and poor. This situation, in which individuals of different rank maintain personal contact, is very different from the situation in our society where differential access to wealth has hardened social groups into economic classes which confront each other in a mute and far from friendly fashion. There is little contact between the white collar and the overall, or even the coronet and the bowler hat. I shall always remember a casual remark made by one of the Bloomsbury group – I think it was Virginia Woolf – about the possibility of enjoying friendly relations with the gardener, but the utter impossibility of enjoying friendship or having anything in common with those millions of people in between who live in the suburbs. This remark, I think, sums up one aspect of the divide between industrial and pre-industrial society.

Much larger state systems than that of the Bangwa used ideas of personal pacts as an aid to governing. Among the Swazi[2] the essential alliance between rulers and ruled was stressed and symbolized by the performance of a blood pact between the king and two elected members of commoner lineages who represented the totality of his subjects, the idea being to unite the monarchy and the people in a friendship pact.

When a king or future king was approaching puberty, two young boys were sought out, boys of the same age who were members of the two most important families of the land. The parents were not allowed to refuse this honour and were forced to show as much pleasure as possible when they were called upon to demonstrate their approval of the royal choice. The ceremony, which took place in private, involved the making of incisions in the right thigh of one of the boys and the left thigh of the other. The blood was mixed with the blood of the king and medicines made of charcoal and herbs, whose names signified 'power' and 'force' and 'loyalty', were rubbed into the wounds. One of the boy commoners was called the *nsila* of the right and the other the *nsila* of the left. After this, the king and the boys became mutually identified, they were complete friends, blood brothers. Everything that happened to one was felt by the other two.

In this manner the alliance of a lord and his subjects was symbolized in a personal way. *Nsila* means bodily secretion, the essence of an individual. Even if it is washed and scraped off the body it remains intimately associated with its owner, to such an extent that anybody who gets hold of it can harm the person whom it came from – the idea of sympathetic magic is at work here. The possession of the king's blood, the king's soul, raised the commoners high above all other subjects. They played an important part during wars and annual ceremonies; if one of them died before the king his death would not be announced and his widows were forbidden to wail his death and go into mourning. This blood pact between two commoners and the king was an alliance, a real friendship, a tie of symbolic clientage between a whole people and their king. Between a king and the *nsila* – who were sometimes called 'twins' – the tie was closer than between brothers. Thus intimacy and a purported equality were expressed in a sitution of political asymmetricality to emphasize the alliance of ruler and ruled.

*

A system of clientage is an economical means of government, since it allows a differentiated social structure to function without the need for coercion and legal sanctions. Of course in these systems the 'premise of inequality' has to be wholeheartedly accepted. The Bangwa and the Swazi accepted the hierarchical *status quo* as the best of all possible worlds. The old African kingdom of Ruanda provides the best documented example of this situation:[3] a society based on class, even caste, groupings with the economic exploitation of one group by another as part and parcel of the system. In this case the rulers, the Tutsi, were less than one-fifth of the population and governed the majority, the Hutu, through a system of personal clientage. The relationship was formed when an inferior person of the conquered Hutu class offered his services and asked for protection and friendship from a Tutsi whose wealth and prestige were greater. He approached his future patron with a jug of beer, uttering the words, 'I ask for milk. Make me rich. Think of me. Be my father, I shall be your child.' If the offer was accepted, the patron bestowed on the client one or several cows and from that time onwards they were formally patron and client, the client receiving the support of his lord in lawsuits or in case of need, while he owed his patron personal service, esteem, and political independence. To call this unequal alliance 'friendship' is perhaps stretching the case too far, particularly as it was a relationship which was hardly governed by choice, since no poor Hutu farmer could survive without a patron. Yet friendship was involved; to live without a friend in high places was asking for trouble since anybody at any time might be confronted with an exacting demand from somebody in a position of greater wealth and power. To have a friend in the upper class, however lopsided this friendship, was the only protection he could depend upon. Clientage between members of these two classes provided society's major cohesion. However, once the 'premise of inequality' was no longer held as good and right – which came about after Belgian colonization and independence – the values of the tenuous friendships turned into hatred and led to the genocide and disasters of the post-independence era.

*

In pre-capitalist or pre-industrial societies where there are extremes of wealth people cooperate, not for a sense of well-being alone, but in order to survive. In the aristocratic situations which we have described for the Bangwa and in Ruanda, each member occupies a relatively fixed position in the social scale and there is always someone above and often below whose cooperation he claims or who may claim his. As a result every man binds himself to several of his fellow citizens either as a client or a patron on the basis of lopsided friendship. Hostility, therefore, is not the norm even in rigid caste societies; whatever the morals of these friendships (and we in the West may be said to have an inbuilt prejudice against clientage and patronage because of a belief in the sanctity of equality) they certainly ease the difficulties of interrelationship between different parts of organic systems which involve inequality and privilege. Patronage or ceremonial friendships convert vague political connections into permanent bonds and provide patrons with a means of assisting a man of lower status, which in another situation (our own, perhaps) would simply be considered the action of a weak and foolish man. And as far as the client is concerned, the element of friendship in patron–client relations allows him the possibility of honourably admitting to an inferior status which in other circumstances would betray his honour and manliness within the community. Even in India the techniques of patronage and friendship crossed caste barriers and the growth of strong, even sentimental ties between individuals of different castes or sub-castes prevented the lower castes from a feeling of complete isolation. In hierarchical societies hostility need not be the norm, in fact patron–client relations which penetrated the lower castes meant that the latter groups were prevented from developing strongly counteractive solidarity.

Am I going too far in suggesting that even the lowest and highest castes were involved in relationships of alliance which involved principles of cooperation and friendship? In India the two poles of purity and impurity are symbolized by the Untouchables and the Brahmins: yet the whole society as a totality is made up of many complementary parts and the interdependence between unequal castes and sub-castes is based on professional specialization, which itself is part and parcel of the caste system. Each sub-caste, for example, has a family of specialists at its disposal for each specialized task, and the relationship between them is permanent, personal, and hereditary and could be said to constitute an interdependence between those who dispose of the means of production and those who do not, an interdependence which is in the end to the advantage of the latter.[4]

For this reason there is, between Hindu castes, a tendency towards tolerance based on alliance. Castes differ in customs and habits but live side by side, with an agreed code which ranks them and separates them. In a hierarchical society, groups and individuals acknowledge their differences, since it is this differentiation which is the principle of the integration of society. Castes and sub-castes are not strictly excluded from one another; one anthropologist[5] shows that in a village with twenty-three castes there are several means of integration. One is expressed through smoking around a hookah, when men of different castes smoke in turn; this would be inconceivable in an ideal caste situation in view of the contact between the lips and hence the saliva – elsewhere a symbol of strong friendship, the ideal substance for creating friendship bonds – with the mouthpiece of the pipe, even if a cloth or a hand is placed between them. The pipe smoked is made of clay without a tube and a cloth is put between the lips and the mouthpiece. In fact there is considerable tolerance, higher castes sharing the pipe with almost all castes except the Untouchables and four other castes. In some cases a different cloth must be placed between the pipe and the lips of the smoker. Between twelve and sixteen castes, therefore, smoke the pipe of friendship, a fact which is of some significance in understanding interaction between castes.

Mayer also offers an example of a more positive way in which persons of different castes are linked in friendship. Groups of young people 'hear Ram's name' together, from their teacher (a guru) and thereby become ritual brothers and sisters – really friends – even if they are from different castes. A person only 'hears Ram's name' from the lips of his guru once in a lifetime and it means that these ritual brothers and sisters are members of a single group. The duties between these friends, joined in ritual, are taken even more seriously than those between kin, particularly in the exchange of presents at special life-crisis rites.

At the festival of Gangaur in the month of Badhon, women who have taken a vow to do so are ducked in the stream by their ritual friends. After this ceremony, the ritual friend and his ritual sister's husband give each other turbans, a common sign of friendship between affines. This connection is kept alive by the girl-friend tying a thread of protection on the wrist of the man at the festival of Raksha Bandhan each year. Mayer stresses that the ties between ritual brothers and sisters are based on friendship, not kinship: 'I must stress that the ritual kin tie is quite distinct from the real kin tie for the membership of a descent group.'

Perhaps I shall be accused of fascist apologetics in discussing patronage in hierarchical societies as friendship and stressing the complementarity inherent even in rigid caste systems.[6] Obviously it is difficult to see in what way the Untouchables of the Indian system benefited in any psychological or practical way from their position in the hierarchy. Nor is it possible to begin justifying South African apartheid by describing the sense of camaraderie between a farm serf and his white boss, or a street cleaner and a white shopkeeper in Durban. I am sure these hypothetical friendships exist. On the other hand, friendship and alliance between individuals in caste societies can be shown to be part of their functioning. Democracy involves the attenuation of individual friendships, despite the claim that in socialist democracies we are all brothers or friends. In a similar way Christianity, in stressing the universal brotherhood of man, is in fact jealous of intense relationships between individuals which detract from a Christian's duty to devote all his love to God.

Members of Western societies are certainly not locked together in dyadic relationships against a hostile external environment. The bonds of affection which we have theoretically extended to the whole society in the name of democracy mean in fact that citizens, instead of making friendships – lopsided, equal, or any other kind – become indifferent strangers to one another, each selling his labour or goods, individually, on an impersonal market. Apologists for hierarchical societies (de Tocqueville and Louis Dumont are possible examples) may with truth point out that democracy breaks the chain of both command and alliance –

hence friendship. Democrats owe nothing to any man and expect nothing from any man. They stand alone and can often survive better that way. Our democracy does not require strong inter-personal bonds between equals since our cult of the free individual allows members of the community to sever themselves from the mass of their fellow men, even close neighbours and members of their families. It is only in a democratic, individual-istic universe – and the capitalist West is the best example – that one can afford to ignore one's neighbour, cousin, and the rest of the world.

6   Friends as Twins

Friendship *functions* – it allies groups, it is the passport for a hot and weary missionary on his way to Lake Victoria from Dar-es-Salaam, it encourages the exchange of humdrum market goods, it sentimentalizes power relations. Yet it is much more than this; I now want to look at exotic cosmologies and symbolic systems to try and grasp a deeper understanding of this universal institution.

Despite the 'friendships' between patrons and clients in hierarchical societies equality and complementarity are friendship's basic attributes. The complementarity of friends is emotional or spiritual as well as practical and for this reason some people are positively attracted to their opposites; we have all wondered at the passionate friendships which can flourish between a middle-aged clerk and a Bohemian adventurer, an aristocrat and a pimp, a dandy and a tramp. In other cases we find complementarity seemingly subordinate to the notion of equality. Mates and cobbers in Australia belong to the same work-group or class and have a cultural and ideological identity. On long-distance trawlers, where there is a hierarchy on board, only deckhands – equals – can be real friends. In prison, Old Pals, 'mates', 'friends', and 'acquaintances' form gradations of friendship which are based on shared experiences and the background of the prisoners outside prison. Azande blood brothers stress their equality – commoners and princes are never partners in a blood covenant. Yet, as we shall see, complementarity and equality are not incompatible: even the assymetrical friendships between Greek villagers and poor shepherds have an equalizing role and friendships flourish between Azande who have some skill or quality to offer each other.

Complementarity and equality find expression in a desire for union, a one-ness between beloved friends.

> Loved, as love in twain,
> Had the essence but in one,
> Two distincts, division none:
> Number there in love was slain.

In these words Shakespeare celebrates the concept of the harmony and fusion expected between loving friends, expressed also in Coleridge's definition of love as 'a desire of the whole being to be united to something, or some being, felt necessary to its completeness, by the most perfect means that nature permits, and reason dictates'. Both sexual loving and friendship can be envisaged as two separate beings striving to become one; a desire for the fusion of two complementary poles into one whole, neither completely masculine or completely feminine. 'Coupling and 'bonding' suggest a kind of spiritual as well as sexual symbiosis between partners – passive and active, male and female This idea of polarity and union is expressed by the concept of *ying*, the feminine pole which is calm, dark, and receptive; and *yang*, the masculine, active, light, and generative. These ideas should not be taken as purely sexual as Lawrence seems to have done in his bisexual philosophy, believing man's nature was dual – not entirely male – and that his male and female elements were continually seeking some kind of balance. Lawrence expresses these ideas when he makes Birkin, fearing his loss of identity in fusion with a woman, say, 'Why should we consider ourselves, men and women, as broken fragments of one whole? . . . In the old age, before sex was, we were mixed, each one a mixture. The process of singling into individuality resulted in the great polarization of sex. The womanly due to one side, the manly to the other.'

Lawrence seems to be referring to the theories of some exegists of the Old Testament who read into the creation of human beings the message that 'God created man, in his image' the meaning that He created him male and female, before the separation of Eve out of the body of Adam. From here we arrive at the currently fashionable, unisexual cult of androgyny whereby sexual differentiation is being undermined and the ideal condition seems to be a human being with the characteristics of both sexes and in whom the roles of man and woman are completely merged. One respected American academic in a book of literary criticism begins with the credo that 'our future salvation lies in a movement away from sexual polarization and the prison of gender toward a world in which individual roles and the modes of personal behaviour can be freely chosen'.[1]

My plea is slightly different: the satisfactions of love depend on human interdependence, the attraction that springs from complementarity rather than the atomistic self-sufficiency of the hermaphrodite. The complete fusion of male and female, the spiritual bisexuality of androgyny, has the perilous potential of turning us into unisexed beings with no emotional or physical needs outside of ourselves – superb material for the machine-controlled society of 1984. The salient point of sexual differentiation, division of labour, and alliances between friends is that they all celebrate complementarity as one of the original elements of culture.

The most obvious symbolic expression of the complementarity and equality of a couple or pair is twinness. Twins, everywhere – two-in-one, one-in-two, half-of-one – are perfect friends. In African cosmologies and classical myth twins symbolize the fusion of the couple, the perfect dyad, the intimate union, Montaigne's 'one soul in two bodies'. Mythical twinness, an almost universal element in cosmologies, may represent not only an original androgyny but through duality the victory of order over anarchy.

The intimacy of mythical twins becomes the ideal friendship. In the Bangwa heaven, souls wander around in pairs and are born as twins or 'best friends'. Pende best friends die together and go to a heaven composed of twins. The origin myth of the Dogon celebrates a primordial twinness which permeates every aspect of their symbolic structure. It is, in fact, a common theme in most cultures. There are hints in our own legends that similar ideas existed. Among the Germanic people pairs of rulers may have been twins – possibly even the legendary Anglo-Saxon invaders Hengest and Horsa. Balder and Hoder were twins. In Biblical religious lore we even find that Cain and Abel each had a twin sister and that their quarrelling began over these girls;

and that Jacob, the twin brother of Esau, had eleven sons, ten of whom were born with twin sisters, whom they subsequently married. In Egyptian myth Shu, with Tefnut his twin sister, comprised the first couple of the ennead (a set of nine gods), created by Ra, without recourse to woman. They themselves gave birth to twins, Geb and Nut, who became the second pair of the ennead and gave birth to Osiris and Isis who were also possibly twins.

In classical mythology Amphion and Sethus, Apollo and Artemis were twins. The most famous pair – recalled even in English by the slang expression 'by jiminy' – are the Gemini twins, Castor and Pollux (Kastor and Polydeukes). The Dioscouri, as they were also known, were thought to be the twin sons of Zeus. In fact, Tyndareus, husband of Leda, played a certain part in their paternity. Zeus, in the guise of a swan, visited Leda and she was brought to bed with two eggs, from one of which issued Pollux and Helen – the children of Zeus. From the other came Castor and Clytemnestra, who were reputed to be the children of Tyndareus and hence mortal. In spite of their different paternity Castor and Pollux both qualified as Dioscouri, meaning 'young sons of God'. Like the Bangwa, far away in time and space, the Greeks attempted to explain the anomaly of twinship by assuming that one of the children was of divine origin. When Castor was mortally wounded in battle the divine Pollux wept over his body – being himself immortal he could not follow his twin to Hades. Zeus was touched by this devotion and authorized Castor to share the privilege of immortality with his brother: thus the Dioscouri continued to live, each on alternate days. Another tradition says that Zeus placed them among the stars, in the constellation of the Gemini.

The Dioscouri became symbols of the greatest love and devotion of friends. They also expressed other complementary relations – the alliance of traders and the friendship of host and guest. Sometimes they are portrayed, dressed in white robes and purple mantles, starred bonnets on their heads, arriving in cities to test what sort of a welcome the inhabitants give to strangers. Once they were entertained in Argos so well that ever afterwards the descendants of the inhabitants came under their special protection. In the same way they were particularly worshipped in Agrigentum because of the hospitality they received there when they visited the town with their sister Helen.

Castor and Pollux were worshipped for their complementarity and their duality. Patrons of almost all the crafts and professions, benefactors of the poor and needy, of sailors and ploughmen, merchants and sailors, their most salient feature was their complementarity as twins – one was mortal and the other immortal – as the result of their dual paternity, spiritual Zeus and material Tyndareus. The duality of twins expresses alliance and exchange and symbolizes friendship in Ancient Greece and in Africa. They are one and yet two.

Twins are not celebrated because of the fact of their multiple birth – triplets are not credited with the supernatural potency of twins – but because of their duality. Nor are they celebrated because they are identical. In contemporary society the fact that twins are the same in all particulars is the main reason for their special strangeness. In Africa and ancient myth twins are not god-like beings because they are identical, so as to be interchangeable, but because they were born as two, from the same womb, at the same time, and are complementary. Castor and Pollux were physically and psychologically different: traditional artistic treatment of the Dioscouri often shows one of them bearded and the other smooth-shaven. There is also an assumption of a division of labour (complementarity) between the strong, tough Pollux who did the hard-hitting and Castor who drove the chariot. The Biblical twins Esau and Jacob, one hairy and the other smooth-skinned, were obviously in no way identical. Most twins are a pair of opposites if they are to have meaning in myth. In monuments of Mithra, twins appear as a pair of children or young men, carrying torches. One of the pair holds his torch down and the other up, in harmony with the common idea of twins being complementary beings. In our own literature of twins – as in Thomas Mann's incestuous story, 'The Mood of the Waslungs' – the emphasis is on the complementarity and difference of male–female twins.

In Western culture we stress the fact that twins are identical; at the same time we stress the sameness – rather than the complementarity and equality – of friends. Today, best friends show off their friendship by wearing identical clothes and having the same hairstyle. Yet it is hard to see how friendship needs can be satisfied by a mirror image, any more than unisex trousers and attitudes improve the sexual complementarity of lovers. Exchange, reciprocity, and friendship all involve an element of rivalry and opposition. Sameness deadens, differences enliven.

In Africa twins are treated with the greatest respect or the greatest disrespect – they are either worshipped or put to death. My suggestion is that such extreme reactions to anomalous births are due precisely to the fact that they are born two-in-one, as two equal persons in a social situation which, however egalitarian, always implies hierarchy, especially in the family. To some people – the Bangwa and the Dogon for example – twins are perfect births, representing a primordial world where twin births were the rule. Others consider twins as imperfect births and are viewed as an insult to the natural order.

The Kaguru attitude to twins expresses the ambivalent attitude to dual births. In the past this Tanzanian people killed twins since they were considered to have dangerous capabilities which would harm their kinsmen if they were allowed to live. At the same time Kaguru men who sacralize their close friendship by making a blood pact are said to become 'one person' by occupying a single social status: best friends have a mutual identity like twins. However in this society equality is a divine ideal and should not be achieved by ordinary mortals. The closest possible human relationship is between persons of the same age and sex, of the same blood – twins who are not separated by seniority and have shared the same womb. Twins in Kaguru were killed because they had rendered themselves dangerous to society by attempting an ideal union that belonged only to God.[2]

The fear and horror of twins expressed by some African peoples was given lurid publicity by missionaries in their reports of the killing of twin babies and the ostracization of their mothers. Mary Kingsley has given her usual vivid and sympathetic account of this situation in south-eastern Nigeria, which I should like to quote at some length:[3]

All children are thrown [into the bush] who have not arrived in this world in the way considered orthodox, or who cut their teeth in an improper manner. Twins are killed among all the Niger Delta tribes, and in the districts out of English control the mother is killed too, except in Oman, where the sanctuary is. These mothers and their children are exiled to an island in the Cross River. They have to remain on the island, and if any man goes across and marries one of them, he has to remain on the island too. This twin-killing is a widely diffused custom among the negro tribes.

There is always a sense of there being something uncanny about twins in West Africa, and in those tribes where they are not killed they are regarded as requiring great care to prevent their dying on their own account . . .

The terror with which twins are regarded in the Niger Delta is exceedingly strange and real. When I had the honour of being with Miss Slessor [a missionary], the first twins in that district were saved from immolation owing entirely to Miss Slessor's great influence with the natives and her own unbounded courage and energy. The mother in this case was a slave woman, an Eboe, the most expensive and valuable of slaves. She was the property of a big woman, who had always treated her – as indeed most slaves are treated in Calabar – with great kindness and consideration, but when these two children arrived all was changed immediately. She was subject to torrents of virulent abuse, her things were torn from her, her English china basins, possessions she valued most highly, were smashed, her clothes were torn and she was driven out as an unclean thing.

Miss Slessor saved the woman and one child, the other having already died from rough handling. A new path was cut for their return to the villages; if they had used the ordinary path it would have become polluted and no one would have travelled over it.

The attitude of the people to the remaining twin is significant:

They would not touch it, and only approached it after some days, and then only when it was held by Miss Slessor and me . . . Even its own mother could not be trusted with the child; she would have killed it. She never betrayed the slightest desire to have it with her, and after a few days nursing and feeding it she was anxious to go back to her mistress, who, being an enlightened woman, was willing to have her, if she came without the child. The woman . . . who would have to live for the rest of her life as an outcast, and for a long time in a state of isolation, in a hut of her own, which no one would enter, neither would any eat or drink with her, nor partake of the food and water she had cooked or fetched. She would lead the life of a leper, working in the plantation by day, and going into her lonely hut by night, shunned and cursed.

... She would sit for hours singing or rather, moaning out a kind of dirge over herself. 'Yesterday I was a woman, now I am a horror, a thing all people run from. Yesterday they would talk to me with a sweet mouth, now they greet me with curses and execrations. They have smashed my basins, they have torn my clothes' and so on. There was no complaint against the people for doing these things, only a bitter sense of injury against some superhuman power that had sent his withering curse of twins down on her.

Many people have decidedly ambiguous ideas about twins – the story of the lapsed vestal virgin, the mother of Romulus and Remus, has been said to be an attempt to explain to a later age the taboo on mothers of twins. Macaulay dramatizes the same feeling:

> Slain is the Pontiff Camera
> Who spake the words of doom:
> The children to the Tiber:
> The mother to the tomb.

Our own ideas on twins may reflect a hint of these extreme attitudes to multiple births. A biologist has suggested[4] that this is because twins provide in miniature a model of man's evolutionary development, embracing his search for identity both as an individual and as a member of society.

This rather grand-sounding explanation of our modern attitudes to twins finds more than an echo in the cosmological ideas of some African people concerning friends and twins. The Bangwa are close neighbours of the Calabar peoples, described by Miss Kingsley, who until the colonial period shuttled slaves from the Cameroon plateau down to the Nigerians, receiving guns and European goods in return. They shared certain art styles and the songs and dances of their popular 'jujus'. All the stranger, therefore – considering their close commercial and cultural contacts – that their attitudes to twins are quite the reverse.

In Bangwa, a woman who gives birth to twins is fêted by the whole population rather than banished from the village. I have seen elaborate sculptures carved in honour of a mother of twins. Villagers bring her food and ask her blessing. A certain number of days after the birth she and the children are dressed in finery, decked out with beads, and paraded through the market where the people congratulate her on her good fortune and press coins into her hands. More than this, a mother of twins automatically becomes a member of a twin-mothers association and is called in to dance at important ceremonies and funerals. I once saw two hundred of these women dance at a chief's funeral. During fertility rites twin-mothers wearing their special insignia – beads, staffs, leaves – 'cool the earth' and offer sacrifices. Twin-mothers are also the most popular diviners and priestesses; having given birth to 'little gods' they are themselves in touch with the divine.

More wonderful than the mothers are the children, creatures to be feared as well as admired. They are demanding, selfish, and cantankerous – half human and half spirit. Most twins are thought to despise the world of humans and special rites are performed to accustom them to the rigours and tedium of a mortal life. These rituals, which last for several weeks and can take place even when the twins are fully grown, are known as 'fattening' in pidgin English and primarily involve the stuffing of the greedy creatures with the best meat and yams available. The word twin is also used for any other person who is at all remarkable, physically or mentally: children born in a caul, or with six fingers, for example. One memorable day I walked five hours to be shown a very special twin who lived with her husband and children far away from the palace in the lowland forest region. Her particular twin miracle was to have been born with no arms and legs. In this way, the Bangwa have a remarkable means of converting the monstrous into the wonderful, the almost-normal. Chiefs, the most wondrous of all beings, may be referred to as twins; a son is frequently chosen to succeed his father specifically because he is in fact a twin – of course in this case the other twin would have to be female or dead.

Most interestingly, the Bangwa call twins 'best friends'. Best friends are known as 'twins' and elevated to the miraculous status of the products of a dual birth. The Bangwa stress equality in friendship – both in 'achieved' friendships (of the heart) and ascribed friendships (of the road) – and the relationship is allowed to cut across differences in rank. If a slave woman has a child at the same moment as the king's favourite wife gives birth, the two children are automatically, inexorably, best friends and twins. Nor is this a formality, since the friendship has its duties and obligations. As among the Kaguru, twins born of one womb are the complete expression of true equality and friends born at the same time approximate this two-in-oneness. Twins in Bangwa are the only persons in a kin group who are allowed to use each other's personal name in conversation and act in a friendly fashion. All other brothers and cousins use the term 'elder relative' or 'junior relative', since age differentiation is as important as social rank and is given full expression in etiquette.

Twins are best friends, therefore, because they are supremely equal and because they shared the same womb for nine months – or according to Bangwa folklore usually longer since twins are well known for having a much longer pre-natal life than ordinary children, roaming in and out of the womb for an indefinite period before finally consenting to being born. This spirit world of unborn children is described by Bangwa as a vast, black cave, peopled by the spirits of babies which float around in pairs and groups looking for suitable parents. The belief is that the supply of children is replenished by the spirits of dead Bangwa who are reincarnated in their descendants. Spirit children who are great friends and always in pairs are choosy about being born again; life with their friends in the spirit world is comfortable and more-over there is the danger of losing one's twin-friend during the journey, since it is rare for a spirit pair to agree to enter a single womb.

When twins are born a special ritual is immediately per-formed both to prevent the death of one of the parents or grand-parents (thus correcting the imbalance in the spirit world) and to persuade the pair to accept their new life on earth. Even when a single child is born and shows a disinclination to live, he will be called a 'twin'. Since it is rare for a spirit pair to enter a single womb – tastes differ even in the world of unborn children – twins are often separated at the last minute. Or some may decide to enter a womb, remaining there quite a long time, before one of them is seduced back to the delights of the spirit world. This renegade torments his 'friend', lurking in the shadows of the fire burning in the mother's hut, trying to make the child die and go away with him.

I once spent a whole day hearing of one old man's pre-natal life. He spent long years travelling in the world of the spirits with his best friend and twin looking around for a luxurious home with agreeable, generous parents. Finally decided, the two entered the belly of a man – this man's father – and from there were eventually transferred in the latter's semen to the womb of his wife. Unfortunately his twin refused to accompany him at the last minute and, furious that he had been deserted, the un-conceived child tormented his friend in the womb, bringing considerable strain and pain to the mother who suffered an agonizing pregnancy lasting two years. Towards the end the unconceived twin went so far as to hide in the woman's eyelid where he formed an ugly, swollen sty. Finally he-she left the pregnant woman's eye and entered the womb of a woman in a neighbouring village who gave birth to a bouncing baby girl the day after the man whose interminable story I was hearing was born.

The point of this story is to show how twinship and ideas of duality are linked with friendship in Bangwa. This man was not so much interested in explaining twins or the spirit world to me as the values of friendship. Children who are born without a twin in Bangwa are considered, in a way, abnormal, at least more abnormal than twins in so far as they are born singly. The pairing of them with a friend of the same age removes any future danger of their being seduced back to the spirit world by a spirit friend or twin.

This need for a partner, a twin, a complementary soul-mate, is brought out in another account given by a friend of mine who was constantly ill as a child. The diviner sought the super-natural reasons for this perpetual state of ailing and declared that he was suffering because his friend had been conceived in the womb of another woman, owing to a quarrel between the children as unborn twins, and they had never been reunited on earth. The other child was found and the two children were formally declared twins, the usual rites being carried out for seven weeks and their mothers assuming the respected status of mothers-of-twins. The children were given names reserved for twins and had their hair dressed in the high twin peaks of 'friends by birth'. A child who shows signs of chronic illness is frequently said to be suffering from the tormenting of his friend, his *alter ego* who lives in the spirit world and delights in attempting to seduce his twin to return and enjoy the carefree, well-fed life of unborn children. The parents of such a child may call in a ritual expert to perform a ceremony to sever him from the malign influences of his friend. An effigy is made of the spirit-twin from a banana stem and a deep pit is dug in the ground. The sick child is placed in it as if for burial, but at the last minute before the pit is filled in the child is whisked out and replaced by the effigy. In this way the unborn twin is foiled and, it is hoped, will cease to prey on his friend.

In Bangwa, therefore, the closest of friends are twins or children who have travelled together in the world of the spirits. Failing a twin, a child is linked by his parents to a child born as nearly as possible at the same time. I had an interpreter who told me that his father, the local chief, considered when he reached the age of five or six that he needed a close friend. When he and his father were walking together in a distant village they found a child of the same age whom the chief swore resembled the son in every respect. They must have been twins, he declared, and the two children were there and then formally declared best friends. Their hair was dressed in the usual style and after a special ceremony they were formally paraded through the market, well-oiled and dressed in fine clothes, like the twins who had 'come out' after the traditional 'fattening' rites. Forty years later these men remained best friends and twins.

The respect for twins and the association of friendship with twins are not uncommon in Africa and have led to frequent discussion among anthropologists; in a series of articles and letters in *Man*[5] the whole problem of abnormality and anomaly as regards twins was brought up once more. Why are twins little gods, little devils? Why are they killed or worshipped? Why are they birds, as among the Nuer? It has been attempted to show that the Nuer associate twins with birds because birds and twins are both associated with God – they are both of the air, the element to which the spirit is likened by the Nuer in metaphor. But Firth points out that twins are physiologically and sociologically abnormal in that they are duplicate personalities or 'one person'; for this reason they are regarded as dangerous and equated with Gods and birds. This may be an interesting and enlightening explanation of Nuer concepts, but as a more universal sociological explanation as to why twins are 'birds', Milner's analysis is more to the point. When a bird is seen with its outstretched wings separated by the mass of its body, there is a perfect suggestion of binary symmetry. Twins, like birds, are composed of two distinct physical entities constituting one social entity. Milner also points out that a bird cannot fly with a wing damaged or missing. Twins are physically separate, but socially unitary and interdependent. That is why in so many societies when one twin dies or marries, and not the other, steps must be taken to avoid the serious consequences of a sudden imbalance.

Among the Bangwa, twins are a primordial and social entity, the perfect union of two parts, expressing communication, complementarity, alliance and friendship. Personal illness and accident in Bangwa may be attributed to a failure to achieve this important balance with another person, symbolized by twins. Moral, ritual, and physical equilibrium is achieved through the presence and devotion of a friend. In the beginning all people were paired as twins in a dual cosmos, equally balanced, complementary halves of a perfect whole. A version of the same kind of mythical thinking has been found among the Pende[6] of the Upper Kwango in Angola where, as we have seen, blood pacts cemented friendships which were likened to the relationship between twins. The two bonded persons, of the same or different sex, were considered to be 'two in one' and eventually died together, being reincarnated as twins. The parallel between Pende and Bangwa ideas is striking – particularly the concept of a spirit world of paired friends or twins; in the Bangwa case, the twins are friends before birth while in Angola two men become twins because they are friends who die together and then continue to exist in eternity as twins.

The study of the interplay of twinship, friendship, sexuality, and metaphysics has been brilliantly extended by a team of French anthropologists working among the Dogon of Mali under the initial stimulus of Marcel Griaule.[7] The Dogon for some centuries have entrenched themselves in a harsh, semi-desert environment on a bend of the River Niger. This region is on the fringe of an immense stone plateau where they have constructed their villages from rocks which have fallen from the overhanging cliffs. These villages are strange huddles of terraced houses and granaries, all with thatched pointed roofs. Looked at from these cliffs, the Dogon appear to be living in a lunar landscape: there is no colour and the contours of the villages are blurred by a permanent heat-haze. Stretching to the horizon, nothing is visible but a plain of sand dotted sparsely with villages. The people cultivate millet and have fields in tiny valleys which divide the plateau into furrows or on the cliff slopes. Some steep farm-gardens are only a few yards long, supported by walls of sun-bleached stones, and can only be reached from the plain by means of a rope ladder.

Dogon burial grounds consist of horizontal faults or breaks in the rock face where there are ruined buildings, now inaccessible, which appear to have been ancient granaries. Many of the houses of the village back on to the rock and a notched pole allows access by means of a 'chimney' to the terrace which forms the lower floor of another dwelling.

Perhaps because they have been somewhat sheltered from major cultural movements they have preserved a unique culture, rich in detailed myths and symbolism, inspired by their religion.

According to Marcel Griaule, twinship has been the rule among the Dogon since the beginning of time – *'en effet, dès l'origine du monde, la règle était de gemelleité'* [8] – and these concepts have been analysed and described with clarity and a wealth of detail by the Griaule team. Twinship symbolizes the complementarity between all kinds of bonded pairs: friends, traders, husbands and wives, a man and his shadow, a man and his placenta. Rich and poor, children of aristocrats and descendants of slaves, become twins once they have gone through circumcision and the ordeals of initiation together, thereby experiencing a new social state. People who form alliances of any kind are seen as a single entity, albeit divided into two parts, like twins. The two parts are not identical but complementary and equal.

Moreover, Dogon ideas on twinness and androgyny have been given some currency in philosophical thinking on dual systems and the androgyne in intellectual circles in France. A summary of the complex ideas found in their creation myth, therefore, will serve as a means of comparing these ideas (and their themes of twinness, incest, and duality) with Bangwa and Pende concepts and also with those found in classical myths which are of a remarkably similar nature.

The Dogon universe issued from an infinity of smallness, created by the Word of a single God, called Amma; this is symbolized today on earth by both the fonio seed (a Sudanese staple grain crop) and the egg of the mudfish; it is symbolized in space by a satellite of Sirius, the star Digitaria. This infinite smallness developed and formed a vast womb, called the Egg of the World, which was divided into twin parts and contained two placentas which eventually gave birth to twin couples, pairs of mixed twins, living and animated beings, prototypes of men, who possessed the creative Word. These beings had the form of the mudfish and are likened by the Dogon to the human foetus in the waters of the womb.

From one half of this egg, one of the male twins, the Fox, was born prematurely. In order to gain possession of the nascent universe for himself, he rebelled against his creator. Tearing off a piece of his placenta which had formed a kind of ark, he climbed down into empty space on it. The torn-off piece of placenta became our planet. He went inside it in order to look for his twin sister, since without her he was powerless to realize any of his ambitions for domination. Walking in every direction he made five rows of twelve holes in the still wet and bloody soil. In this way he set out the first field of the future, with its sixty plots. When his searches on earth came to nought, he went back up into the sky. But Amma had given his twin to the pair in the other half of the egg so that the Fox should not get hold of her and had put the rest of the placenta out of his reach by turning it into a sun – that is, burning fire.

The Fox, the archetypal rebel and trickster, then stole eight seeds of cereal created by Amma and sowed them in the earth; the humidity of the placenta, which had not yet entirely dried out, caused one of the fonio seeds to germinate and to become red and impure. The premature intervention on the part of the audacious Fox, the incest he had committed by penetrating his own placenta (that is, the womb of his 'mother'), and above all his theft and planting of the fonio seed (the 'sperm' of his father

Amma), permanently disturbed the order of creation and made it incomplete and impure. Amma, in order to remedy this situation, had one of the twins in the other half of the egg castrated and offered in sacrifice to heaven. This twin shed his blood to purify the universe; he was given the name of Nommo and his body was cut into sixty pieces. One by one these pieces were thrown into space at the four cardinal points; some of them fell to earth and were transformed into plants, symbols of the purification wrought by this sacrifice.

Nommo, however, was brought back to life as a human couple – a man and a woman, made from the stuff of his own placenta. With the same material he created four pairs of mixed twins, who were the real ancestors of mankind, the sons of Nommo, who is considered their father. In another version of the creation myth, Nommo, male and female himself, drew two outlines on the ground, one on top of the other, one male and one female. Nommo stretched himself out on these two shadows of himself and took both of them for his own. The same thing was done to create woman. Thus it came about that each human being, from the first, was endowed with two souls of different sex, or rather with two different principles corresponding to two distinct persons. In the man, the female soul was located in the foreskin and in the woman the male soul was the clitoris. Each person then had to merge himself in the sex for which he appeared best fitted and circumcision and cliterodechtomy are seen as the removal of external femininity and internal masculinity. An incestuous act in creation, therefore, had destroyed order, based on the principle of twin or androgynous births, and order was only restored by the creation of human beings; twin births are replaced by dual souls. Dual souls were implanted in each newborn child by Nommo who held them by the thighs over the etched outlines in the ground.

From the union of the original Dogon ancestors, mankind grew apace and life became organized on Earth. Meanwhile the rebel, the Fox, a single being without his twin sister, was incapable of achieving his wished-for domination. He was fated to pass his time vainly pursuing his lost twin who was at the same time his female soul. Nommo's role as a complete being, a pair of twins, was to limit the disorderly activities of the Fox and to do this he divided up all the constituent elements of the universe, placing them in categories and keeping them under his constant control.

The Dogon myth, so bleakly summarized here from material in the works of Dieterlen,[9] Paulme[10] and Griaule,[11] clearly brings out the importance of duality and twinship in Dogon thought. Most elements of Dogon cosmology refer back to this myth – the griot (of a caste of musicians and praise-singers), for example, and his twin sister were made from those parts of the placenta where the sacrificed Nommo had fallen. The blacksmith and *his* twin sister were made from the umbilical cord of the victim and the blood which came from the castrated genitals of Nommo and from the cord. Incidentally the Dogon blacksmith is the twin *par excellence*,[12] a fact which is attested by different versions of the creation myth which explain the origin of his magical powers. The Dogon say, 'Nommo and the blacksmith are of red blood, like a resplendent ball'; and 'Nommo and the blacksmith are twins; both are red like copper; the heat of the fire and the charcoal at his forge have blackened the smith.' The smith, like all the first living creatures created by Amma, God, shares the privileges and powers of twins, including their sacred character and a certain intangibility. It is for this reason that the blacksmith can successfully invoke God when he prays for rain – rain is the sperm of the sacrificed Nommo, his twin, whose sexual attributes have become the tools of his forge.

Not only blacksmiths but also Dogon traders are twins in the sense that twins invented trade, their father finding in their shrine the cowrie shells which became the currency of Dogon commerce. (In West Africa, cowries are commonly symbols of twins, wealth, and fertility.) The spirit, Nommo, placed the eight cowries in the place of the hands of the first trader because, man *qua* trader counts with his fingers. He placed only eight because when man first began trading he counted in eights – eighty, for example, is a round hundred in Dogon thought, as it used to be in France. Cowries are linked to words, which are exchanged and communicated in the making of speech; and cowries, through being exchanged, bring about trade and hence social life. A mother of twins has special magical advantages as a trader; and twins themselves receive bonuses when they buy goods in the market – 'People give to twins in order to gain something of their luck.' In setting up twin shrines, cowries are given and placed in two piles: the two heaps symbolize a buyer and a seller. The pall for the dead, on which these cowries are placed, is also a symbol of commerce, for the twins who made the first exchanges sat on it, and it is made of black and white squares of equal number.

Centres of trade and commerce among the Dogon are established under the permanent sign of twinness. At the end of the long rituals following a dual birth the twins, as sponsors of the ritual multiplication of commercial cowries, are carried to the market-place and put near those areas where the circulation of money and the exchange of goods is being carried on most vigorously. A sacrifice is then made at the market altar set up for Lebe, whose 'skeleton outline cast up by the Nommo spirit is formed of the eight ancestors, the eight paired ancestors, patrons of twins. It is they who drink the blood of the sacrifice and with them come the dead twins of all time, including the first twins, the inventors of trade.'[13]

Among the Dogon, therefore, twins stand for exchange, complementarity and equality as well as duality and order and as such they symbolize friendship and alliance. Twinship is even expressed in the violent friendships between the Dogon and the Bozo, a fisherfolk on the banks of the Niger; the two people exchange wild jokes and insults (see p. 220) in token of an ancient friendship. The Bozo are 'fish' and in mythical times the mudfish and man (i.e. the Dogon) were twins. The Bozo are of the water and the Dogon traditionally refer to them as 'walking fish', while the Dogon are of the land. The friendship pact between the two peoples, who are by no means near neighbours, has always been expressed in insults and joking, the Dogon believing that once upon a time a part of the vital force of each group was deposited in the other. Thus each Bozo possesses in himself part of a Dogon and *vice versa*. In their relationships, each party acts on that part of himself which is in the other – his twin and his friend – and this forms a sort of foundation in the other person on which he can work.

What about actual Dogon twins? Like Bangwa twins, they are

delicate creatures who must not be grumbled at or they die. They are visionaries with second-sight and can see the forest spirits and the recently dead, who fly around the village. Again like Bangwa twins, they lose their second-sight and their fragility once they become adolescents. Dogon twins are also given special names and a year after their birth there is a ceremony on exactly the same lines as that which takes place on the installation of the Dogon priest-chief, the Hogon. Both the twin ceremony and the installation of the priest are beneficial to soil fertility and human prosperity in general. The twins are given necklaces of eight cowries and a special pointed hat like the priest's bonnet, with cowries sewn on it.

For both the Bangwa and the Dogon the ideal and perfect birth is twin birth. Single children upset the social and cosmological order of things. The Bangwa associate them immediately with another 'friend' or 'twin', a single child born as nearly as possible at the same time. Among the Dogon, at every childbirth the intermediary spirit, Nommo, prays to God for the birth of twins but Nommo's prayers are not always answered, of course, and that is why he has given two souls to every child. A child's body is one, but his spiritual being is two. And until his initiation rites he remains spiritually, symbolically, and physically androgynous (until puberty dual children retain foreskin or clitoris, their masculinity and their femininity thereby remaining equally potent). For a girl the clitoris is a symbolic twin, a male makeshift with which she cannot reproduce herself and which also prevents her mating with a man. She has it removed, since anyone trying to mate with an unexcised woman would be frustrated by opposition from an organ claiming to be his equal. Similarly when a boy is circumcised and his foreskin is transformed into a lizard, he loses both his femininity and his twin.

The duality and complementarity of male and female is associated with the duality and unity of twinship. Twins correspond to the number two. Duality between male and female corresponds to the opposition between the masculine symbol, three, and the feminine, four, which added together gives seven, the Dogon symbol of the complete being. Twinship here is a useful concept for understanding the relationship between two people who are symbolically one, and the androgyny of the male and female parts of a single person, made up of two. In this complex and original way twins have been converted by the Dogon into a mode of thought; among the Kaguru and Calabar peoples twins are an offence against the divinity because they attempt to imitate his godlike duality.

The closest the Dogon can get to perfect union is twinship, expressed both in their creation myth and in their belief in the original duality of all things. Twins as an ideal unit also express the alliance and duality of friends, traders, joking partners, and husbands and wives. Each member of these dyads has in a sense found his other half. Most people are nevertheless born alone and to compensate the Dogon for this misfortune each child is linked with an animal who represents his unknown other half – his unborn twin. This animal-twin himself has a twin, another taboo animal, and so on, and so on, thus connecting the aggregate of Dogon families with the whole animal kingdom through the essential notion of twinness.

Twinship, alliance, complementarity are intertwined in Dogon thought with bisexuality and hermaphroditism. The Greeks also revered twinness and bisexuality – Hermaphrodite as well as Castor and Pollux provided a symbol of conjunction and unity. In our own culture, opposite sex twins have a strong hold on our imagination – 'complementary, different in heredity and sex, but identical in birth experience, the two seem to encompass between them complete human possibility'.[14] In the lore of opposite-sex twins, the two are depicted as an original unit which split, a unit which strives to be reunited by sexual love.

Myths of origin throughout the world, like the Dogon legend, describe the original pair as twins born at a miraculous birth and destined to be lovers. Even Genesis suggests this, although in Jewish tradition the twin theory was removed to the next generation; all Adam's sons were born with a twin sister whom they married. In Greek mythology the beginning of the world involved androgyny and twinness. The first births included that of Night, a twin who was born bisexual and fissiparously, at the same time as her male twin Erebos. Night herself gave birth to Day and, unaided, engendered the children of the Night, among whom are Sleep and Death, a pair of twins, one black and the other white. In Hindu mythology, Shakti was the female element of Shiva, and Ardhanarisvara is a composite figure, half man and half woman. Mitra and Varuna, a spiritual dyad like Castor and Pollux, were dual gods, possessors of the power which formed the essence of the Kshatriya caste. Mitra and Varuna maintained universal order, Mitra presiding over friendship and ratifying contracts and Varuna looking after oaths. Tacitus, writing about the 'Adam' of the Teutons, said he was called 'Mannus' (man) and his father and mother was Tuisto, meaning 'two-sexed being'.[15]

Thus in Christian, Egyptian, Greek, and Hindu cosmology, as well as in that of the Dogon, we have a pattern of symbolic relevation of a dual order of reality, of the complementarity of the first human beings which is androgynous in nature. Among the Bangwa, these ideas are expressed in a much less high-flown way by their special regard for twin births. This duality and original androgyny are ideas which express love, exchange, and friendship – the very nature of man. Plato in the *Symposium* places these ideas divertingly in the mouth of Aristophanes, who suggested that in the prehistoric world, 'in the old age, before sex was', there were three kinds of person: male, female, and hermaphrodite. All of them were said to have been circular and double in shape with four hands, four feet, and one head with two faces; but Zeus, in order to punish these original, androgynous beings for their intrepidity in trying to scale the heavens, decided to crush them by cutting them in two ('like sob-apples ready for pickling or as you might divide an egg with a hair'). At the same time he gave each of them the desire to find their own other half and restore their original unity. Men who were halves of those combined beings called hermaphrodites were said to be inclined towards the love of women, while women who were halves of primitive women were said to love other women, while the male halves of the third group went off in search of their other male half.

For Plato this myth glorified and justified the attractions of sexuality and the wonders of male love. Love, however, was not merely the desire for bodily completion: if a man encountered his other half, the pair would be lost in amazement and friendship and intimacy. The ideal of joined male friends was that they should never leave each other, night or day, and should become such a close partnership that they could lead a common existence together as though they were one being; and after death they would still be one in Hades. Plato, in the words of both Aristophanes and Diotoma, tells us that men of thought and action desire to return to the original condition of man, which is unity. Diotoma, talking to Sophocles, says that love, the great mediator between the mortal and immortal, seeks not so much to win back the lover's other half, but to restore a state in which they were not distinct, when they were one. Plato's arguments are applicable to heterosexual as well as homosexual or 'platonic' love. Eros becomes the aspiration of our mortal nature towards immortality and is therefore impatient to procreate. There are, however, two kinds of procreation, one of the body and the other of the spirit; Platonism, which is concerned with the latter, suggests that truly divine mortals whose fertility resides in the soul become teachers, go in quest of beautiful adolescent boys, 'marry' in a far closer union, and have a more intimate friendship than those who beget normal children, for the children who are their common offspring are immortal and fair.

Despite Plato's pederasty and the parody inherent in Aristophanes' account of the hermaphroditic, androgynous beginnings of the world, it is clear that we have here a fictive, cosmological answer to a theory of friendship and alliance which has much in common with Dogon thought and which is germane to this book. The idea of two being present in one individual, the notion of twinness, is a major element in the cosmology of many peoples – the belief in an original unity and duality has in fact been incorporated into the very social structure of some peoples in the form of moieties.

From my point of view, the lesson to be learned from the theme of twinship is that it expresses in a clear-cut manner the need in men and women to complete their individual being. Man is a dual being seeking his complementary other half: the male needs the female for perfect sexual union; friends seek in each other the qualities they lack. In one sense, the image of twins is also a narcissistic one, the pair of friends only trying to mirror their own identity in each other, at the same time seeking in undividedness an attempt to repeat the unity of the mythical androgyne. The rupture of the original duality of man is seen in myth and life as a degradation resulting in chaos and disorder, which is only to be repaired by seeking the union of the sexes, of twins or of friends.

7   Business Friends

'Exchange' – the business of transferring goods, ornaments, wives, Christmas cards, greetings – is institutionalized in all societies, not least in our own. The Polynesians exchange food to express bonds of friendship and kinship. We take wine or vegetables from our garden when we visit friends and they do the same when they pay us a return visit. Why is it that individuals and self-sufficient groups exchange goods which have little or no economic value? Since Marcel Mauss's study of gift exchange we know that these presentations are made to express, cement, and create alliances between individuals and groups.

Moreover, pure commerce, involving profit, is rarely pursued without an injection of altruism and sentiment, the degree of affect between traders varying from the total emotional commitment of the Trobrianders when they lovingly exchange their ornamental armbands and necklaces (see p. 159 ff) to the warily amicable exchange of vodka and grain between Russia and the United States. In our own local communities, a bottle of whisky at Christmas, an interest in your client's children or his hobbies, a game of golf, may seal a commercial pact. A group of men in a Yorkshire club or a Soho restaurant would seem to be indulging in a purely convivial routine of gin-drinking, food-exchange, and backslapping – in fact they are having a 'business drink' or a 'business lunch'. George Brown is trying to sell Bill Menotti four thousand pairs of shoddy Moroccan shoes – but before he does so he tries to make him his friend.

'Business friends' – this is not an entirely euphemistic phrase for cut-throat competitors. Business men dote on their clubs, their Rotaries, and their Freemasonry. Insurance men, publicans, and cold-cream manufacturers have their annual dinners. The notorious 'expense account' oils the wheels of business by allowing potentially inimical individuals to form friendship bonds through the symbolic process of sharing food. After the ritual meats the men are on Christian-name terms and begin to exchange jokes and reminiscences. It is no longer pure business – the buyer softens towards the manufacturer and the friendship makes it less painful for George to exploit Bill.

In this chapter we shall be looking at the way other societies deal with trading relationships. Sometimes it seems that a non-profit-making exchange, based on friendship, becomes more important than the commercial transaction. In the Pacific, Trobriander business partners pay much more attention to their personal appearance and the exchange of economically worthless ornaments than to the profitable exchange of food and tools they have brought with them. Cosmetics and hairstyles are aimed at impressing their partners. Do we not also consider our clothes, our hairstyles, even our wrinkles, when we wish to impress our client or our boss? Like the Melanesian who arranges his hair and smooths his skin with coconut oil, we pay as much attention to external appearances, our youthful good looks, and our friendly, frank attitudes as we do to our knowledge of the job in hand or the goods we are about to sell.

Dale Carnegie was aware of the personal element in business relations. According to his bestseller, *How to Win Friends and Influence People*,[1] a budding millionaire must look smart, assume a friendly attitude, smile continually, and flatter his business associates. The competitive spirit (you 'win' friends) must be dressed up in lovingkindness; and a friendly interest in a man's new tie or his daughter's school report gets you a better job, sells more shares, and undercuts more colleagues than any amount of intellectual preparation or ability. 'Fifteen per cent of one's financial success is due to one's technical knowledge and about eighty-five per cent is due to skill in human engineering – to personality and the ability to lead people.' Friendship has helped Dale Carnegie's myriad readers to break strikes, bamboozle chain-store managers, sell insurance, and become likely Presidents of the United States. It is of course an interested friendship, the demonstration of amity being more pretence than real. The Carnegie student is told to enter the office of a boss he wants to impress telling himself: 'I love him, I love him. I must smile and talk about his interest, make him feel important, and above all not argue with him. He is my friend.'

Using ethnography, I want to show that instead of using a show of friendship in order to do business, business itself may really be a way to permanent friendships. The personal alliances set up through the exchange of goods often become of much greater value than commercial relationships. In this book we have seen that one of the most common expressions of friendship – between blood brothers, patrons, and clients, co-god-parents, twins – is the exchange of gifts and services on an obligatory or voluntary basis. Love does not exist in a vacuum and, unless the exchange is a sexual one, Christmas cards, telephone calls, and birthday gifts are necessary to maintain a dyadic bond founded on affection. In small-scale societies reciprocity between groups as well as between individuals is basic to the functioning of the whole community and there is usually a moral obligation for members to be personally interested in the welfare of everyone. Cooperation is thought to be good and right and is expressed in the exchange of courtesies and gifts. Commercial exchanges are a kind of proof of friendship and a gift to an enemy may automatically convert him into a friend – even the abductor of an Eskimo's wife paid compensation (the gift) and the two men became friends due to this interchange. The more transactions between friendly individuals and allied groups (in-laws, linked clans, bond friends), the more close-knit the society. And these exchanges of gifts or trade goods are usually made on a face-to-face basis, which means that all social action is thought of in terms of immediate or delayed reciprocity. As a result of exchanges of this nature individuals are forced to regard each other as persons who become subjects of on-going rights and duties; what is reciprocated is not merely an economically useful article or even a tangible expression of friendship, but a whole series of courtesies, rites, feasts, and symbols – Mauss's *prestations sociales*.

Even in a straightforward market relationship, most people prefer to inject an element of friendship. We chat to the Welsh lady in the dairy, haggle in the Mediterranean market, and the heads of government of Russia and the United States put on friendly smiles and hug each other in the interests of trade. The

147

notorious expense account, involving the friendly eating together of business associates, is another example. In China there used to be a traditional relationship between merchants and also between landlord and peasant which was known as *kan chi'ing*, friendship, despite the business basis of the bond and the difference in social level between the parties to it. It implied 'affection and sentiment' and as well as being a technique to reduce social distance it was used by merchants to 'make friends' – secure connections – with guild members and bureaucrats by giving dinners and making gifts.

Old prejudices about primitive man – that he was promiscuous, fetish-ridden, without a past, innately aggressive, 'pre-logical' – are slowly being removed by detailed studies of institutions and attitudes. One of the longer-lasting preconceptions is that primitive man (and this was always a definition of primitiveness) lived in closed societies of the Ancient Hebrew type (see pp. 204–5). Civilized society is 'open' but primitive society lived walled in from outsiders by taboos, endogamy, and linguistic and social barriers. It was – and still is to an extent – axiomatic in textbooks that different tribes saw each other almost as different species, with whom they could not and would not communicate in any way. Neighbours of primitive tribes were untouchable 'barbarians', those who lived beyond the magical frontier; 'we are the men', while the people along the path, over the river, or beyond the mountain are not quite human. Fantastic notions circulate about neighbours who walk on their arms instead of their legs, who eat disgusting rubbish like tadpoles, raw blood, or the pig, who cannot stand upright because their heads are so heavy. Even Lévi-Strauss, arch-proponent of the importance of primitive exchange, writes that 'the most primitive peoples consider the tribe is a kind of wide family and that the frontiers of mankind stop with the tribal bonds themselves'.

This is true of both civilized and primitive peoples – it is doubtful how far our enemies in war or the victims of pogroms are considered human. Nevertheless this picture of primitive society, surrounded by a dark cacophonous forest of unknown semi-human neighbours who were only good for head-hunting and head-shrinking, is a distorted one. Even the most isolated, warlike, and cannibalistic people maintain some kind of cooperation with their neighbours, even those who look different and act differently. Although the boundaries are there, they are not impenetrable. The most inimical tribes agree to certain possibilities of traffic across their frontier zones or set up neutral areas where men may occasionally meet for the exchange of goods, ideas, and ceremonies.

The societies are rare which exhibit a nervous fear of international friendship – America during its isolationist days, the ancient Hebrews, Japan up to its defloration by Western powers, are exceptions. The exchange of goods and people between the most timid societies is carried on by some means or other. In the well-known situation of 'silent trading', for example, there is a commercial alliance between two stranger groups where there is no verbal exchange and where the partners need not see each other. Herodotus has recorded these shy transactions between a peaceable and unarmed people in East Scythia and their wild nomadic neighbours. The Carthaginians also traded 'silently' with an African people down the west coast of that continent.

Beyond the Pillars of Hercules [the Straits of Gibraltar], there is a spot where people live, to which they sail with their goods which they unload and set down in rows on the shore. Then they go on board again and make a fire that gives much smoke. And when the natives see the smoke, they go down to the shore, lay down gold beside the goods and go away. Then the Carthaginians land again, look at the gold and if they consider it equal to the value of the goods they take it and sail away; if on the other hand, they think it is too little, they enter their boats again and wait. Then the others come and lay more gold there until the sellers are satisfied. But none of them harm the others, nor do they touch the gold until it is equal to the value of the goods, nor the others the goods until the gold has been taken.[2]

Similar kinds of trading have been recorded all over the world. The Pygmies used to 'steal' bananas from their Bantu neighbours and leave game in exchange. Farmers and smiths among the Vedda also exchanged 'in silence'. However, although widespread, the examples are rare enough since few known societies see personal contact as an undesirable aspect of trading exchanges – on the contrary.

As far as institutionalized 'silent trading' is concerned, it should be remembered that even without contact a personal (friendship) factor enters into the exchange since it is good faith between the mute partners which guarantees the success of trade.

Most people trade openly and without fear – with great pleasure, in fact. Even nomadic hunters are not always self-sufficient and exchange their meat for farm products, while proud and self-contained pastoralists, like the Fulani of West Africa, give local farmers milk in return for grain. One tribe may produce a surplus of a speciality not found in another region and trade it with neighbouring peoples – those living along the coasts send fish inland, for example. In Chapter Three we had an example of the Azande who travelled long distances to acquire *banga* wood used in divining rites and established blood friendships with the inhabitants of these far-off regions in order to do so. One of the most 'notoriously' primitive peoples of the world, the Bushmen, traded their delicately wrought beads with their Bantu neighbours and among themselves; centrally placed groups played the role of intermediaries, obtaining from their northern neighbours supplies which they bartered further south, and *vice versa*. In this trade, eggshell, beads, and tobacco, because there was a steady demand for them, had a fixed value by which other goods could be 'priced'.[3] The Eskimos, traditionally considered as living in isolated, self-subsistence communities, in fact travelled hundreds of miles to exchange commodities such as soapstone and foodstuffs.[4] Similar evidence from European prehistory shows that shells found in Upper Palaeolithic deposits of Southern France could only have come from as far afield as the Eastern Mediterranean. In such cases it appears that the trade was seen as 'good in itself' since the objects exchanged were often not necessities. The imperative is to trade for the sake of the exchange, to interact with people by exchanging goods of purely ceremonial or decorative importance. Until fairly recently many archaeologists, historians, and anthropologists have explained any sign of culture contact between neighbouring and distant peoples by an invasion hypothesis. The discovery of similar artifacts or cultural patterns in different parts of Europe or North America were said to have been the result of conquest, followed by a mass migration. According to this theory, when future archaeologists dig up twentieth-century Scotland and find that 'porridge-eaters' were being replaced by 'cornflake-eaters', they would have to postulate an invasion of a 'Kellog's people' from the American continent in Ford cars. Ethnography has shown that most contact between societies is friendly and continuous, not aggressive and sudden: the simplest societies foster friendly alliances through internal and long-distance trade.

Australian aborigines are great traders and the desire for social intercourse is a contributing factor in actuating trade. Friendly relations are also set up ceremonially in many areas by reason of the fact that a special raw material is obtainable by barter. At all the ceremonies where barter takes place, opportunities are seized to settle grievances between distant tribesmen and fulfil social obligations so that ceremonial trading is facilitated, especially when distrust or hostility has interrupted cordial relations between groups. Trading exchanges foster peace. Moreover, ceremonial goods are traded for the mere pleasure of the exchange: various tribes assemble to dance and sing and obtain objects whose value has increased through the ceremony of an exchange which may extend over hundreds of miles. Among the Yaralde in South Australia, two boys belonging to distant and hostile communities, are brought into a special friendship by the exchange of their respective umbilical cords a certain time after their birth. In this way a sacred and permanent alliance is initiated. When they grow up they enter into a regular exchange of gifts which provides the machinery for a sort of commerce between the two groups to which they belong.[5]

Friendship, reciprocity, and trust, therefore, provide elements of credit and a guarantee of honesty in a situation where there are no legal contracts. Commerce and gift exchange not only bring people into friendly contact, with mutual interests leading to toleration, cooperation, and peaceful alliance, but the values of friendship may override the values of the commercial exchange. The efforts which trading partners make to exchange a piece of stone or a magically important piece of wood would seem quite out of proportion to the value of the object, or its necessity. Sometimes it seems that a scarcity is almost 'invented' for the purpose of an exchange between self-subsistent peoples in order to keep the peace. Exchange becomes a kind of social imperative and an expression of friendship.

Even in London's Pentonville prison, where relationships between groups are determined by sentiments of mistrust as much as cooperation, an elaborate system of contractual relations is an essential feature of the prison sub-culture and consists of a whole range of illicit enterprises based on exchange by which the prisoners create goods and services for each other or allocate those which are provided by the prison authorities.[6]

In Pentonville, the degree of intensity of friendship relations is variable and the integration and cooperation does not come from the mere fact of shared interests – criminality! 'Any man who thinks there is honour among thieves should be choked to death when he says it.' Cooperation and friendship depend to a large extent on the functional interdependence of individuals who make exchanges, which are primarily based on tobacco. These exchanges are of prime importance and are the only means by which a prisoner, living in a world with no social charter, can make his way through the often treacherous currents of prison life. Prison rules are so comprehensive that any relationship initiated by a prisoner could theoretically constitute an offence. 'Unauthorized' articles are not permitted, while any service by one prisoner for another is similarly unlawful.

The ceremonial exchange of tobacco seems to be an example among prisoners of the imperative to cooperate: the exchange is always mutually agreeable, although (unless the exchange takes place between mates) it is basically economic and involves an immediate, rather than a delayed return. It is also a bond which lacks continuity unless it is between the Old Pals, members of a kind of prison freemasonry among old-timers who believe themselves to be a limited and socially superior élite within the prison community. One of the dominant characteristics of the Old Pal network of friends is that goods and services, normally obtained by illicit economic exchange, are the subject of genuine giving.

Despite the commercial nature of the tobacco exchanges, among all prisoners the need to communicate and exchange within this comparatively complex economic system creates a considerable interdependence between individuals and is a means whereby an inmate may enter into face-to-face relations and communicate with men in other parts of the prison. Groups which might otherwise remain *incommunicado* are linked by runners, and routinized techniques of communication serve to buttress the structure of inmate society. The importance of this exchange on the morale of the prisoners is recognized by the administration since it is accepted by them, at least negatively.

The peaceful amity of commercial exchange is symbolized in some societies by ceremonial friendships between traders, in others by the sanctity of the market-place; in England, by the market-cross. In Dogon land, we have seen that Dogon twins express the perfect union of the androgyne and the complementarity of exchange. Dogon twins are celebrated as the inventors of trade – the binary attraction of twins is viewed as a symbolic expression of ties between allied groups, stranger and guest, partners in commerce and joking partners who exchange fish and grain. The market-place itself is protected by a shrine of clay or stone which is associated with twins. Once a year the village priest offers sacrifices, asking God to send as many strangers as possible. Even in this isolated and traditionally inward-looking tribe, cosmology – involving the spirit Nommo, the First Word, cowries and twinship – celebrates the notion of exchange, alliance, and commerce. In fact the whole social rhythm of a village takes its measure from the market cycle – there is usually one market every five days and since the distance between each is rarely more than a day's journey, traders can visit each one of them and establish friendly commercial contacts.

Everywhere the market is a centre of internal and intertribal exchanges where social communication takes place and rituals and ceremonies are performed. Among the mercantile Bangwa, the peace of the market is symbolized by a sacred tree planted in the centre of an open space by the local chief, who sacrifices a goat and allows its blood to seep down to the roots. The chief is personally responsible for the safety of people who attend his market; there is a strong taboo on any kind of violent argument and no weapons of any kind are carried. The chief, as protector and 'owner' of the market, is not allowed to set foot in it on market days but sits on a raised platform outside the palace with a retinue of wives, retainers, and cronies and receives the tribute and compliments of his subjects as well as their complaints.

Buying and selling seemed to me only one aspect of the crowded and exuberant Bangwa market. People spill down the narrow paths leading to the palace from the earliest morning hours, loaded with raw and cooked food, wine, oil, woven mats, bundles of tobacco. Small boys tug at snorting pigs and reluctant goats. Women set up countless palm-wine bars and Ibo traders arrive from yesterday's market in a neighbouring village bringing their cloths and 'fancy goods'. Purchases are quickly made and the rest of the time is spent greeting friends, exchanging kola nuts, or drinking a cup of wine with a relative or an acquaintance. The low chatter of barter increases to an incredible din as the day wears on. I used to come to dread the joyful camaraderie of market day as all my friends, unrecognizable in their market-day finery and their market-day extraversion, greeted me, shouted at me, took me hither and thither to meet their friends or to a 'quiet' place to tell me the latest scandal. And in the midst of this wildly gay chaos, ceremonies would be performed: a splendidly buxom girl, glistening with red-dyed oil, celebrates her coming-out after nine weeks in a 'fattening' enclosure; a group of masked men rush through the crowd swinging a bell and shooting off ancient flintlocks to announce the death of a local notable; some boys accused of witchcraft are being made to swear their innocence in front of a fetish. And by the huge slit gong, Mafwa usually sits grandly with her friends in a strange oasis of peace, smoking her pipe, discussing her own business and social affairs – the amount of a girl's bridewealth, preparations for a funeral, the shortage of beans.

The Bangwa enjoy their markets. According to the chiefs, nervous of the innocence of their young wives, they enjoy the markets much too much. Sometimes I would see a servant parading through the market, beating the royal gong, sending everybody back to their homes and farms before it got dark and dangerous – he reminded me of Charlemagne's complaint in ninth-century Europe that 'this continual running around markets' would lead to the complete decline of agriculture.

Fortunately for Bangwa farming, the men who haunted the markets did not have to farm – their wives did it. They were therefore free to visit as many markets as they wished as long as they were within walking distance of their compounds – and the Bangwa would walk five or six hours to attend a market. In this way the 'unemployed' men could keep themselves busy for all of the eight days of the Bangwa week. On most days there was a choice, since every chief or sub-chief worthy of the name had to have a market in front of his palace, under the sacred shade-tree. Sometimes it only amounted to two or three old women sitting patiently on the grass with some freshly boiled groundnuts or an egg or two. Many of the markets seemed to offer more in the way of prestige and social intercourse than economic opportunity.

Nevertheless, the Bangwa are a mercantile people; their very presence in the mountains occurred in order that they might take over as middlemen in the trade between the high savannah lands and the low forest. From the advantageous position of their eagle's-nest villages they shuttle salt, oil, palm wine, livestock, and smoked fish up and down the escarpment. In the past the fortunes of the Bangwa chiefs were made by buying slaves from the grasslands and selling them for guns and currency to their neighbours, who purveyed them to the peoples of the coast and to the Europeans. The fortunes made in the past were sunk mostly in women. Rights in women – as sources of bridewealth – are still tenaciously held by them (see p. 173).

In all these exchanges the Bangwa, like Western business men, use the ideology of friendship. Only friends trade – sell palm oil, carvings, or European goods. And in the past only chiefs who were friendly allies exchanged the slaves and guns and special 'king things' which were royal monopolies. In the interests of trade, friendships were made with traditional enemies and against what would seem to be the greatest of odds. The Bangwa despised their democratic forest neighbours with the *hauteur* of a mountain aristocracy but in order to enjoy the profits of the slave trade an alliance had to be made between the respective chiefs. The Bangwa chief let it be known to his people that his son and heir had been sold by mistake to a distant tribe and it was only through the good offices of the forest village head that he had been found and brought back. The gratitude of the people was so immense that a friendship pact with the despised forest chief was feasible and trading was permitted.

Once they had become friends, the two chiefs exchanged wives as a symbol of their alliance. They were also believed to share witchcraft activities. In Bangwa, only friends and allies attend the same witchcraft covens where they are thought to share the most precious fruits of their commercial activities and their witchcraft depredations – the metaphorical 'eating' of their choicest subjects, who are exchanged with gruesome and colourful formality. Chiefs – or their *alter egos* – meet each other at well-known witching spots where they play competitive games, leaping like deer over mountain and valley, sliding down red-earth landslides, the winner presiding over the friendly cannibal feast. When the sport is over the friends travel home together through the 'forest of the night', protected from danger on either side by a gorgeous and replete team of titled palace servants, favourite wives, and princesses.

More prosaically, friendship expresses commercial relations in other societies we have already discussed in this book. Although the Saraktsani shepherds of Greece seem to put a premium on *not* making friends, believing that the interests of unrelated families are opposed and mutually destructive, nevertheless their honour, pride, and spirit of intense competitiveness allow them to set up friendship relations with those 'foreigners' in the village with whom they are involved in commercial relations. The sponsors of their marriages and baptisms are the merchants who buy their wool and cheese. In the Andalusian pueblo, most economic dealings – the selling of grain and flour, charcoal, game and eggs – are done between friends. They are conducted in private and there is no need for middlemen: business fits into the scheme of friendship, which creates or fulfils obligations. Even economic relations between villages are carried on through friends; there are in fact no other institutions apart from friendship which exist on an individual basis and which can bring about cooperation between separate communities.

In Guatemala, the Chinautleco are an independent people, each family preserving its physical isolation by keeping its property separated from that of its neighbours by marking it off with cactus-like plants which serve as a high fence. Yet these Indians, as adults, seek friends among themselves and also among the Spanish-speaking Ladinos, the enterprising business men and middlemen at the town markets, where the Indian women sell their pots. To an Indian, Ladinos are normally 'selfish, greedy, ambitious, proud, and unscrupulous', and Ladinos consider the Indians as 'filthy animals, ignorant and uncivilized', but once a Ladino and an Indian become involved in commercial exchange and friendship these attitudes are forgotten. A Ladino who acts as a middleman for the Indian potters often becomes a close friend, either through the institution of compadrazgo or straightforward patron-clientage, interpreting to Indians what is taking place in the wider political and economic sphere, as well as helping him in times of need.

The Pacific rather than Africa or Europe provides the best examples of the interconnection between trade and friendship. New Guinea societies have been isolated from the world market economy until relatively recently (unlike Africa) but they have certainly not been cut off from each other. Intricate trading networks linked and still link mountain tribes with the coast, and mainlanders with islanders. Some of these people have been described as primitive capitalists – passionate traders who use many different kinds of money and ceremonial currency to buy goods, rituals, and dances which they trade with other communities, many of whom are traditional enemies who were once engaged in savage and endemic wars with the traders.

Throughout the islands and the mainland of New Guinea, manufacturing centres for important commodities are localized in different geographical areas so that groups trade over distances of more than a hundred miles for special pots, stone implements, and valued ornaments. The Motu, for example, used to sail some hundreds of miles from Port Moresby in heavy, unwieldy canoes with their characteristic crab-claw sails, bringing pottery, stone blades, and ornaments to the peoples of the Gulf of Papua from whom they obtained sago and heavy canoes. The Motu call their Papuan trading partners their 'best friends' and make much of them, decorating them with personal ornaments, giving them shell armbands and accompanying the exchanges with much embracing and protestations of love.

The most extensive and well-described trading network in New Guinea embraces not only the islands near the east end of the island, but also the Lousiades, Woodlark Island, the Trobriand archipelago, and the d'Entrecasteaux group. Malinowski[7] has made it clear that trade, though important, is not the only incentive in this complex exchange system known as the *kula*. Since the kula has become an ethnographic classic and admirably illustrates my theme that there is an intimate link between trading, alliance, and the imperatives of friendship I wish to go into some detail about the ceremonial and social aspects of the kula exchange of valuables between these communities.

The exchange system is carried on between members of related communities and also between culturally and linguistically separated peoples who inhabit a wide ring of islands forming a geographically closed circuit. On each island in the ring, a more or less limited number of men take part in the kula, receiving the ornaments, retaining them for a short time, and then passing them on. Members of the kula network, therefore, periodically receive an ornamental armband or necklace, which is then ceremonially consigned to a further partner at a later date – armbands travelling in one direction and necklaces in the other. It is an exchange backed by myth, law, and rite as well as popular sentiment and it depends on trading partnerships and friendships which bind thousands of individuals in a circular alliance. The exchange is in no way a free one since a man who is in the kula has only a limited number of people with whom he exchanges. The friendship between trading partners is lifelong and involves various mutual obligations and privileges; it is symbolized by the exchange of purely decorative objects which have a ceremonial rather than a commercial value.

The kula network, therefore, is a wonderfully clear expression of interpersonal relations based on friendship which are found, although usually in a more attenuated form, in most societies. The whole kula ring forms an interlocking community of allies, men living hundreds of canoe-miles away, bound together by direct or intermediate partnerships, exchanging gifts, getting to know each other, and meeting at regular intervals. Closest friends within the ring are partners from the same village or island. The overseas – the international – friend is seen as an ally in a land of danger and insecurity, where witchcraft, sorcery, and more tangible dangers are to be feared. After a long and dangerous ocean voyage and arrival in a foreign island to exchange necklaces or armbands as well as ordinary trade goods, a man's special kula partner is his main guarantee of safety, providing him with food, company, and shelter.

The basis of the relation between kula friends is reciprocity, but it is a delayed reciprocity since there can never be a direct exchange from hand to hand. An armband is handed over but a man must wait until his friend makes a return visit before he receives a complementary necklace. It is gift exchange between friends, not commerce between traders, since the equivalence of the objects exchanged is never subject to discussion, bargaining, or computation. Nevertheless, of course, there is always much longing and sighing for the best ornaments. The more famous bands and necklaces each have a personal name and provenance and as they circulate around the kula cycle their appearance always creates a sensation. All the friends of a man with a specially wonderful necklace in hand will compete for it and try to obtain it by blandishments, promises of the gift of a pig, axe-blades, or food.

The exchange exists for the sake of the exchange. Here is a world where not only food and manufactured goods (trade goods), but ornaments, customs, songs, art motifs, and all kinds of other cultural influences travel from island to distant island. It is a ceremonial exchange between friends which finds elaboration in myth, in the rituals embellishing canoe-building, and in feasts associated with the kula. The magic made when a group leaves on an expedition is aimed at success in the exchange and is directed at the partner's emotions – it aims to make him soft, unsteady in his mind, eager to hand over to his friend the best kula gifts, not the largest and cheapest yams.

The relationship between kula friends and partners is brought out clearly in a detailed description by Malinowski of the arrival of a Trobriand expedition in the enemy island of Dobu. There is less intimacy with kula partners the more distant and foreign they are and a Dobuan is separated from a Trobriander on both counts. In Dobu, the Trobriander sailors only disembark from their canoes when they have performed extensive rituals to ensure the success of their visit and have made themselves irresistible to their friends through the use of spells and cosmetics. And whatever the normal state of enmity between the two groups of islanders as a whole, kula partners always show the utmost friendship.

Arriving in their great canoes after a long journey, the Trobrianders rest for a while before beginning to undo their baskets. The older men murmur their magical formulae, they all wash in the sea and rub themselves with medicated leaves to make themselves beautiful and attractive to their Dobu partners. They break open coconuts, scraping and medicating them before rubbing their bodies with oil to give their skin a shining appearance. Before arranging their hair, they chant spells over their combs. With a crushed betel nut mixed with lime, some draw red designs on their faces, while others use an aromatic resinous concoction to draw ornamental patterns in black. The sweet-smelling mint plant, which has also been chanted over at home before the voyage, is taken out of its little receptacle where it has been preserved in coconut oil. The herb is inserted into the armlets – ornaments they have brought as gifts – while a few drops of oil are smeared over the body and over a special magical bundle of trade gifts.

All the magic which is uttered in the canoes before landing in Dobu is 'personal beauty' magic, and the main aim of the spells is to make each man irresistible to his kula friend. In Trobriand myths there is often a description of an old, ugly, and ungainly man transformed into a radiant and charming youth through this kind of magic; the myth is an exaggerated version of what happens every time the beauty magic is spoken on the beach at Dobu. As one Trobriander put it, 'Here we are ugly; we eat bad fish, bad food; our faces remain ugly. We want to sail to Dobu; we keep our taboos, we don't eat bad food. We wash; we charm the leaves; we charm the coconut; we anoint ourselves; we make our red and black paint; we put on our . . . smelling ointment; we arrive in Dobu, beautiful looking. Our partner looks at us, sees our faces are beautiful; he throws the ornaments at us . . .'

Of course the belief in the efficacy of the cosmetics and spells makes them effective, since the trader – like the modern Western woman dependent on Helena Rubinstein and Elizabeth Arden –

has the conviction of being beautiful to his friend and the magic provides this assurance, influencing his behaviour and deportment. In the transactions between the two kula partners it is the manner of soliciting which matters most. The beauty magic will make a man's friend and partner hug him and 'take him to his bosom'. In the spells he and his friend are likened to a pair of pigeons and a pair of parrots, birds which symbolize friendship to the Trobrianders. Wearing these cosmetic preparations the visitors will sit on their partners' knees and take from their mouths the betel-chewing materials. 'My head is made bright, my face flashes, I have acquired a beautiful shape like that of a chief; I have acquired a shape that is good. I am the only one; my renown stands alone.'

The ferocious Dobuans on shore have a general taboo on strangers which is waived for their trading friends, but the Trobrianders still feel the necessity of bridging this taboo by magic. At certain periods of the year the visitors are received with a wild show of hostility and fierceness and treated as intruders; this attitude ceases as soon as the visitors have carried out a ritual of spitting around the village. The Trobrianders express their feelings in this situation characteristically: 'The Dobu man is not good as we are. He is fierce, he is a man-eater. When we come to Dobu we fear him, he might kill us. But see! I spit the charmed ginger root and their mind turns. They lay down their spears, they receive us well.' A remarkable example of the achievement of friendly feeling against all odds, in the interest of exchange.

The Trobriander canoes are ranged in a row facing the shore. After the ritual spitting the histrionic moment of tension is over, the Dobuans in their warpaint shed their weapons, smile welcomingly, and listen to the leader of the Trobriander group as he harangues them, telling them to give the visitors a large number of valuables and surpass all other islands and past occasions. After this, his own partner blows his conch shell and offers the first gift of valuables to the master of the expedition from the Trobriands. Other blasts then follow and men disengage themselves from the throng on the shore, approaching the canoes with necklaces for their special partners. The necklaces are always carried ceremonially, tied to a stick with the pendant at the bottom. The fleet of canoes then sails round the island, stopping in front of each hamlet where the Trobrianders have their partners.

At each stopping place no visitor can eat any local food, yams, or coconuts, before he has received all his gifts. The Trobriander continues to try and soften the heart of his partner; he will feign illness, remaining in his canoe and sending word to his partner that he is suffering from a terrible disease. If this fails he may have recourse to magic again, magic to seduce the mind of the man on whom it is practised, magic to make him silly and amenable to persuasion, numbing all his faculties: in fact the same rites are performed when a man is trying to seduce a woman. When the ceremonial exchange is finished the partners meet to chat and exchange food, and trade is carried on between visitors and local natives who are not their partners though they must belong to the same community as those with whom the kula is made.

Back home in the Trobriands there is not the same degree of ceremonial between kula friends when they exchange valuables locally, since the partners in this case know each other well and speak the same language: they are close friends, not allies from foreign tribes. There is no need for 'danger magic' and relations between visitors and hosts who inhabit neighbouring villages are free and easy, although some 'beauty magic' is used and not all ceremonial is absent. On entering a neighbouring village, a party will march briskly in without looking to right or left, while a small boy blows frantically on a conch shell and the men let out a ritual scream. Others throw stones and spears at the ornamental carved and painted boards running in an arch round the eaves of the chief's house or yam house. Even the gifts are handed over to their friends in an aggressive fashion. They are thrown down fiercely and almost contemptuously. Nevertheless, despite the rivalry the partners are true friends.

The kula is unique but only in its elaboration of the exchange cycle and the extent of its sociological and geographical significance. An intratribal and intertribal exchange system unites a vast area and large numbers of people, binding them with definite ties based on reciprocal obligations, and with a highly developed mythology and ritual. Exchange is carried out between partners who are friends, at least for the period of the kula. The valuables symbolize the importance of the exchange, and of the permanent alliance between individuals and groups. The individual member sees the relationship between himself and his immediate partner as the important aspect of the kula, not the whole cyclical structure described by the anthropologist. He will know the names of his partners' partners and possibly his partners' partners' partners, but beyond that the kula exchange is a misty dream. Nevertheless, the kula does serve the purpose of welding a number of tribes together and it embraces a complex of activities which are woven together through interpersonal relationships to form an organic whole. The imperative is the exchange and through this exchange each Trobriander achieves a status, which depends on having a network of friends both at home and abroad. The kula is the main means of establishing amicable links between unrelated and even hostile neighbours; it sanctions an individual's assertion of his personality outside his village and clan.[8] Along with this assertion of individuality we have the relationship of two persons bound up in a continual give-and-take, in activities which continually stress reciprocity, equal return, generosity, and honour between friends. During an overseas voyage a man is on his own, away from ties of kinship and village responsibilities. He is seeking an exchange purely for himself, through the favour of his opposite number on a distant island.

The ritual and magic prepare the man for his alliance, by washing from him his corporate identity as a member of the home community. During a Trobriander's few days ashore with his friend, it is every man for himself and ritually licensed as such. Washing and anointing himself, a man makes himself irresistible to his friend, but at the same time by acting as an individual he is enjoying his own emotional satisfactions, becoming a person outside his lineage or village. The central ceremony of the kula is the symbolic gift-giving which expresses the friendship between two men whose respective districts are in a state of latent hostility.

The kula symbolizes the kind of reciprocity which sustains life at home and maintains vital alliances abroad; both intra-community and international relations are maintained through friendships between individuals. Moreover it symbolizes a tendency among the Trobrianders to create social ties through the exchange of gifts. It is an impulse which is fundamental to men in society – the display of affection, the desire to share goods, for no other reason than that of making friends. Exchange is a basic human need and the Trobrianders have institutionalized it in friendship pacts between partners in a gift-exchange cycle where the relations of equality, complementarity, and alliance, rather than those of social or economic gain, are emphasized. The Trobrianders, like most societies, find cooperation good and right, and through relationships with other individuals they develop social sentiments of friendship which find expression through gift exchange. Reciprocity expresses a principle of equity based on the recognition of the moral equality of persons, even strangers, who cooperate in certain ways. The kula, compadrazgo, twinship, and blood pacts are all in their different ways a means of establishing bonds which unite two individuals in permanent friendship. There are countless other means of institutionalizing this need for cooperation – possibly the most common is the exchange of women (sisters, daughters, or marriage wards) as wives, between allied individuals and groups. In the next chapter we shall consider these relations of affinity as another manifestation of friendship.

8   Friendly In-Laws

In many, if not most, cultures marriages are not made to suit two individuals, but to please the families or the clans of the bride and groom. All over the world, past and present, people have accepted unions for political or social reasons which seem to us both unnatural and injurious to the marital wellbeing of the couple. We have already seen in this book that children may marry adults, women marry women and even men marry men. We Westerners, however, do not marry minors or – at least until recently – members of our own sex. Nor do we marry our own brother or sister, our incest laws making sexual connection with certain relatives inconceivable, sinful, or legally punishable. Yet there is nothing inherently right about our own legal and moral attitudes. The prohibition of incest specifies that parents and children or brother and sister cannot have sexual relations or marry each other. Yet in some historical and ethnographic cases (Ancient Egypt and some African and Polynesian kingdoms) incest was defined far less strictly than elsewhere, always for very practical reasons; incestuous marriages were often limited to a minority group to keep wealth and power in the hands of the few.

In our society, marriage is a matter of free choice – we fall in love or at least find an amenable mate and settle down to parenthood and companionship 'till death do us part'. Yet even in Europe marriage may be a practical affair which concerns less the bride and groom than the wider community. This is the *raison d'être* behind European royal marriages with their strict attention to genealogy and 'blood', the distrust of morganatic marriages, and the alliances of first cousins. Among royals,[1] marriage must determine the rank of children who will become kings, queens, emperors, and tsars and it must maintain royal status through the correct form of kinship filiation. Within each royal family individuals are ranked in a complex hierarchy of significance for succession and marriage negotiations. A wrong marriage debars them from the throne or may remove them from the royal hierarchy altogether.

More importantly, marriage alliances are used to bind together various royal families and their countries in peace and in war. Royal marriages tie one family into a network of relations with a number of often antagonistic royal families – once established, these marriage bonds influence a multitude of political and personal activities. The need for offspring to ensure the succession is also always implicit in the marriage of those in line for the succession and for this reason a major condition of a royal marriage is that the royal spouse should be of equal rank. Children of royalty are always primarily considered as potential successors to royal office and only secondarily as children of their parents.

Royal marriages in Europe are therefore practical affairs, like marriages in a primitive society. A good example of this is the practice of transferring fiancées if the heir apparent dies after a political marriage has been arranged but before it has taken place; the fiancée marries the new heir apparent, as in the case of Mary of Teck who married the future George V of Great Britain when his elder brother died in 1892. In the case of King George and Queen Mary we have a close parallel with the African institution of widow inheritance, whereby the bride or wife of a deceased man is inherited by his successor.

Even further down the European social scale there are many examples of arranged marriages, among the wealthy middle classes as well as among landed peasants, and we are aware of the benefits of making alliances. In many non-Western societies, however, the practice of setting-up alliances through marriage is universal and no marriage is ever allowed to become a matter of free choice – marriage becomes part of a structured system of exchange.

The exchange of Christmas gifts or spondylus shell ornaments forms part of a basic principle operating in human affairs – you have been given something and you must return it or cause offence. Gift-giving occurs on the level of the individual, the community, even the nation, and if the gift is not reciprocated in some way you have refused friendship and become a beggar. Reciprocity is the support of man in society. There is evidence that in the beginning prehistoric man, true primitive man, did not survive through war and greed for land but by exchanging goods and symbols – one of the most convenient of which must have been their womenfolk. Does the imperative of reciprocity explain why the Trobrianders go to such lengths for the purpose of exchanging useless armbands, why Africans and Americans import food when they are self-sufficient, and why most peoples go abroad for wives when they have plenty of women at home?

Incest prohibitions serve the interests of this social exchange of marriage. The reason for the universal taboo on sex with close relations is not that incest biologically weakens or psychologically damages a species but that all groups derive benefit from offering to other men the women they must refuse themselves. Lévi-Strauss quotes Amerindians on the practical advantages of incest prohibitions: 'If you marry your sister you will have no brother-in-law. Who will go hunting with you? Who will help you with the planting?'

In refusing to remain a biological group like the apes and procreating with his mothers and sisters, primitive man created a truly human culture. Through a system of exchanging sisters and creating friendly relations with brothers-in-law, in-laws, or affines, he set up an ongoing system of related groups. This is the significance of the Biblical text: 'Then we will give our daughters unto you, and we will take your daughters to us and we will dwell with you.'

'Again and again in the world's history,' wrote the nineteenth-century anthropologist Tylor, 'savage tribes must have had plainly before their minds the simple practical alternative between marrying out and being killed out.' Marriages based on women exchange establish alliances between groups and in so doing limit man's aggressive behaviour; it is a cultural achievement which places him far above his so-called brother, the ape. Palaeolithic bands must have exchanged women as a token of peace and friendship. It would then have become the rule that one band became dependent on the other for its women, and thereby permanent, inherited bonds of friendship and alliance were formed. Women became the symbols of a communication and exchange system as well as items of value.

We may also suppose that at some stage goods became more elaborate, women ceased to become the group's only asset, and the direct exchange of women could be converted into the exchange of goods for women. But even when bridewealth is the norm in these exchanges there always remains the idea that the woman is the symbol of the alliance or the peace pact. In these systems, it follows that marriage between a man and a woman could never be a private business – left to individual choice as it is in modern society – since the most important reason for marrying was not to have a sexual partner or a companion but to establish relations with another group. The elementary exchange of women implies relations of equality and friendship between allies; men marry, as we have seen, to have friendly brothers-in-law as much as to have wives. Special rules are normally followed in the choice of a spouse and for this purpose the whole kinship field becomes a kind of complex game, members of groups being distributed between different categories. Usually the category of the parents defines, either directly or indirectly, the members of the group or another group into which they may marry.

In the simplest system of exchanging women – elementary exchange – the children of brothers and sisters continually remarry over generations; this is true bilateral cross-cousin marriage. In this system, of course, there are no real in-laws since all one's in-laws are kinsmen and all one's kinsmen are in-laws. Your father-in-law is your uncle (or mother's brother) and your brother-in-law is your cousin (your father's sister's child). Nevertheless, the relationship between kinsmen through a marriage is converted into a special bond of affinity and friendship. In other societies, marriages do not link equal groups, but like lopsided friendships serve to make alliances between groups with different access to the symbols of wealth and power. In these cases a superior class gives women to an inferior class, women passing down the system and men up. Complex systems like our own do not constantly renew links in this manner, but distribute women widely throughout society.

For anthropologists, the exchange of women in cross-cousin marriage has been given the greatest attention since it reveals an elementary form of reciprocity between men and groups, which is man's way of meeting the confusion of the natural order in a primary way and transcending it, to assert his culture and his humanity. Lévi-Strauss[2] has made the enlightening distinction between the realms of nature (hunting and hunter, war and aggression) and culture (exchange and alliance). Within nature, sexuality is the most social of instincts, but if it is expressed randomly it results in promiscuity and incest. The orderly exchange of women between groups through marriage resolves this problem. By making women the elements of exchange between men, a cycle of reciprocity is set in motion that is the main means of distinguishing and allying social groups, by setting up a definition of their otherness. In other words, the original we–they distinction in human society was set up by rules of incest coupled with the laws of reciprocity.

At this stage I must bring up themes of perennial fascination to the social anthropologist, although the technical-terms – quite distinct from the jargon – may present a stumbling block to the lay reader. These terms, concerned primarily with kinship, descent and marriage, may be explained quite briefly with the use of the diagram on page 170.

In most societies apart from our own, *descent* is the basis for the formation of important social groups. Unilineal descent is a distinct reckoning of descent – when reckoned through males, exclusively, it is called patrilineal or agnatic descent – the ancient Romans were an agnatic people; when reckoned exclusively through females it is called matrilineal or uterine descent – the Iroquois and the Ashanti of Ghana are matrilineal peoples. Bilateral descent traces descent through males and females equally – the English are a bilateral people, this system permitting daughters to inherit from fathers and a princess to succeed to the throne.

In the diagram overleaf, the men (triangles) and the women (circles) included in the area marked X are patrilineally related; they belong to a patrilineage and trace a genealogical connection to A; they are agnatic relatives. The men and women in the section marked Y are related through women; they form a matrilineage and trace their descent from B; they are uterine relatives. In

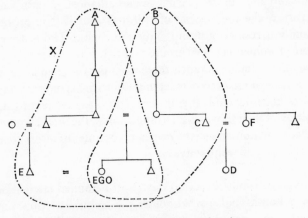

X —·—·— Patrilineage—people related through males

Y —————— Matrilineage —people related through females

△   Males

O   Females

EGO   Reference point individual

Kinship and descent

= married

— descended from

A – ego's agnatic or patrilineal ancestor

B – ego's uterine or matrilineal ancestress

C – ego's mother's brother and uterine kinsman

D – ego's cross-cousin, but not a uterine kinsman. The relationship
     is matri*lateral*, not matri*lineal*

E – ego's parallel cousin and agnatic kinsman and brother-in-law (or
     affine)

F – ego's mother's brother's wife, his affine or in-law.

some rare societies an individual, *ego* on the genealogical chart, may belong to both lineages – X and Y – a patrilineage through his father and a matrilineage through his mother. In the usual case, where only one line of descent is reckoned, he will still have important relations with the kin of his mother, if descent is reckoned patrilineally; or his father, if descent is reckoned matrilineally. These relationships traced through the parent who does not determine descent are called matrilateral or patrilateral and are based on general (lateral) ties of kinship and not distinct (lineal) ties of descent. Kinship is traced through related persons, indiscriminately, without reference to agnatic or uterine descent. The kinship relation through the parent who does not determine descent is sometimes called complementary filiation – it is a filiation which complements the all-important descent tie.

In small-scale societies, because of the importance of descent and kinship, individual relatives beyond the immediate family have great structural importance and for this reason they must be defined in exact terms. There is no point referring to C in the diagram as an 'uncle' of ego; he must be called the mother's brother to distinguish him from the father's brother. The former is a matrilateral relative and the latter is a patrilateral one. Similarly, with regard to cousins, it is important to distinguish between two classes. Parallel cousins are the children of two siblings (brothers or sisters) of the same sex (ego and E in the chart are parallel cousins); cross-cousins are children of two siblings of the opposite sex, that is, the father's sister's child and the mother's brother's child (ego and D are cross-cousins). It will be noted that parallel cousins belong to the same lineage (ego and E are agnatic relatives), while cross-cousins do not (ego and D are not matrilineal relatives since D belongs to a matrilineage through her mother, F). In Western society, where descent is bilateral and of little significance in the formation of corporate groups, the differentiation between cousins is of little importance. However, among European royal families, where descent is traced bilaterally but with a preference for agnatic succession to titles – sons before daughters – it is interesting to note that close-kin marriages occurring among royals show a marked preponderance of cross-cousin over parallel-cousin marriage, a situation which might be predicted by an anthropologist in view of the political functions that royal marriages have been shown to entail. Marriage to a cross-cousin repeats and reinforces an alliance made in an earlier generation with another royal house – parallel-cousin marriage is merely marrying within the extended agnatic family.

However elementary or complex the system of exchange, and whatever the units involved – be they families, lineages, classes, castes, or tribes – men enter into relations of exchange with each other and form friendships, symbolized by relations between brothers-in-law. Even if a woman is not exchanged for a woman, the bridewealth which is obtained for a man's sister gets him a wife eventually and a chain relationship between brothers-in-law is set up, a cycle of friendship not very different from that between kula partners or blood brothers.

Brothers-in-law in New Guinea are allies, exchange-partners, and friends. Among the Kuma[3] this situation is brought out clearly. 'It can be said of the Kuma that marrying and giving in marriage involves a process of exchanging the most highly valued and scarce goods – women. Sister exchange is the ideal although the sisters exchanged are usually clan sisters.' The relationship between brothers-in-law is the only one in which friendships can develop in a way which renders personal devotion, rather than the fulfilment of material expectations, crucial in determining the actions of one man towards the other. Brothers-in-law are mutually obliging and generous, treating each other as age-mates, attending the same courting ceremonies, and helping each other in tasks such as house-building. After marriage, brothers-in-law become firm friends if they have not been so before; they are always in each other's company; at gatherings they are seen standing together in the casual embrace common with age-mates. Men frequently exchange visits with their wives' brothers and their sisters' husbands, to talk as cronies and enjoy the easy hospitality always available. 'The strongest bond between two men is the relationship of brothers-in-law.' And two men who are best friends but unrelated will call each other 'brother-in-law' to emphasize the element of bond friendship in this relationship which owed its origin to an exchange of women.

*

In Bangwa, in-law relations express much the same principle but are fiercely complex – I have in fact written a whole book about them.[4] Girls are traditionally betrothed to their future husbands soon after birth – in this polygynous society girls are a scarce resource and a girl may even be promised to an anxious future husband *before* she is born. While the girl is growing up, the man makes a series of presents to his in-laws, particularly his mother-in-law. On marriage, a bewildering selection of relatives receive their share of the goats, hoes, salt, and oil which make up the considerable bridewealth although today these symbolic gifts are carefully converted into Cameroon currency. Small gifts are given to the bride's close relatives – the groom's brothers-in-law and sisters-in-law, but the bulk of the money, which may reach £300, is shared among four men known as the girl's 'marriage lords' – her father, her mother's father, her mother's mother's father (or their successors), and her *tangkap*, or 'money father'. Tangkap needs special explanation – in Bangwa ideology everybody is descended from an original woman slave and the successor of the man who owned this slave is the tangkap or 'money father' and takes the bulk of the bridewealth when all her female descendants, traced through women, marry. These rights in women are 'what the chiefs feed on', since it is they who have most of the pecuniary rights in their female subjects. It is an institution which causes much anger among the young men in Bangwa today – they feel that if the government would only deprive the chiefs of these rights, which are a left-over from the slaving days, they might be able to marry before they approach middle age, which is the situation for a lot of them today.

The Bangwa, therefore, have two kinds of in-law or affine; he has those relations between close kin of the husband and the wife, and relations between the husband and the bride's marriage lords (more an alliance between a client and his four patrons). At the formal gathering of these relatives for the settling of the brideprice, the distinction between the two groups is quite clear. Elaborate preparations are made to receive the four marriage lords who are given special stools covered with fine cloth, and plates of kola nuts and jugs of wine. The close kin of the bride and groom, on the other hand, scurry around serving food, showing suitably obsequious behaviour to the four lords. The first payments are made with great formality – each lord receives money representing a 'stool' – money to persuade him not to take home the cloth-covered stool prepared for him; 'dew' – to compensate him for having walked through the early morning dew-laden grass to come and collect his money; 'cork money' and 'food money' to persuade him to drink the wine and eat the food prepared for him. The other in-laws receive small presents of 'oil' and 'salt', apart from the mother-in-law who receives a large 'hoe'. The bulk payments ('goats') given to the lords are handed over after hours of the most tedious and violent haggling carried out by go-betweens, since the marriage lords are much too grand to take notice of such mercenary matters!

Obviously, it is towards the first category of in-laws, his wife's closest kin, that a man feels any degree of real sympathy and friendship. Between these in-laws the relationship is equal and complementary and permits the exchange of friendship. Moreover it is a relationship which will be converted into a kinship bond after the birth of children to the couple. A man's brother-in-law becomes the children's uncle, their mother's brother. Between a man and his wife's marriage lords, on the other hand, the bond is a legal one, not one of affection, involving financial payments between wife-givers and wife-takers, a relationship which is inherited by the children of the union.

In-laws are equals and friends; between brothers-in-law the reciprocal term is *nse-ga*, which translated literally means 'my water' and beautifully expresses the togetherness and common substance of this category of affines. Marriage lords are called 'my lord' and relations are tense. In-laws have a relaxed, equal relationship. They are also seen as paths to alliances with new groups – and the furthering of contacts through brothers-in-law is so sought-after that there is a strong taboo against marriages between a man and a woman who are already in-laws. You may marry fairly close patrilineal kin, but not affines since they are the means of making new friendships. Chiefs marry from all classes and categories of society, spreading their network of political friendships to families of retainers, commoners, sub-chiefs, and foreign chiefs.

Brothers-in-law are friends to be trusted. In some parts of Africa where there are widely dispersed clans, a traveller far from home stays with anyone bearing his clan name. The Bangwa, however, always makes for a compound where he has a brother-in-law since he knows he will be entertained with more warmth and spontaneous generosity. Brothers-in-law witness each other's wills, arrange burials, receive confidences. Brothers-in-law, like friends but unlike marriage lords, are never involved in witchcraft attack, since they are automatically free, as a category, from accusations of sorcery. Close kin and marriage lords are dangerous witches.

In other societies, it may well be argued, brothers-in-law are not the friendly allies I have been making out, linking groups through the exchange of women on a basis of equality and amity. Clearly, wife-exchange has never meant perfect accord. Some people even declare that they only 'marry their enemies' – 'we marry those we fight'. In some cases brides are taken from their own people by means of a ceremonial capture which has real overtones of violence and may end in actual fighting. However, even in these situations solidarity is the rule: rivalry is an important element in friendship and the fact of being 'locked in conflict' is still a kind of integration. The fact that the capture is ceremonialized is a sign of the restraint that intermarrying introduces into two enemy groups. Communities may be both permanently hostile and permanently friendly, through the intermarriages which maintain the continuity of the relationship. For whatever way a wife is won, once a group gives you a woman you are in their debt and once the debt has been repaid a temporary balance is achieved.

Even between brothers-in-law there are indications that in-laws are both friendly and hostile; to begin with you may regard your husband's group or wife's group as strangers, even potential enemies, but at the same time they have to be treated as friends. The relationship is ambivalent, but on the whole the relations between brothers-in-law, technically equal and usually of the same generation, tend to be affectionate and cooperative. It is not so easy for a man and his wife's mother; although friendship is required, there is often a strong undercurrent of antagonism. Between a man and his mother-in-law complete avoidance is often the rule. In the Andaman Islands the parents of a bridegroom and the parents of a bride treat each with the most careful respect 'because their children have married' and they had become 'friends'.

This ambivalent relationship of hostile solidarity is often extended to the whole affinal group, which brings us to a hoary anthropological theme – the mother's brother and the sister's son in agnatic societies. The mother's brother is both an in-law and a kinsman. He is not only an uncle and a close relative but also a representative of the group – usually a lineage – which gave a man's father his wife. In the societies we have so far discussed in this chapter this relationship of mother's brother – wife-giver – to his sister's son – wife-taker – is extended to the patrilineal kin of each group. Thus any single person is related to a whole group (his mother's group): he is a sister's son to all of the men and they are his mother's brothers. There are therefore many mother's brothers and many sister's sons, the terms being used in anthropology to denote both the real uncle-and-nephew situation and the relationship of friendship and alliance between kin groups, one of which has provided a wife for the other. These groups, 'mother's brothers' and 'sister's sons', are known as classificatory relatives.

Between classificatory mother's brothers and sister's sons in Africa there is a hierarchical relationship explained by the system of generalized exchange of women and implying a constant superiority of wife-givers (mother's brothers) over wife-takers (sister's sons). Generalized exchange is to be distinguished from elementary exchange (see pp. 168-9), where women are directly exchanged between groups.

The major point is that in Africa and elsewhere a mother's brother is both an in-law and a close kinsman of his sister's son. He is the representative of a group which provided your own paternal group with a certain commodity, a wife; and he is also one of your closest relatives. (It should be remembered that I am not discussing the special case of matrilineal societies where the mother's brother is often the head of the extended family.) This ambivalence of being an in-law and a kinsman has to be resolved in some way: how do you behave to a person who is at one and the same time a sentimental relative linked to you through your mother and an affinal relative who received bridewealth when your mother married? How do you reconcile descent and alliance? In Bangwa, for example, the mother's brother is the most important member of a person's intimate kin group, more nurturing even than a father. He looks after his nephews when they are ill and drives away witches if they are preying on them. However, a mother's brother is also head of a man's mother's paternal group, who sacrifices at the ancestral skulls and, as marriage lord, receives payments when his sister marries. In one aspect the mother's brother is a sentimental kinsman and in another he is an ally with formal expectations which are legally and supernaturally sanctioned. The mother's brother as an ally and marriage lord is frequently accused of bewitching his sister's children: this is a relationship based on debt and law. Yet as the mother's brother he is supposed to protect his sister's children from witchcraft.

How are these conflicting roles resolved? How do you behave towards a man who is both a friendly uncle and a stern bewitching member of a different group? In Bangwa this potential conflict is usually avoided by separating the two roles. Due to a very high polygyny rate, your real mother's brother – who is your father's friendly brother-in-law and your friendly uncle – is not the same man as the mother's brother who is head of your mother's paternal group and your sister's marriage lord. In this way a mother's brother and his sister's son may enjoy a relationship of easy familiarity and friendship. In other societies, however, the latent antagonism between mother's brother and sister's son conflict with the overt expression of friendship (as it does between brothers-in-law) and this ambivalence is nicely sorted out through an institution known in anthropology as 'joking relations'.

In some parts of the world friendly in-laws and classificatory mother's brothers and sister's sons do not meet with embraces and handshakes and warm words of welcome, but hurl insults and even filth at each other, topping off this unseemly and violent behaviour with mocking references to their impotence or their mothers' private parts. Joking friends molest each other physically, even pretend to abduct each other's wives; commoners swear at chiefs and even small boys mock their elders and snatch food from their hands.

What is the meaning behind this institutionalized and permanent April Fool's Day situation between certain categories of kin and affines? For in-laws, joking may be an alternative to the extreme respect of complete avoidance – the possibility of conflict with the mother-in-law being removed by avoiding her. Among the Dogon, joking occurs between a man and his female in-laws of the same generation and below, although he shows respect and *quasi* avoidance to his parents-in-law. The explanation is that both friendship and extreme respect are requirements of these roles. The relationship between a man and his wife's family involves both attachment and separation; avoidance or joking eases an ambivalent situation. In Ghana[5] one man surprised a European observer when they were drinking beer in a compound, by throwing down the price of a pot of beer before a paternal half-sister: 'Take this and push it in your vagina . . .' explaining later that 'you can abuse your equals'. We found similar examples between blood brothers who are also equals (see p. 84). The remarkable things about the insulting and joking to an outside observer is the strong contrast it makes with the restraint which normally exists in these societies between persons of different rank.

Joking, therefore, is a means of combining friendliness and antagonism, and involves behaviour which in a normal context would express and arouse hostility. It occurs between mother's brother and sister's son in many patrilineal societies, or between relatives connected by a similar, though more distant, matrilateral connection. In Dogon the mother's brother shows great indulgence when his nephew criticizes him for meanness and makes inordinate demands; and on ritual occasions, nephews are allowed to 'diminish' their uncles by running off with his cattle and foodstuff. Any visit which the nephew makes to his house is a pretext for levying small amounts of goods and this is done with a great deal of shouting and joking, with insults directed at the uncle's wives.

'All those things,' the Dogon say, 'which the *mangou* nephew (joking relative) steals from his uncle, it is because of his mother: it is because of the anger which he feels at the idea that there has been no marriage between his uterine uncle (his mother's brother) and his mother. If the nephew insults his uncle's wife, it is because she has taken his mother's place. The symbolic anger he feels towards his father is because his mother did not marry his uncle.'[6]

According to Griaule, the focal point of interest in these statements is the non-realized, but ideal union of a man's mother and his uterine uncle, between a brother and a sister. As we have seen in our discusion of twinship, the mythical union is between a pair of twins whose prototype came from the egg of the world. On a more practical level, joking relations among the Dogon reveal an element of ambivalence: the mother's brother and his poor, insulted wife, must not be offended by the coarsest abuse. In doing this the intimacy between the mother's brother as the representative of one patrilineal group and the sister's son, from another, is stressed. Mangou share relations of mutual assistance as well as insulting, stealing, and mocking.

The ambivalent alliance – both friendly and hostile – between the mother's brother and sister's son is brought about by another kind of stealing which takes place on the birth of twin calves among the Dogon. The district concerned becomes the scene for comings and goings, which may last for weeks. Everyone capable of walking makes for his mother's brother's compound in order to tell them the news and receive a 'present'. Old men who are incapable of walking must be content to visit relatives of their mother's brother in their own village or watch out for others coming to the market. However, since everyone has a 'mother's brother' – classificatory or real – and is a mother's brother to other groups of people, the money received at the end of the long trek to bring the news of the birth of twin calves, must in the end be handed over the next time to those who come begging with the announcement of a similar piece of news. Thus money is exchanged between allied groups and a man who does not put himself out to visit his mother's brother is the loser since later he will have to give without receiving. Twinship again – this time of calves – symbolizes exchange and parity between friendly groups.

Joking relations are seen in terms of the complementarity between twins and between traders. These groups (of Dogon mothers' brothers and sisters' sons) are paired like twins and have similar prerogatives and duties. The joking and obligations are based on the basic need for friendship and alliance which permits the exchange of women, peaceful relations between people who might otherwise fight, as well as commerce. Exchange and reciprocity is basic to joking partnerships, trade and twinship. The Dogon themselves see the relationship between joking friends as an economic rite and insist on the obligatory exchange of gifts, services, and reciprocal assistance.

Reciprocity and alliance between sisters' sons and mothers' brothers who are joking partners is expressed most strikingly at funerals. At a Dogon funeral ceremony the mourners arrive wearing their best, ceremonial clothes, but the matrilateral kin (sisters' sons) of the dead man's family run on the scene as a group, dressed in rags, their oddest and oldest hats, the women disguised as old men with false beards of goats' hair and carry millet stalks as spears. Throughout the ceremony they giggle and insult their friends, parodying the ritual and the sad gestures of the mourners – as if a group of carnival maskers had run into a church burial service. They rush into the house, nagging the mourners, the kin of the dead man, mocking their poverty and their stinginess, tumbling about and pushing into people, knocking over the vats of porridge and beer which have been prepared for the invited guests. Others arrive and try to steal the dead man's clothes while the sons and brothers of the dead man defend them. They may even get hold of the corpse, itself, as it is being carried to the burial place. These joking partners, the dead man's sisters' sons, are trying to carry away with them his vital breath, thus removing his spirit from the paternal group to return to the maternal group as a new-born child. The struggle and buffoonery is then followed by a sacrifice as the male kin buy back the breath of the dead man by giving a goat to the matrilateral kin.

The same thing happens at the end of the mourning period, which is celebrated several months or years after the funeral; those who participate take the opportunity of indulging in feigned violence, raiding cattle and foodstuffs which they carry off to the young men's house in their village ward where it is eaten and shared with their age-mates.

Funerals are frequently occasions for persons who are friends, but not closely related to the dead man, to perform important roles. Among the Azande, blood brothers carried out autopsies; in Bangwa, it is the brother-in-law. In other societies best friends or compadres wash the corpse as in the case of the dead Chinautleco child (p. 101). They are performing pre-eminently 'friendly' functions, which kinsfolk cannot do and which in our own society we have relegated to the neutral hand of the state or funeral directors. It is probably true in all cases that these joking relatives, friends, and compadres are all outside the range of persons who might, through witchcraft or sorcery, be supernaturally responsible for the man's death. Moreover, these friendly outsiders serve to restrain excessive grief; through joking they assert the needs of the living over the dead. The joker is a friend, who expresses his friendship by stealing and wild behaviour. The joker is immune to the pollution of death, as well, because he is not a close kinsman.

What about the joking itself? We have established that two friends in an ambiguous social position joke in order to maintain their necessary alliance. Has the joking its own purpose to fulfil? Obscene joking has to do with pollution: otherwise it merely represents a temporary suspension of the order of things, a kind of catharsis. A joker at a funeral controls the situation and is given immunity. He is confident of his position as a sister's son and the disruptive comments which he makes are in a sense the comments of the social group upon itself. The joker expresses a consensus and within his peculiar role he lightens for everyone the oppressive reality, demonstrating its artificiality particularly at funerals. Freud saw the joke as an image of the relaxation of conscious control in favour of the subconscious, and this is probably a clue to the appreciation of joking and buffoonery between friends and at funerals. The excitement of the joke lies in the suggestion that any particular ordering of experience or society may be arbitrary. It provides an opportunity for a sudden intuitive realization that an accepted pattern is not necessary. It is frivolous, producing freedom in the form of sudden exhilaration. The jokes also connect different fields, destroying for a moment the usual hierarchy and order and permitting uninhibited friendship. The joke, explains Mary Douglas, says something of value about individuals as against the value of social relations and community. The role of an individual, or the ego-oriented view of life, is bound up with friendship and is enough to warrant joking between members of separate categories. [7]

On the other side of the African continent from the Dogon similar customs prevailed between matrilateral kin who are allies. A joking partner in Tanzania must rush to his friend's burial, loudly and indignantly denying the truth of the death, even with the corpse stinking before him. He demands to be buried alongside his friend, if his kin insist on burying a 'live corpse'.

At an Ambo funeral, a joking friend arrives with curses and maledictions, accusing brothers and sisters of bewitching him, and closing the eyes of the dead. 'You devil,' he screams at the corpse, 'get up from where you lie. You only pretend that you have died; you are alive. You are only worrying people by seeming to be dead, but you're not.' And to the mourners at the funeral of a woman, he shouts, 'You devils, why do you cry over her when you have killed her and eaten her? You have not killed her to throw her away, because you have got your meat.' Then the joking partners curse and call out the word for genitals. Joking partners wash the body and anoint it with castor oil, binding strings of beads around the neck. During the funeral they cook food for the grave-diggers and after the meal they sweep away the ashes of the fires lit in the yard by those who watched during the night – thereby sweeping away the pollution of death. (This example stresses again that a 'sister's son' as a member of a matrilateral group can well be a woman, since the categories 'sister's son' and 'mother's brother' may refer to both sexes.) In Tanzania, if a man dies an evil death his joking partner is called in to burn all his belongings since he can expose himself to pollution without danger. In the past, a joking partner could also be called upon to kill a man's cursed, abnormal children.

In most parts of Tanzania, the relationship between joking partners is known as *utani*. It links individuals, clans, and even tribes who live at great distances from each other. It first came to the attention of white missionaries and administrative officers when they noticed the extraordinarily violent relationship which sometimes manifested itself in the market between two so-called 'joking partners'. A man might begin to embrace, pummel, and otherwise lewdly assault a respectable woman in the market or main street and she would have to accept this unseemly behaviour complacently or give as good as she got. However, the institution seems to be dying out since modern women are sometimes not aware of the traditional role expected of joking partners; such a joker has more than once been hauled before European magistrates for assault. When you slap someone and call them a 'filthy baboon', is it a traditional rite or assault and battery?

Whole clans are related through this joking relationship. Among the Ambo such a relationship exists, for example, between the Iron Clan and the Goat Clan – supposedly because the Goat was always antagonistic to Iron; and between the Grass Clan and the Penis Clan, who became friends and joking partners because people urinate on grass. Joking partnerships between different clans cut across clan barriers and provide services and opportunities for trust which are not normally found; members of other clans are entitled to common courtesies but are kept at a distance for fear of offence, court cases, and witchcraft[8] (see pp. 219-20).

Joking relations between different clans among the Gogo, also of Tanzania,[9] are as significant as those between categories of kin, such as mothers' brothers and sisters' sons. The origins of clan joking here are said to be due to conflict in the past over the ritual leadership of the clan, once usurped through trickery and treachery. These joking partnerships are the expression of friendly alliance between different clansmen and perform the straightforward function of easing the strain of meeting strangers while travelling, or when in search of distant grazing land. The possibility of sex and marriage between these clan joking partners is constantly referred to: and marriage between them, although an ideal, is in fact rare. The important thing is that these unrelated members of different clans become potentially assimilable to the status of in-laws.

Rigby explains all forms of joking among the Gogo as a means of allying separate categories of people or of expressing this alliance. Joking between structured groups allows alliances between clans and lineages. Joking between partners expresses a boundary image across which friends are able to form alliances. In a society like the Gogo, there are two principles at work. There is the social structure, based on lineages or clans; and there is the general community, a solidary group of all the people. The boundaries between the structured groups are connected by alliances. In-laws become joking partners, form close ties, and become friends.

In most cases joking is associated with affinal relations, complementary filiation (an expression denoting the relationship between mother's brothers and sister's sons) and cross-cousin relationships; it is an institution which links corporate groups. In an agnatic society, the structure of social units beyond the domestic group may be based on non-agnatic kinship, as it is among the Gogo – that is, on affinal, matrilateral ties, in which there is a kind of dependence of the same nature as we described for in-laws. This is the basic significance of the anthropological term, 'complementary filiation'. The relationship between these groups is not one of substance or corporateness (as it is within a clan or lineage) but of alliance, friendship, and compacts based on some kind of exchange, usually of women and bridewealth. Relationships between joking tribesmen, joking clansmen, and joking in-laws are characterized by mutual cooperation, whether they like it or not. Ritual interdependence (as at funerals) and aggressive joking occur between those categories of persons whose relations are ordered outside the basic structural categories. Within a basic structural category of this kind – such as a patrilineal clan – there is an unambiguous classification of members. However, between groups linked for other purposes there is ambiguity and this ambiguity, which derives not from the need for cooperation but from the separation of categories, is resolved through joking.

Joking mediates the relations between two groups whose mutual friendship is necessary in order for women to be exchanged, goods to be traded, and rituals to be performed. In joking relations, as in blood pacts, there are general obligations of mutual aid and the sanctions are usually moral or supernatural. Joking relatives in Tanzania, for example, chaff each other and at the same time consider each other as great friends with far-reaching obligations for hospitality and the sharing of property, performing special functions at funerals and with certain *quasi*-magical powers over each other. Joking is not merely permissive behaviour, but ritualized behaviour of shared disrespect which enjoins friendship. Joking partners are equals: 'A man's [joking partner] is his *alter ego* – nothing is resented and nothing is refused. And if you cross your friend, the rollicking leg-pulling fellow may become a sinister creature endowed with power to imprecate the worst evils and his curse has the force of law.' In West Africa, a similar concept of the *alter ego* is found among the Malinko where joking between a whole complex of interconnected persons from in-laws to caste groups has been recorded.[10] The word for the relationship, *sanāku*, can be translated as 'duplicate' or 'double' and joking partners share obligations of reciprocal assistance. Or again: 'Sanāku is a kind of twin – inside him there is a little piece of his partner, and *vice versa.*'

Clearly, therefore, joking institutionalizes a kind of alliance between persons who would otherwise have been enemies or at least strangers. It expresses a need for friendship and reciprocity in a situation where inequality or hostility may also be present. Grandparents and grandchildren are 'friends' and enjoy a relaxed relationship, although the age difference is great. Joking reflects the fact that the partners are separated in some way by the social system, so that some of their interests are divergent and there is always the possibility of hostility. This is how we should see the joking relationship between a mother's brother and a sister's son, between a man and his uncle, who is a close relative and also an in-law. The friendship between the two is something different from the solidarity and mutual help found between members of a lineage, two brothers, or associates in a club. Through his mother's brother a man is in direct relationship with individuals of his mother's group, which may have interests which are inimical to his own and belong to a different, even hostile clan. Among the Bangwa, such a mother's brother has taken bridewealth in exchange for his sister's son's mother and expects a large share of the bridewealth when his own sister's daughter marries. Here we have hierarchy and equality, which is part and parcel of a system of exchange. Hostility is not permitted with members of a man's mother's group and, through joking, friendly relations may be maintained, even if it is not a friendship based on complete mutual trust and loyalty but a negative obligation not to take offence when excrement is thrown at you, your beer-mug is snatched from your hand, and insulting references are made to your virility – or your lack of it.

Joking relationships are ambivalent, since a taboo on being offended by the coarsest of insults makes it obviously impossible for conflict to arise while at the same time joking stresses the intimacy between the partners. Like all weird customs, a close look shows that insults and raillery between joking partners are perfectly comprehensible in their social context. In Western society most people have their joking partners, people we pummel and slap on the back, people we throw things at, people with whom friendship is expressed mainly through teasing. In some cases a relationship has a certain unease that makes straightforward, honest comradeship impossible. A kind of tension existing between different categories of workers in an industrial situation has been shown to have been eased by similar joking.[11] Nevertheless, between joking partners the friendship is real, no less than friendships between partners in blood pacts, in gift exchange, and in compadrazgo are real. They are all alliances based on friendship, formed with the aid of different models, none of which amounts to a completely contractual relationship since it is an alliance lacking legal sanctions.

9 Friends in Common

In this chapter I want to leave the discussion of exclusive personal relations and look at the interplay of men and women as members of groups. Friendship may be a blanket category applied to all the members of a gardening group, a local trade union, or a darts club. Some people find it easier to enjoy this kind of togetherness, in which emotional satisfactions are derived from the values of the group itself rather than from interpersonal relations. In fact there may even be a feeling that exclusive friendships are somehow wrong – communes are certainly supposed to work better without them, and close-knit friends are the revolutionaries of well-run clubs. At the present time we can observe a growing inclination for people to form associations of like-minded persons, classes of persons with the same political and sexual inclinations rather than the same access to economic wealth. From my point of view, it is wrong to seek total emotional satisfaction in such group activities. It may be comforting to enjoy the friendship of an Englishman because he is an Englishman, a birdwatcher because he is a birdwatcher, a woman because she is a woman. But only through special, particular friends – this is the point of the phrase 'best friend' – can the true values of friendship be appreciated and a personal note be injected into our more and more depersonalized worlds.

If gay ganders provide a frivolous parallel for the friendship of Australian mates (see pp. 72-4), the behaviour of apes has given more than one student of animal and human behaviour some ideas about the qualities of friendship between men in groups. In descriptions of the behaviour of groups of baboons, for example, a kind of gang togetherness has been noticed, a certain number of adult males constantly associating and tending to support each other in aggressive interaction with other males. In some cases baboon males associate so continuously and closely that they are scarcely observed acting independently. From this kind of observed behaviour between apes in groups – trios or larger – some quite remarkable theories have been advanced about human interaction: that men join groups by a kind of hereditary compulsion; that attraction spurred on by a shared instinct for aggression keeps them together; that women by their very nature are incapable of this kind of bonding; and that men who lack the satisfaction of these group activities – in hunting bands, street gangs, or football teams – suffer psychological deprivation and a diminution in the quality of their life.

Group bonding in animals and men is necessary for practical survival and Lorenz has suggested that personal bonding of this kind evolved because of the imperative for members of a group to cease fighting each other in order to combat outsiders more effectively. Amity is therefore part and parcel of aggression: 'Intraspecific aggression is millions of years older than personal friendship and love ... Intraspecific aggression can certainly exist without its counterpart, love, but conversely there is no love without aggression.'[1] Less mildly, Robert Ardrey maintains that apes and humans have founded their complex social institutions on the simplicity of an instinctive territorial drive: 'The stranger must be hated, the fellow protected. For the foreigner there must exist no measure of tolerance or charity or peace; for the countryman one must feel at least rudimentary loyalty and devotion. The individual must protect the group; the group the individual.'[2]

Therefore we should consider group activities as the result of innate aggressive desires, territoriality, and xenophobia. There are groups – or rather gangs – which encourage an all-inclusive kind of friendship; emotional bonds bind the group, the group stands against the world, both human and physical. People join for the sake of the group, not for the sake of a friend, and everyone becomes an undifferentiated pal or mate of everyone else. Antagonism between members of the group is suppressed and this sublimation of internal antagonism sets the group against like units or against some superior stratum. A purely physical environment is apparently insufficient to preserve this group solidarity and the redirection of aggression towards other human groups is an essential fact in its survival. 'Expedition choler' or 'polar disease', a kind of nervous madness and hypersensitivity to the mannerisms of one's companions, often attacks groups of men completely dependent on each other against a hostile environment. Nevertheless, friendships between soldiers, miners, fishermen, and other people occupied in dangerous professions derive from the perilous nature of their work.

Australian mates certainly form aggressive groups which strictly exclude the female. The platonic companionship of two bushmates provides the myth for all kinds of shared sentiments – between diggers, workmen on building sites, in drinking parties in the garden suburbs, as well as in communities of escaped convicts, and the unemployed in Melbourne in the 1890s. From the gang mentality of bush rangers and 'larrikins', we have the exaltation of a patriotism which is suspicious of outsiders to a quite fanatical degree – the White Australia policy was one example of it.

The dangers of the non-human and human environment played a part in the shared sentiments of soldiers who had faced the hazards of war together, of goldminers engaged in a dangerous occupation, of escaped convicts who faced starvation, and the larrikins who banded together because of unemployment. A gang mentality replaced the wholehearted sacrifices of devoted bushmates – all that the members of these miscellaneous groups could hope for was that a 'good fellow' would divide his beer or his loot and not give evidence against a mate. Bushrangers have been glorified in Australian folk literature as the inheritors of mateship, but in fact they were mostly selfish, violent bands of ruffians – examples of loyalty were rare and seldom even a part of the group's dogma. The city larrikins were groups of unemployed who flowed into the towns looking for work and adventure after the fizzle-out of the Australian gold rush; their behaviour had much in common with convict groups in that they formed intolerant, exclusive gangs to fight law and authority. There was a group of loafers known as the Cabbage Tree Mob which infested the towns of Melbourne and Sydney at the turn of the century. These frustrated and disappointed goldminers, the larrikins, were a nineteenth-century version of Hell's Angels, notorious for their violence and their sadism against enemies; but they showed a remarkable sentimentality in group values – and, unlike the Angels, towards their womenfolk. Yet while mateship may have been the model for most of their values, brutality and selfishness were so common that there was an almost complete failure to maintain the ethics of loyalty which are basic to traditional Australian ideas of mateship.

More effectively and more sincerely, these ideas were used in developing workers' consciousness throughout Australia – 'by practising, at every opportunity, unity in individual cooperation, mateship in all things, we will pave the way for the spread of brotherhood and the annihilation of the present competitive, selfish social warfare' (the General Secretary's report to the General Labourers Union, 1893). D. H. Lawrence took up this theme in *Kangaroo*,[3] showing how the aggressively masculine, homoerotic element in workers' and diggers' associations led not to democracy but to a mystic, well-nigh Fascist, sentiment. Lawrence glorifies the feeling of male togetherness – 'the lean, naked faces of the ex-soldiers gleamed with a smiling demon light' – and in his book Australian mates become mysogynist gangs of romanticized and romantic hooligans.

This is the story of mateship – from close friendship to a gang mentality. Nowadays in Australia everyone has to *be* a mate, not *have* a mate. Strangers are automatically called 'mate' – 'How y' going, mate' – although here the word contains a vague threat rather than a promise of friendship. It means 'Be like us and you'll be all right, mate'. In extending mateship to the whole Australian ethos, 'being mates' means being Australian as opposed to Australian or English and has resulted in a crude and rather smug brand of xenophobia.

Heroic self-sacrifice between mates in the bush or cobbers on the battlefront provides a sentimental picture of the past which has become pure nostalgia, and among town-dwellers mateship has degenerated into an idiotic, sporty brotherhood of toughs. Emotional friendship between mates has become a fake he-manliness which has little in common with the older tradition – the close, even passionate, friendship of a David and a Jonathan or a Pedro and a Juan would horrify those Australians who still melt into drunken sentimentality, conjuring up mateship in the bush, the mines, and the trenches – indulging the same need for expressing male bonding which is found in all societies, modern or ancient, primitive or civilized.

Gangs, associations, and clubs. The Bangwa have their secret societies of warriors, headhunters, anti-witchcraft priests, witches, royals, commoners, slaves. In Guatemala, male groups were a feature of village life in Chinautleco, young men forming street-corner gangs in each canton, their close bonds encouraging aggressive attitudes to outsiders. We saw in the episode between Juan and Pedro that one such male group used physical force in an attempt to challenge the youth who intruded into their canton and was trying to court one of the girls. If the intruder had not had a friend to serve as pacifier in the canton he was visiting, he ran the risk of severe physical punishment. In Chinautleco, male groups played an important role during a youth's courting days since they would help one of their number to successfully conclude his affair, after which the young man would withdraw from the bachelor group immediately and completely.

Are these male groups an expression of an innate male tendency to bond in order to survive? Are they frustrated soldiers and insecure delinquents, or (as scientists like Tiger and novelists like Lawrence suggest) real men who have come to terms with their animal selves? Ardrey would go further and maintain that they were demonstrating basic instincts to fight, to steal, to assault, and to kill. It is suggested that male groups of this kind offer psychological rewards to their members which the rest of society cannot enjoy; their members are happier than their soft-centred, conforming brothers since they find security, self-expression, and physical satisfaction among their own kind. For Ardrey, gangs recreate the universal animal institution of territoriality, as well as evolving a moral code and satisfying a need for a man to be loved by a man. These gangs have not been rejected by society but have rejected society: 'In its territorial combats, the gang creates and identifies enemies, and [a man's] need to hate and be hated finds institutionalized expression. Finally, in assault and larceny, the gang and its members enjoy the blood and loot of the predator. And there is always the weapon, the gleaming flick-blade which the non-delinquent must hide in a closet, or the hissing, flesh-ripping bicycle chain which the family boy can associate only with pedalling to school.'

This glorification of the brutality of gang life is as infantile and seductive as the most sadistic pornography. As an anthropologist I have been unable to find any other examples in any culture whatsoever – however primitive – which sentimentalizes in this glib way the violence of a deviant group. Headhunting, ritual cannibalism, annual wars with outside groups are all examples of aggression, but they are always limited by treaties, friendship pacts, trade, and intermarriage. In all societies killing, like utterly promiscuous sexuality, is controlled in the interests of happiness and order. Among the Bangwa, physical assault within the community was both a crime and a sin as heinous as witchcraft and brought supernatural sanctions on to the heads of the whole society.

Less emotionally than Ardrey and with a recourse to more scientific data, Lionel Tiger[4] has investigated the behaviour of men and animals in groups and has concluded that men's behaviour does in part reflect an underlying biologically-transmitted propensity, with roots in human evolutionary history: 'The recurrent though formally varied pattern of male bonding may depend upon or is a function of a biologically and socially learned component of the male life cycle.' Tiger argues that such a universal, although culturally varied, feature of human behaviour as male aggression, coupled with female exclusion from male groups, may in fact derive from a genetically determined need for males to form defensive and foraging units. This genetically transmitted male bonding behaviour is of the same biological order for these surviving functions as is the female–male bond for reproductive purposes. The details of their organization may depend, says Tiger, on genetically programmed sub-systems.

This argument suggests that male friendship is a propensity only to be elicited and manifested by real and close social and physical contact between males. Thus the exclusion of women from certain categories of all-male groups reflects not only a formalized hostility to females and the political domination of men, but a positive stress on attraction between males which shares elements of the relationship between the ganders Kop-schlitz and Max in Lorenz's pond (see p. 73). Tiger suggests that homoeroticism, a kind of submerged homosexuality, is a special feature of the general phenomenon of men's desire to get together in groups, whether these be street corner gangs, chess clubs, or freemasonry.

Thus when male baboons come together in gangs they share certain prejudices and standards in terms of which they become friendly. The kind of behaviour of Melbourne larrikins and Chinautleco bachelor groups is not therefore a uniquely human development, but a direct consequence of pre-hominid ecological adaptation – which, by the way, means an incredible time gap, scores of millions of years, between the pre-hominids and our-selves. This group behaviour grew from the hunting of large animals, where the cooperation between males would have been a necessity. The specialization of men in hunting widened the gap between males and females and the male–male friendship patterns for hunting purposes became programmed to ensure equal non-randomness in the conduct of social relationships.

The objections to this simplistic approach to human be-haviour have been made by qualified ethologists. First and fore-most, despite the undoubted attraction of comparing the antics of ducks and apes with our own, any transference of observation and theory from the animal to the human world falters on the vital single fact of man's ability to learn and adapt to new environments at an incredibly fast rate; apes and ducks are much more dependent on instinctual and hereditary factors. If female apes do not form emotionally satisfying groups for work and play, is it a sufficient reason for maintaining that twentieth-century European women are not clubbable? In any case, fanatical aggression theorists choose from the vast material on animal behaviour details which suit their theories. The details which contradict them are just as many. Lorenz himself points out that there are some animals which are totally devoid of any aggressive behaviour, instinctive or otherwise, yet which keep together in firmly united bands or flocks. Street gangs in our own society might be said to provide an example of allied, aggressive groups of individuals, joining forces to defend a territory against outsiders. Monasteries and communes are examples of another type, in which there is a sense of 'in community', for life, and where strong personal friendships between members are discouraged as much as enmity in the interests of the group. Lorenz also notes that animals which live placidly in flocks are not predestined to develop permanent friendships, either; their association, like that of monks or hippies in a perfectly-run monastery or commune, is all-inclusive and anonymous.

Leaving aside the vexed questions of territoriality, aggression, and instinct, it is none the less true that groups of men are formed, united together against like groups or against the world, and achieve their solidarity through culturally developed rituals which have rightly attracted the attention of zoologists and ethologists as being analogous to but not identical with the way some animals maintain themselves in groups. Among certain occupation groups, particularly fishermen, miners, and warriors, social progress means a straining towards equality and a free-flowing camaraderie which may, to outsiders at least, have a homosexual tinge. In Newfoundland, for example, groups of fishermen have immensely strong relationships which are glorified as a means of protecting them against the rest of the world – even against their own womenfolk, who are considered polluting objects if they come aboard the fishing boats.[5]

In prisons, bonding between men is temporary but is still backed by some form of ceremonial behaviour. In Pentonville prison[6] the interdependence of individuals in a system of exchange – of tobacco – has been developed as a means of transcending the difficulties experienced by men living together in face-to-face relations not of their own choosing. Even in prison, bonding between members of a group is essential, otherwise individuals would be out on a limb. Tobacco exchanges link them to a community through routinized techniques of communication which buttress inmate (note the word) society. Other groups like the Sicilian mafia bands and German brotherhoods achieved group unity through formal blood pacts or oaths. In prison society, however, the prisoners have ties which do not spring from shared criminality alone, but from a sense of interdependence between individuals whose cooperative

activities are directed towards lessening the pains of imprisonment. In Pentonville, groups of close friends develop who share
common interests deriving from their background outside the
prison. A close community of interest depends on a cultural and
ideological identity – being fellow-prisoners is not enough. As
one inmate said: 'There are mates, friends, and acquaintances.
Mates you do anything for, you give them anything they want,
and if they are involved in a punch-up you go in.' 'Friends you
lend but you don't give.' And if a friend is in a punch-up you
think about what might be involved before you help him.
'Acquaintances you don't want to know and you couldn't care
less what happens in a punch-up.' This man had two mates, a
dozen friends, and 'thousands of acquaintances'. His attitude
towards his mates is an example of true friendship, such as I
described in the first chapter. His attitude to friends exemplifies
a gang mentality, while that towards his acquaintances might
provide a cynic with a demonstration of the impossible obligations of Christian fellowship.

A prison is a 'total institution'; another is that of a Hull-based
trawler crew[7] – a group of men engaged in an extremely
hazardous occupation not dissimilar from that of primitive
hunting, coal-mining, or Australian stockraising. They work in
tough conditions off the coasts of Russia, Iceland, and Greenland
for relatively low wages. The crew is made up of about twenty
men, twelve in the deck hierarchy and two in the galley, four in
the engine room and the radio operator – plus the skipper and
the mate. Above deck is the officers' territory and they eat in a
different room from the rest of the crew. The skipper and the
mate occupy a special position, since they receive a percentage
of all profits – they are entrepreneurs rather than salaried
officers. All the deckhands, as in an African hunt, receive payment by results, so that the quickest and best workers get on to
the best and newest ships. For the deckhands, work is intense,
for twenty-four hours a day at times, fighting storms and cold,
hauling the gear, operating the winch which drags the net.
Normal outlets such as sex and drink are not available. Deckhands, conservative and fatalistic, see life on board ship as a
ritual world. Among them there is a strong sense of community

feeling, a oneness relative to those 'above deck', and friendships grow up between individuals.

Deckmen are equals on the Hull trawlers and everyone above deck is regarded as an officer. In situations where we have no such feeling of identity and equality between groups, we usually fail to get friendships and bonding. In the Norwegian merchant marine, for example, there is a near taboo on personal friendships.[8] This is not because the bonded community sees itself as an undifferentiated whole, like a convent or a gang, but simply because there are no relationships of equality between men in groups, as there are among the Hull deckhands. Individual merchant seamen, whatever their rank, stand on their own. The top positions in the merchant marine are only reached from the bottom and they can in theory be reached by anyone: consequently there is competition at all levels, not solidary friendship. There is also the fact of a high rate of turnover in personnel and people concentrate almost solely on their work roles. Here we have an ambivalence between people 'being in the same boat' and each man being in a unique position through pay, shift arrangements, and chances of advancement.

Most examples of inclusive friendships between men as members of groups are found in situations involving a high element of risk or danger; among Australian convicts and bushworkers, deep sea fishermen and criminals, coal-miners and soldiers, there is a high premium on solidary group friendships. *People of Coaltown*[9] describes an American community with a long history of violence and self-help, antagonism and fighting, heavy drinking and shooting matches; it is a society with little or no emphasis on personal friendships or networks of cooperation, but rather on a traditional and bitter hostility between individuals, particularly between the local inhabitants (the natives) and immigrant workers who arrived in the town during its coal boom. It is remarkable that down the mines the individual hostility which was the rule in the town could not be kept up. The hazardous occupation seemed to be the cause of the number of examples of enduring, loyal friendships even between native and immigrant. The miners themselves admitted that these bonds sprang almost entirely from the dangers they encountered in their work, although they were furthered by the hostility the miners felt in relation to the mining management – in the same way that the Hull deckhands felt emotional bonds as a group of low-paid workers in relation to the skipper and the mate, who represented the trawler's owners.

In Coaltown during periods of catastrophe the most rigid barriers were dropped and arch-antagonists came to the aid of one another as well as the families of the injured. 'Men form close friendships. It is surprising that they argue about things but when a man gets hurt, all come to do what they can. It is an unwritten law. You are good buddies and you never forget them. Just like in war.' All of the coal-miners saw themselves as buddies to a certain extent. If one man meets with difficulties the collier next to him, or a collier who is a quick worker, will help him out, although if any individual consistently fails to fill his quota and needs help all the time, the colliers tend to exclude him from their team. A man must also be a good miner before his work-mates feel they can trust him. Community feeling in the mine is also bolstered by strong and permanent alliances between pairs of men, some of them sticking together for long periods.

Coaltown provides an example of what sociologists call an anomic situation, where all social relations outside the pit were uncertain and where no one trusted anyone else. Yet even above ground people became friendly to a certain extent during a crisis when the mines closed and during a serious depression. 'When the mines began playing out, everyone became somewhat closer because we had to share a common tragedy.' These sentiments recall the breakdown of class antagonism and individual isolation during the London blitz, as well as the strength of friendly emotions felt by comrades-in-arms.

In ethnography, examples of male bonding are legion: secret societies govern stateless societies through possession of cult objects; hunting groups meet for communal hunts protected by a ritual which even a woman's shadow would spoil; warriors are organized in age-grades or associations; 'leopard men' roam prairie and forest and terrorize women and children; circumcision converts children into men and through this common rite they are ranged forever against the woman's world; men form associations to perform cooperative tasks – farming, dancing, carving. Countless books have been written to show that men form groups and become merged in solidary units specifically set apart from women and children.[10]

Despite evidence to the contrary we deny women not only the right but also the capacity to bond in groups. Club activities have been given a genetic and homoerotic flavour – male groups preponderate in society, not through the persistence of historical and cultural patterns and the need for cooperative action in war and hunting, but because men must come together through a biologically determined propensity. This is a new claim for Women's Liberation to cope with. Tiger suggests, along with Ardrey and Morris, that aggressive behaviour is directly a function of male grouping and maintains that any hindrance in allowing opportunities for male bonding, such as co-educational schools, may prevent the search for a comprehensive and satisfactory male individual experience. Men, to fulfil themselves as men, must meet in clubs for Men Only. As for women, they can neither bond as close friends or as members of groups. They are loners, eminently unsociable beings, who do not form groups because of their sexual situation and their reproductive functions. According to Lorenz,[11] 'Associations between women are rare and must be considered weak imitations of the exclusively male association.'

Women, it is claimed, lacking the hereditary requirements to form gangs and protect their territory to the death, are lone appendages of their menfolk and babies because they are programmed that way. They have even been excused their wild behaviour in prison on these grounds: 'Women have more difficulty in adjusting themselves to prison than men do. The reasons may be that they themselves are an even more anti-social selection than men, or women take less kindly to institutions full of nothing but women.'[12]

Ardrey, as usual, popularizes the scientific hypothesis: the modern woman 'is the product of seventy million years of evolution within the primate channel in which status, territory, and society are invariably masculine instincts, in which care of children has been a female preserve, and in which social complexity has demanded of the female the role of sexual specialist. Yet she must somehow struggle along in a human society which idealizes in her behaviour every masculine expression for which she possesses no instinctual equipment, downgrades the care of children as insufficient focus for feminine activity, and from earliest girlhood, teaches her that a rowdy approach to the boudoir will bring her nothing but ruin. Should she attain the analyst's couch walking on her hands, it would be little wonder, for she lives in an upside-down world.' In their revenge, women become 'psychological castrators of husbands and sons' and 'the unhappiest females that the primate world has ever seen'.[13]

There is, as usual, some truth in this. Men do like to be together and in many cases exclude women – but this is the situation in our culture, not a universal trait based on genetic inheritance. An English coal-mining group provides an example of a fairly common modern situation.[14] Groups of mates who work together down the pits provide the most significant feature of life above ground. Men continue to take part in male groups from the time when, as boys of school age, they form groups to play together and, later, gangs to go to dances and make forays into neighbouring towns. This group feeling, inspired no doubt by the strong feeling of solidarity experienced by men in the mines, is threatened above ground when the time comes for young men to marry. In his twenties the young miner starts courting and to escape from his male group into wedlock is quite a battle, with his mates putting up a good deal of opposition. In Ashton, although links to the group are weakened after marriage, it is a point of honour among men to continue for some time drinking and attending sporting events with their mates. In middle age, when children have grown up, expenses are less, and when the novelty of marriage has long worn off, men return once more to the company of their peers in club, pub, trade union meeting, or betting office.

Groups such as these certainly isolate and deliberately exclude women. Germaine Greer writes: 'Every wife must live with the knowledge that she has nothing else but home and family, while her house is ideally a base which her tired warrior-hunter can withdraw to and express his worst manners, his least amusing conversation, while he licks his wounds and is prepared by laundry and toilet and lunch-box for another sortie.' The fact that men enjoy themselves and express themselves among men is fought tooth and nail by many wives as an encroachment on the all-inclusive marital relationship.

The Bangwa have their clubs, associations, secret societies, and dance groups and since Bangwa is a male-dominated society these associations are dominated by men. Is it, as has been suggested, a kind of homoeroticism that causes men to come together in groups, a biological propensity rather than the need for cooperative action or political control? Men derive enormous pleasure from their joint activities – dancing, trading, hunting, drinking, eating. Yet not one group excluded women as a matter of course: warrior associations used women as emissaries; Mafwa as a princess made hunting magic and attended the most secret sanctums of Bangwa governmental associations. Nor were there any taboos on women attending rites, ceremonies, or dances and all the most important societies had some special status reserved for women.

African societies more frequently divided men from men than they divided men from women. Men and women of special rank played music, danced, performed ceremonies and rites. Some powerful Bangwa societies were said to be taboo to women and children, but when they had their meetings in the sacred copse outside the palace and the women and children had to hide in their huts, most of the male population – formally classified as children – also had to hide, while certain titled princesses entered the copse with the male members.

In Bangwa, some women entered into all-male spheres. And once one woman is welcomed as a full member of the darts club or the hickory lodge the theory of male exclusivity is breached. In Chinautleco, men formed strong personal friendships but the major village associations, known as *cofradia*, were connected with formal celebrations of the various saints which were in their custody; each association was made up of men and women between whom there was the utmost cooperation. In the strict hierarchy of officers there are both male and female counterparts, each with their staffs and symbols. The intense and emotional service and celebration of the saints is shared between the sexes and there is not the slightest indication that women are seen only as shadows of their menfolk.

Moreover, women form groups where femininity and female-ness are prized and enjoyed. Women may not hunt or form trawler crews but they have their secret societies, their age-grades and their craft groups in which femininity is celebrated by symbol and mask and serves to separate their world from that of the men. Bangwa women organize themselves into groups: to work together on the farms, to form a savings society, or merely to get together and learn new dances. They have associations with elected officers, and their special costumes and sacra, and they perform at funerals and festive occasions. Women have now organized themselves into political cells under my friend, Mafwa. These women's groups did not ban men – in fact there was usually a special role reserved for a man. Nevertheless, their meetings revealed a delight in each other's company as women and a pride in things concerning women. They sang, danced, ate, and drank; they put on their ceremonial finery, wearing their women's masks, and performed exuberant round dances, show-ing their enjoyment of each other's company in demonstrative phrases and embraces.

The women farm together, singing and chattering to relieve the tedium of the work. In polygynous compounds they are also organized into groups, meeting under a senior woman to discuss problems and grievances. I have watched a powerful chief cowering in his sleeping-hut because one of his wives had been unjustly reprimanded and her 'colleagues' had simply gone on strike. These women are proud of themselves as women, of their role as providers – the agricultural economy depended entirely on them – and they have many opportunities to fulfil themselves in roles outside the purely domestic sphere. Interestingly – and this makes the Bangwa a special case – menstruating women are not secluded or even banned from the most sacred rites.

Is this the kind of recognition of femininity that Germaine Greer is seeking – 'she must know her friends, her sisters and seek in their lineaments her own'? Women come together in groups, seek satisfactions together and glory in their role of life-giver, a role which rivals in significance that of their menfolk – erstwhile hunters and warriors now frequently relegated to the role of baby-sitter while their wives march off to the farms or the market.

In the Trobriands, the women as well as the men make sorties to neighbouring villages for amorous purposes (see p. 233). In Bangwa, women join forces to preserve their own territory and their own dignity, to the extent of badly hurting one poor man who unwittingly polluted their farm by shitting on a freshly-hoed garden. Women in other parts of the Cameroon are equally conscious of their identity as women and if necessary protect their rights in a flagrantly militaristic way. The Kom have a female practice called *anlu* which is a punishment meted out to men for offences against women – for uttering such obscenities as 'Your vagina is rotten', for beating a pregnant woman, or causing a nursing mother to become pregnant. Anlu is started by a woman who gives out a high-pitched scream; any woman who recognizes the sound leaves what she is doing and joins the group which soon swells and becomes a mass of dancing women, singing impromptu stanzas to inform the people of the offence which has been committed. They pour into the compound of the offender, relieving themselves anywhere and everywhere, and exhibiting their private parts, until the man repents. He is then taken and immersed in a stream – and the incident is closed.[15]

Another Cameroon people uphold the female world in a similar way, defending the sanctity of the vagina – Miss Greer will be gratified to learn – against men's insults. The Bakweri have a verbal category, *titi koli*, a word meaning a woman's vagina and also the action taken by a group of women if one of them is insulted, through a reference to her 'stinking vagina', by a man. If a woman is insulted in this way, she calls together her women friends, relatives, and neighbours and they converge, in military array and with special plants tied around the waist, on the guilty man. The village head is brought into the dispute to prevent violence and the women *as a group* are given a pig as compensation. The women then surround the man and sing sexual songs in an aggressive fashion, accompanying them by normally shocking or obscene gestures.

As Shirley Ardener points out, the Bakweri women are acting as a group in defence of their femininity symbolized by the vagina. The insult, *titi koli*, is thought to concern all women and therefore the women are demonstrating not only on behalf of the insulted woman, but on their own behalf as a sexual group. The obscene songs are apparently a retaliatory threat to men's position. In order to have men respect them – as women – they behave in a socially depraved manner in order to demonstrate that they will not recognize men's power to make them conform to his world. While women in Europe and America may be finding it necessary to question the basic assumption of the female stereotype and to search for new models in a world which has turned them into poor imitations of men, Bangwa, Kom, and Bakweri women in their traditional roles have worked out a satisfactory outlet for their feminism – women are separate from men but need at least their respect. The Bakweri, by focusing attention on the vagina (rather than hiding it away in an erotic fashion as we do, or banishing it altogether in the sweet scent of deodorants), are demanding respect for their sex. Feminism is about being women – and has nothing to do with economic opportunity or relative status between the sexes.

Men act in groups and women form bonds. And even men and women join together in closed groups against other closed groups. Patriotism in its extreme form is the conversion of this group feeling to a whole nation, so that insiders become suspicious of outsiders to a fanatical degree. In *Christ Stopped at Eboli*, Carlo Levi[16] describes all the young people becoming *compari* – friends – of St John, binding themselves into a relationship based on a mixture of love, friendship, and brotherhood, with the village itself as the fount of moral sentiment. This Catholic rite provides an additional link for villagers not related through kinship. However, the dangers of strong group bonding are shown in the tendency of communities to erect boundaries against outsiders, which derives from an exaggerated feeling of oneness with insiders and fear of outsiders. Australians, including new Australians from Italy and Greece, should all be mates united in the defence of Australian values, which until recently included the White Australia policy. Xenophobia and isolationist policies follow in extreme cases. The United States during her isolationist period refused to explore a network of commercial or political alliances and encouraged instead a pathological fear of the great enemy – in this case Russia – even to the extent of banning names like Alfred because of the implications of the last syllable. Patriotism in such a situation leads to assertions that everything from one's own country is automatically best and everything from outside evil.

Sociologists have even attempted a classification of social systems according to the degree of cosmopolitanism they permit. Fascist Germany allowed very little; contemporary Britain, traditionally receptive to outsiders, is becoming less and less so as immigration restrictions are tightened up. Anthropologists have pointed out that a feeling of group belonging is reflected in our need for classification and categories – in some societies totems fulfil the need for setting one human group apart from another, so that each group sees itself almost as a different species.[17] Mary Douglas[18] has suggested that the higher the boundary between one culture and the next, the more that culture will divide up its natural world into friendly and hostile species. The contrast between social groups will be paralleled by contrasts between men and nature. If outsiders are threats to the common togetherness of the group and all exchanges and alliances are suspect, then certain aspects of nature will be singled out to represent the intruder who breaches boundaries that should be kept intact. There are also fascinating parallels between the self-sufficient individual and the attention which he gives to his body: 'Formal social relations call for relaxed posture, free movement, casual dress, uninhibited speech . . .' The group may be envisaged as the body. If a man recognizes strong allegiances to group and group alone, the body orifices are to be carefully guarded – since inside and insiders are good and outside and outsiders are evil. In members of a closed group, therefore, we might expect excessive attention to toilet training and an austere attitude to the good things of life.

Douglas has suggested a relationship between exclusive group behaviour and natural symbols of deviance such as monsters and freaks. To the Israelites, for example, all hybrids and mixtures were worrying, even abominable – the creeping things of Leviticus, along with the pig, the hyrax, the hare, and the camel, and others that neither cleave the hoof nor chew the cud. They were abominable because they did not fit into the neat pattern of their classification system. The Israelites needed something from nature to abominate – since most outsiders and exchanges were suspect, Douglas argues that the pig came to represent the abominable intruder who breaches boundaries that should be kept intact.

Is this condition a primitive one, or a special psychopathic state? The Ancient Hebrews are the most widely known example of a closed group, outside the Indian caste system, which has closed its boundaries to people, foreign gods and ideas instead of extending the limits of its culture and ensuring a wider network of alliance with friends, neighbours, and foreign tribes. Primitive society may welcome strangers, foreign wives, traders (see pp. 215–16); the Bangwa had no totems, no monsters, no forbidden fruits, no unclean sex. The Ancient Hebrews, on the other hand, even preferred to marry their cousins – their fathers' brothers' daughters. This marriage system tends to preclude the circulation of women, which in most societies is a healthy means of encouraging relations between families and groups; women, instead of forming part of the general communication system, are considered as part of the patrimony of the group, to be shared exclusively within the narrow grouping of kin. The Hebrews preferred to keep their boundaries intact and reckoned any attempt to cross them as a hostile intrusion, expecting no good to come of external or internal exchange and having no rules to facilitate it. This was the American situation before the *rapprochement* with Russia and China. Among the Ancient Hebrews such a marriage system, together with a complex fabrication of animal categories which were considered taboo or polluting, cut them off as a group from neighbouring peoples.

Closed groups of this nature are rare, although black and white in South Africa are seen and see each other as different as cats and dogs. Yet even caste groups are not entirely closed and chinks are made in the armour of caste by special friendships (see pp. 117–20).

In this chapter we have looked at interpersonal relations as they are played out in sex groups, communities, and closed societies. Membership of such groups satisfies both emotional and practical needs, but it would be wrong to suggest that belonging to a group is a biological imperative or that the kind of bonding which is enjoyed is the primary relationship between friends.

Real friendship is an affair between individuals and has its satisfaction in the close interaction of two people who complement one another's personality and provide mutual emotional rewards of quite a different order from the safe, anonymous sentiments of group interaction or the biological pleasures of sex.

In Africa, the need for strong individual friendships is recognized even within an association of men. Among the Didinga[19] strong emotional friendships between two persons of the same age-grade system were positively encouraged by the institution of special friendships between warriors of different sets. As soon as a junior warrior set was formed, each of its members had to find a 'best friend' among the ranks of the senior warriors. The two young men, the elder about eighteen and his friend five years younger, may already have been friends. This ceremonial friendship, with its practical military function, is publicly ratified and acquires a lifelong social and emotional value, incurring responsibilities on both sides. In Sparta, institutionalized friendships between soldiers were strikingly similar: there, the senior friend instructed the junior in military behaviour and assumed responsibility for his conduct in times of crisis. The junior warrior was also expected to look after the prestige of the older man and in no circumstances let him down – in or out of battle. Both among the Didinga and the Spartans, 'best friends' became passionately devoted. The ethnographic and historical examples may serve to illumine better-known literary friendships between warriors – Achilles and Patroclus, Orestes and Pylades, Roland and Oliver.

My point here is that although members of groups may feel secure in each other's company, particularized friendships between individuals – seen as satisfactions in themselves or as a means to further alliances – are of greater value both to the persons concerned and to society in general. The rest of this book, using mostly ethnographic material, will pursue this idea in some depth.

10 Lovers, not Warriors

One of the underlying themes of this book is that love and friendship – or cooperation and reciprocity, exchange and alliance – are as important, if not more important, for personal wellbeing and the survival of culture as aggression. For some people it has become embarrassing to recognize or admit a basic need for love and for many of them it may be impossible to accept that a person's identity as an individual, society's character as truly 'human', and our survival as members of that society, may depend on anything so vague, so *unstimulating*, so humanistic, as love and friendship. Good deeds, altruism, the aesthetics and business of exchange, and the communication of women between groups are all a far cry from the exciting themes of violence, war, and sexual attack which have been uppermost in hundreds of books, plays, and pseudo-scientific tracts which have appeared over the past twenty years.

The emphasis on man's non-peaceful nature has had a long history. One of its prophets was Freud; there is little in the history of the analysis of human relations starker than the account, put forward by Freud in 1914, of the libido as narcissistic excess. Love equals self-love and the libido has no need or wish to go beyond the bounds of inner self. Love in libido theory is an enforced remedy because the primary desire of the libido is towards ingestion of all realities into self. The id becomes the repository of all the untamed, instinctual cravings which surge within the human body and soul, a kind of undifferentiated sexual energy which is rooted in the body with its unalterable, hereditary constitution. This volcanic, impulsive id is only held in check by culture and society whose controls become our conscience, our super-ego. Civilization or culture were seen by Freud as repressive forces, holding down our 'naturally' aggressive libido, through the authority of the super-ego. Freud denied any basic need in human culture for love and friendship and insisted on the importance and universality of the sexual urge, interpreting the socialization of man as merely the overcoming of sexual jealousy, regarding hate as a more spontaneous urge, a more ineradicable appetite than love; an interest in art, literature, and music was merely a substitute for sexual gratification. In *Civilization and its Discontents*,[1] he wrote: 'The truth is that men are not gentle, friendly creatures wishing for love, who simply defend themselves if they are attacked but that a powerful measure of desire for aggression has to be reckoned with as part of their instinctual endowment.' It might, of course, be argued that what Freud took as inborn hostility is in fact an acquired form of nineteenth-century European behaviour following on the frustration of the human organism's satisfactions. Love, for Freud as for Lorenz (see p. 21), grows from aggression and hate. We love in order that we should not become ill – *endlich muss man beginnen zu lieben um nicht krank zu werden.*

Freud saw human beings as so many atoms, each looking after his own exclusive interests. The most usual criticism of Freud is that in many of his studies, from which he hoped to make conclusions valid for men and women everywhere, his raw material was taken from the Viennese middle class. However, there is a more important and pertinent limit of which one needs to be aware. Although some scientists like to think of themselves as cosmic exiles, searching out pure knowledge in the isolating conditions of a neutral laboratory, they are as influenced as the rest of us by the culture and social conditions in which they live the rest of their lives. The late nineteenth century was the heyday of self-reliance. The middle classes had come into their own as a result of the expansion of industry and trade and could exist independently of the ownership of land. If the middle classes, by hard work, could make good for themselves, why shouldn't everybody? This view provided an invisible 'atmosphere' which nearly everybody breathed in without question. In the biological sciences, Darwinism, the theory of the survival of the fittest, provided confirmation that this was the true picture of the way the world worked.

It is only a small dimunition of Freud's massive achievement to say that he too was influenced by this view and that, in part at least, his emphasis on man's innate aggressiveness, which he overtly describes as being the result of the sex drive, was the result of this. Today, we are more inclined to question the over-riding virtues of self-reliance – the institution of the Welfare State after the Second World War is a simple item of evidence so far as Western consensus politics is concerned, while the rumbling aftermath of the Love Generation revolt of the late sixties is another.

We are, however, viewing Freud with hindsight and only slowly beginning to put him into correct proportion (and let it be said that we too are undoubtedly breathing in unquestioningly an atmosphere permeated by ideas and assumptions that our progeny may question).

Freud was the bearer of a capitalist ethos. His insistence on the importance of the father figure meant a denial of tenderness both filial and parental and an excessive emphasis and universalization of sex. The whole idea of a child's socialization-process involved the overcoming of sexual jealousy and fear. In Freud's work, pity for others is inconceivable and love an egoistic exercise.

More recently, psychologists and animal behaviourists have begun to admit the existence of innate bonding instincts between individuals. Animals living in groups keep the peace and in-dividual animals even form friendships. Whether instinctual or not, bonding mechanisms in individuals derive from a basic trust deriving from bonds established in early childhood, usually with the mother, and from this trust we derive our fundamental attitudes of sociability and our capacity for commitment to people. Investigation has shown that we are exceedingly friendly beings, and Tiger's work suggests that these roots of sociability are more deeply seated than aggression. Our most important signal of friendship is the smile and there are many others. A need for love and a need to love are basic. Post-Freudian psychologists like Melanie Klein have stressed again and again that without love a child cannot acquire an identity: 'We must in fact for our peace of mind either feel ourselves loved or in a position to be loved.'[2] And people who do not receive a modicum of love end up in violence or mental homes. Nor are sexual drives a sufficient explanation of love – 'the roots of love are not in sexuality, although love makes use of it for the secondary strengthening of the bond'.[3] I myself would go so far as to make the unfashionable suggestion that sex, especially when it is associated with a romantic passion, is destructive of real love.

Despite ethnography and the re-working of Freud's views, we have been told over and over again in the last ten years that man is a naked ape, with an instinct for aggression. Desmond Morris has written of man as an upright, ground-living ape, with a swollen head and brain, no snout, feeble teeth, a reduced sense of smell, excellent eyesight, great dexterity, and the power of speech – placing, let it be noted, man's greatest achievement, that of communicating through symbols, last. Along with others, Morris has maintained that man's aggressive nature is inherited as a behaviour pattern from animals because of its survival value and is genetically transmitted to children. We are therefore predatory, competitive, and aggressive by nature and any idea of living without violence and war is a fantasy; we are condemned by so-called science to the war of every man against every man. Konrad Lorenz also sought significant parallels in human and animal behaviour, beginning modern ethological studies with his amusing and sympathetic observations on the greylag goose – here aggression was shown to establish the dominance of the most powerful males, a dominance which by selection produces, cares for, and protects the stronger young. Dominance serves the purpose of spacing animals out over the available ground and preventing over-population within the group. It also makes for order by establishing the authority of the stronger males, the weaker being arranged in a pecking order, thus securing a powerful hierarchical social structure.

However, man is no goose. Nor is he an ape. The remote ancestors of both man and the modern ape branched out into two divergent lines some thirty-odd million years ago, one line leading to the anthropoid apes (the chimps, gorillas, and orang-outangs) and the other to the *hominidae*, leading through Australopithecus to modern man. It is a scientific fact, not stressed by Morris, that *hominidae* developed along totally different lines for this huge period of time. We should also remember that the entertaining comparisons of Morris and the dire predictions of Robert Ardrey are mostly made by establishing similarities between apes and men whose behavioural patterns are taken almost exclusively from middle-class Euro-American society – that is, the readers of their books – in much the same way that Freud generalized for the whole human race from the behaviour of nineteenth-century bearers of Viennese culture. Human culture is in no way universally the same and to ignore the behaviour of the rest of the world, or even the varied past of our own society, is to present a distorted and not to say far-fetched picture. I have tried to present in this book some examples of non-aggressive human behaviour outside of our own Western capitalist, aggressive, world.

I should like to stress here that whatever man's culture potential, it is not dominated by instinct as it is in animals. Man's needs are satisfied in all sorts of ways, while instinct by definition is a fixed response to the same stimulus. People communicate, plan, store learning, teach each other, live in the past, present, and future, change from one belief to another, to a far greater extent than any animal. As Marx wrote, 'What distinguishes the most incompetent architect from the best of bees is that the architect raises his structure in the imagination before he constructs it in reality.' Direct comparisons of the behaviour of man with that of animals offer little more than poetic interest, since the evidence about the bio-social nature of man does not support the notion of human instincts. Man's uniqueness lies in the fact that he has freed himself from most of those predeterminants which condition the behaviour of animals. We can learn aggression as we learn cooperation and friendship, but we are not born with either. Deductions from coral fish and apes are unscientific primarily because most aspects of human behaviour – eating, loving, killing, and believing in God – are learned activities. Leave a pair of immature dogs on a desert island and they will survive to produce puppies which will grow up into recognizable dogs. An infant boy and girl in the same predicament would not even survive and find food, much less breed and rear a family, since we are totally dependent on learning in order to crawl, stand up, walk, talk, copulate, and feed ourselves.

Supporters of the theory of man's innate aggression agree that

men finally have to cooperate, but they suggest that this cooperation is nothing more than an agreement not to fight and results
from fear and coercion. Amity, for them, derives only from
enmity or from the hazards of the environment – a coal pit, or the
ocean (see pp. 194–7). Even Bertrand Russell[4] maintained that
for a peaceful state of things an external enemy was necessary
in order to provide the cohesive force of society, so that a 'world
state, if it were firmly established, would have no enemies to fear
and would therefore be in danger of breaking down through lack
of cohesive force'. Lorenz, from a different angle, maintains that
aggression is a necessity and through an insufficient discharge of
the aggressive drive we shall suffer neurosis – like American
Indians and African tribes, once their wars came to an end.
Amity only persists as long as there is enmity, in the form of
hostility or aggression: once an alliance achieves its purpose or
has been permanently frustrated, friendship comes to an end.
Without a joint purpose to channel their energies into a friendship relation, aggression theorists maintain that individual men
and animals will return to a normal state of mutual animosity
unless rewards are presented to arouse a further desire for friendship. This is the kind of argument which is used to explain why,
in wartime, the extra enmity from outside – between the British
and the Germans in the 1940s, for example – also produces
additional qualities of friendship. I agree that hazards and the
need for defence are important factors which bring men together
– into both groups and pairs – but it is not the only reason why
men, for the most part, live in peace and form friendships.

Neither men nor animals are always at war. From students of
animal behaviour we have as many reports of cooperation and
bonding as we have of hostile aggression. Apes are not predatory
killers, of course, but peaceful vegetarians; Jane Goodall's
chimps[5] seem to found their community life on little else than
good nature and although there is an order of dominance, it is
not all aggressive. When bands meet in the forest or the savannah
there is a great outburst of excitement but antagonism is absent
and all may quite happily feed in the same trees. Violence only
occurs on the most exceptional occasions. Even Ardrey sadly
admits that we have to reckon on some degree of amity in the
primate potential, although he insists that the soft-hearted

chimp has been confined to a few remote African areas due to his lack of 'drive'. Nor are apes unique examples: most animals live peaceably together and intraspecific aggression is rare among them except under abnormal conditions such as overcrowding. Animals are only predatory towards animals they feed on and in any case it is well known that a lion when it kills is never angry.

In my researches I have found that cooperation between members of a society, along with a tolerance of outsiders, is more the rule than the exception. All societies, for example, recognize a duty of hospitality to strangers and a respect for messengers, even from their enemies. Strangers are usually converted into guests and guests are universally treated with honour, given food and shelter and sometimes sexual privileges. In some groups, permanent host-friends look after traders and strangers and provide havens for them in foreign countries. In Rome, the *jus hospitii* gave the guest protection through custom and religion. In Greece, strangers were protected by Zeus – and the Dioscouri – and given the honorary title of 'friend'. Is it not odd that our supposedly violent and aggressive primitives should have been so uninhibitedly welcoming to strangers when missionaries and traders arrived in their islands? How does this attitude to strangers tie in with our ethnocentric ideas of innate aggression and territorial imperatives?

The friendship offered to strangers reflects a need to trade, to exchange cultural ideas, to communicate. Exchanging names, shaking hands, rubbing noses are all techniques of proving goodwill. Among the Igbos, the kola nut is the traditional medium for welcoming guests and reassuring the hosts themselves of a stranger's peaceful intentions. The kola nut is the symbol of hospitality and friendship and to be presented with a kola nut is to be made welcome as a friend and a temporary member of the community. With its intertwined segments, which are broken open by friends and shared, the kola is an expression of personal interrelationships. 'Among us the kola nut is a highly valued and indispensable product. It commands our respect in a way no other produce has done ... Kola nut is a symbol of friendship. Its presentation to a guest surpasses any other sign of hospitality which any host among us can show, even though in some places it costs only a penny.'[6]

Primitive societies are not prone to constant aggression and internal and external violence unless they are in a state of acute disturbance. For some reason, however, the views that aggression and hate are natural to human culture have been accepted with a strange amount of blind voracity. The acceptance of our aggressive nature seems to come as a relief, excusing our own ruthless ambition, our involvement in genocide and war, our obsession with violence and sex. In fact, ethnography shows that the simplest societies are usually the most peaceful and the most cooperative. Even hunting bands, such as the Australian aborigines and South African bushmen, usually live at peace with their neighbours. Moreover, within their groups they even allow the greatest power to the physically weakest members, the very old men who, at least in the Australian case, monopolize food and other scarce resources such as women. Hunting itself as an activity does not imply predatory or aggressive attitudes since the bushmen, the pygmies, and the eskimo, all hunters, are the least warlike of peoples and show little actual hostility to their prey.

War has never been a permanent threat in primitive societies; and if it happened it was rather like a recurring ritual or ceremony, not a constant series of interminable hostilities. Fighting and aggression occurred, of course; among Australian aborigines, ceremonial duels and intertribal warfare took place but violence as such was in direct opposition to the peaceful values expressed in their magical and religious ceremonies. Furthermore, there is no archaeological evidence that warlike behaviour was the norm among prehistoric groups.

Primitive society, therefore, cooperates as much as it fights. From one angle social behaviour may be viewed as two-faced and calculating, but from another it may be described as considerate and sympathetic to the needs of others, even outsiders. Social life may be precarious but man does not always behave as though his neighbour is about to impinge on his territory. On the contrary, the condition of man in society has placed a high premium on his being able to communicate peaceably with his fellows, particularly in hunting and food-gathering societies which are often very small – from twenty to a hundred individuals in a band – and out-and-out aggressive individuals or stranger groups could not be allowed to flourish. Competition and a perpetual attitude of defence against possible aggression are not the hallmarks of society. Primitive and civilized cultures are aggressive or friendly, or both, according to their system of values but in almost all cases alliances are set up with neighbours and peace is kept for the greater part of the time. Even the most xenophobic peoples have discovered that society profits more by establishing some kind of *modus vivendi* with neighbours and strangers than by killing them. Men, therefore, cooperate because they would destroy themselves if they didn't, even if temporary survival were achieved by redirecting aggression away from their nearest and dearest. This is why men have *learnt* techniques for associating or coming to terms with the most remote outsiders – the Trobrianders and the ferocious Dobu, the Dogon and the 'walking fish', the Bozo, the pygmies and their giant Negro neighbours.

If we look at the records of early travellers in Africa, the Pacific, and South America, we must be struck by the initially friendly actions of the peoples they encountered. Despite one or two gory exceptions and the perennial joke of the cooking-pot and the cannibals, explorers and adventurous missionaries who have found themselves at the mercy of isolated tribes have usually been treated with hospitality, kindness, and respect. Normally this continues until their land has been appropriated by the visitors, their women prostituted, sexual illnesses introduced, and their children sold into slavery. The Tasmanians – extinct for these very reasons – were described by Cook as a friendly people with 'benevolent expressions' who had a gentle confidence in the weird, pink-skinned monsters who arrived in floating wooden islands and came ashore with sticks that exploded and killed without any visible force. The sailors who landed in Tasmania must have appeared much stranger than any Martian would appear to us, since we at least suspect there might be life on Mars while the Tasmanians thought they were the only men in the universe. Yet they received their 'guests' with open arms and a positive friendly interest. In Hawaii the respect given to the European amounted to worship as far as Cook was concerned

– friendship and adoration at first sight. Hawaii's first missionaries were greeted by the poor unsuspecting Polynesians with a supine admiration for the words and wisdom of these over-dressed American Puritans that ultimately led to their cultural extinction.

The most warlike of peoples, at least in the popular imagination, are the recently acculturated hill-tribes of New Guinea. Yet probably the most striking traits shared by these diverse people are an acute interest in novelty and a desire for strange goods and the ways of strange men. Instead of hanging their heads and hiding or getting out their poisoned arrows and headshrinking equipment, New Guinea boys and men who have never before seen a white woman show an unquenchable interest in their clothes, their equipment, and their language, and a great eagerness to acquire these things for themselves from the representatives of the colonial takeover.

As we have seen, the Melanesians are avid traders as well as famed warriors. How is it possible for warfare and alliance, violence and amity, to go on at the same time? For New Guinea's warlike reputation is not a mythical one: before 'pacification' a constant state of warfare existed between neighbouring communities, even those of the same culture. Among the Dani, for example,[7] all men were fighters and most old men had war wounds. The Dani were divided into some dozen groups, each of whom was a potential enemy of the others. Warfare, however, was a rather stately and ceremonial affair. Between traditional enemies who were neighbours there was a no-man's land, marked out at each end by tall wooden look-out towers, a few minutes' walk apart, from which frontier-guards kept watch. This ceremonial fighting might only last one day. After magical rituals, there followed some fairly fierce fighting at which as many as twenty clashes took place; at the end of the day the members of each side sat down on their own edge of the zone marked out as a no-man's land and roundly abused their foes. These wars were part and parcel of the people's way of life; in a large measure their health, welfare, and happiness depended on the pursuit of aggression against traditional enemies – as it is with English soccer fans! Wars also served a religious end, since in particular rites the offering of a cannibal victim caught in war was an essential part of the ceremony. Yet at the same time the Big Men who were battle leaders were also traders and undertook trading voyages through and into enemy country and made pacts with the tribes they fought. It may seem strange to us that warfare and friendly exchange can go hand in hand, although the amount of trade between the bitter enemies of the Cold War would have surprised many people in Europe in the fifties and sixties. Among the Hagen,[8] also a New Guinea people, the Big Men were also warriors and traders and competition was expressed both by fighting and an elaborate ceremonial exchange known as the *moka* in which communities tried to outdo each other by the size of their gifts of valuable shells and pigs. Exchanges are specifically made 'to keep the peace' and payments of shell valuables and pigs are compensation for allies or ex-enemies who have become exchange friends as a result of their losses in past warfare. In practice, these war indemnities lead to reciprocal exchanges between partner communities which continue over the years and are said to be between allies and friends, although a latent aggression or rivalry is expressed in the competitive size and splendour of the gifts. Gift-giving, therefore, can satisfy the same aggressive feelings as war!

In many other societies war is a kind of ritual sport, a game, where the actual killings, from revenge or for special prestige status, were few and far between. Among the Australian aborigines fighting was confined to rare expeditions which were socially sanctioned and which had a specific purpose – to avenge a death or to punish an offender, often as the result of a quarrel over a woman or an accusation of sorcery. The immediate aim of most fighting was that the enemy should be made to suffer an equal injury. It was not fighting for fighting's sake or to satisfy an instinct. There are, however, plenty of examples of warfare which seems to have got out of hand – among the North American Indians after years of depredations from European settlers, or as the result of unassimilated social change; and among the West African tribes which had been corrupted by the pernicious effects of the Atlantic slave trade initiated by Europeans. Yet common sense must make it clear that continual raiding, headhunting, and endemic warfare would hardly permit the survival of local groups, either attackers or attacked.

The Bangwa are a good example of a 'ferocious and warlike' tribe, the reputation attributed to them more by the colonial powers than their neighbours. According to the British district officers' reports on the Bangwa, they were lusty cannibals and headhunters who fought their neighbours for women slaves to marry and men slaves to eat. They describe the Bangwa *juju* with their beaded human skulls, the grotesque masks covered with human skin, the violent, bloodthirsty dances of warriors carrying spear and sword. In the history books they are only known as the murderers of their first white visitor, a murder which led to savage German reprisals and even more savage Bangwa counter-attack.

The reality is rather different. The Bangwa had occasional skirmishes with their Mbo neighbours, but the quarrels were regulated by permanent trading exchanges and peace pacts, as well as immigration from Mbo to Bangwa lands. The Bangwa were much too astute as merchants to eat prisoners of war who could be sold as slaves: in any case the slaves they sold were passed to them by tribes up in the grasslands and they never made war to get captives. The closest they got to cannibalism, as far as I know, is related in the story of the boiled fragments of a dead enemy soldier which were given as an enema to an ailing prince. The skulls they dance with are ape skulls. And the skins they use for their masks are antelope skins. I have already told of the hospitality and friendship with which the first German agent was received by the Bangwa and how he repaid it. In the German records this man was not even shot by the fearful Bangwa but shot himself when he tried to escape and was recaptured by them. The German reprisal, merely for the imprisonment of their agent for a few weeks, was to attack the Bangwa people with modern guns (including machine-guns), killing women and children as well as soldiers, burning down the palaces, looting valuables and ritual objects which were sent to German museums, and exiling the dead agent's friend, Chief Assunganyi, for twelve years.

Ethnography is a wonderful source material – according to his needs, the theorist chooses material to suit his purpose. Whether man's basic impulses are thought to be sexual, aggressive, friendly, or submissive, the supporting material is always at hand. This is possibly the reason for the recent glorification of the anthropologist – what the people want to hear at a certain time, the fashionable myth, the anthropologist can provide, whether it be functionalist, existentialist, structuralist, or aggressionist. Polynesians gave us 'sexual promiscuity' in one generation and a society hedged in by incest taboos and marriage prohibitions in the next. The New Guinea highlanders are both 'friendly traders' and 'vicious killers'. The African king is a cruel despot and a kindly *primus inter pares*. And as for myself, since my book is about cooperation rather than fighting, I want to look at the way groups, communities, tribes, and nations get on together rather than decimate each other. More seriously, I would like to show that, even granted aggressive instincts or drives, human culture has invented countless ways to counteract the anarchy of violence and out-and-out territoriality.

Joking relations have already been dealt with as a means of allying groups of affines within a tribe; they were also extended to establish positive and permanent relationships with neighbouring peoples, or with unrelated clans and castes within society, the joking serving to counteract natural suspicions between disparate groups. As we have seen, the Gogo (pp. 183–4) joke with their matrilateral relatives, affines, and members of different clans. The same institution also links the Gogo with strangers. The origin of such a relationship involving joking, insults, and hospitality is usually attributed, mythically, to an original state of warfare which was converted into a tradition of rather fragile friendship. Not all international relations, however, derived from enmity – the Nyamwezi, living much too far away from the Gogo ever to have fought with them, also share the obligation to joke, exchange food, and generally provide hospitality. The Nyamwezi traded between the interior and the coast of Tanzania from the beginning of Arab and European contacts and one of their major routes ran through the heart of Gogoland. Joking friendships here facilitated trade (as blood friendship did for the Azande traders of banga wood) and provided hospitality and refuge for the Nyamwezi in a foreign land. It was rather as if Italian ice-cream sellers or fish-and-chip shop proprietors in

Scotland had set up an institutionalized joking relationship with the whole Scottish nation for the purpose of selling ice-cream and fish and chips to the Scots, at the same time receiving hospitality – the relationship being extended reciprocally to all Scots and Italians, even several generations after the Italians had ceased selling ice-cream and living in Scotland. The two countries would not fight, and if a man from Aberdeen met an Italian in a Norwegian railway station they would begin to throw the ash-trays at each other, pummel each other, and insult the memory of their dead mothers before sitting down to a friendly chat and a meal together.

A similar situation in West Africa has already been mentioned. The Dogon have institutionalized relations with neighbours of different race and language, usually for commercial purposes, even though the interests of the Dogon and their neighbours at first sight seem diametrically opposed. Cooperation was sought between Dogon and Dioula traders; between the Dogon and the Bozo, a distant tribe of fishermen on the Niger; between the Dogon and cattle-herding Fulani; and between the Dogon and endogamous caste groups and leatherworkers in their own society. Cooperation between these diverse groups was seen as a permanent necessity and in most cases potential conflict was avoided by joking relationships. The beauty of this institution is that ethnic differences can be openly recognized, the joking providing a rationale for friendship and alliance between potentially hostile groups. In each of these international and intranational alliances there is always an ambiguous relationship, half hostility and half solidarity, and both the friendship and the separateness of the two groups is recognized. Joking – involving the usual raucous insults, references to the private parts of close relatives, horseplay, and the throwing of rubbish – restrains open conflict in the same way as it smooths the way for cooperation between matrilateral and affinal groups.

Whether man is innately aggressive or not – and I personally believe he is not – it is clear that he has always had the means to control his violence and hostility and cooperate with other members of his species, particularly as he lacks those instinctive controls over aggression which animals apparently possess. Most societies and groups of societies have produced a state of affairs in which members have agreed to cooperate and not to fight: the kula, the peace of the market, joking partnerships, alliances between affines have all shown this. Man in society needs the favourable attitude of his fellows and has a personal interest in their welfare and happiness. Rousseau called it the general will; Kant, the moral law. Durkheim maintained that common sentiments were at the basis of society, while Talcott Parsons saw the social system as a system of roles, with harmony resulting from the more or less universal agreement about the behaviour expected in each role. Here we have a belief that the norm involves conformity to rules, values, and the expectations of others, and that conflict as such is a negative force which may disrupt the normal functioning of society in abnormal times. Every society has institutions to restrain and resolve conflict. More than this, it would appear that man desires the good of those with whom he comes into contact – all things being equal, of course. Adam Smith, in his *Theory of Social Sentiments*,[9] maintained that all moral sentiments arose from sympathy, the principle of which leads men to enter into the situation of other men and to share with them those passions which some situations have a tendency to excite. Adam Smith found that sympathy itself was the basis of the fabric of society and that friendship had an essentially moral character.

Thus, while not denying man's capacity for aggression – that capacity is obviously enormous – I have been more impressed that man, arriving on the scene with warlike tools and a developed brain, did not wipe himself out. The human species developed capacities for fighting and efficient methods of killing in the struggle for survival but they also solved the problem of not using these means if they wished to survive.

The various means by which he achieved this end have provided the theme of this book. Men in groups have always exploited the resources of their territories and lived in peace with their neighbours, exchanging women, making peace pacts, and generally forming and enjoying reciprocal relations.

11 Primitive Passion

This book has so far avoided the vexed and fascinating subject of sex. Its nature, the forms of sexual activity, and the problems of sexual relations have been assumed to be the same all over the world, yet we have no Kinsey Report of the primitive world, no serious depth-studies of the expression and repression of sex in any one small-scale society. I have been concerned to describe friendship and platonic love rather than overt sexuality and the accompanying universal themes of incest, adultery, and homosexuality. The prime bond of friendship is a moral, even spiritual one and whatever the element of subconscious sexuality in the relations between David and Jonathan and the Nzema husband and his male wife, their love is not expressed physically. We must not equate friendship with sex.

When we come to the subject of romantic love, however, the element of sexuality cannot be ignored even if it is completely suppressed or wonderfully sublimated. The combination of spiritual love, frustrated sex, and marriage is a uniquely Western contribution to the evolution of human relationships; a comparison of romantic passion as we know it and as other cultures experience it will surely throw some light on our exotic attitudes. Do primitives experience anything like the romantic love syndrome, which lifts people to the heavens and drives them to their doom? Are we the only culture which requires, at least in theory, romantic love plus chastity as a prerequisite for a happy marriage? If the answer is yes, why is this so?

Freud maintained that the pleasure principle (sex) underlies all cultural action; consequently it would not be far-fetched to suggest that Freudians maintain that amity derives from sexual instincts. Once Freud had established the libidinal components of the ego, it became clear that all instinctual impulses had to be sexual. The fundamental layer of the psychic structure, the id, the domain of the unconscious, strives for the satisfaction of instinctual needs in accordance with this 'pleasure principle'. The ego, as the mediator between the id and the external world, has the task of representing the external world for the id and so saving it. For the id, blindly striving to gratify its instincts in complete disregard of the superior strength of outside forces, could not otherwise escape annihilation. In fulfilling this task the chief function of the ego is to control the instinctual impulses of the id, 'dethroning the pleasure principle' and substituting for it the 'reality principle' which promises greater social security. Freud also maintained that a third layer of the psychic structure, the super-ego, originates from the long dependency of the infant on his parents; the parental influence remains the core of the super-ego which establishes morality and the 'higher' things of human life. The external restrictions imposed by the parents and then society become a person's conscience; henceforth the sense of guilt, the need for punishment generated by transgressions or by the wish to transgress these restrictions, especially in the universal oedipus situation, permeates mental life.

Friendship need not derive from an unconscious sexual drive but a cultural imperative to exchange ideas, sentiments, and goods. Social action does not derive from biological instincts alone; and neo-Freudians such as Fromm have switched from an emphasis on biological instincts to the study of the effect of culture on personality. Some 'universal theories' run the risk of being primarily applicable to the society of their inventor – in Freud's case it was the middle-class European society of the beginning of the twentieth century. The Europe of the seventies would seem as exotic to Freud as a South Sea island. Where, for example, is the patriarchal, tyrannical father today? With changes in social and economic structures even our libidinal needs change. Fromm has shown that the libidinal impulses and their satisfaction (or deflection) are not the result of a universal social condition but are linked to the interests of society and become a stabilizing force, binding the majority to the ruling minority. Anxiety, love, confidence, even the will to freedom and solidarity within the group to which one belongs – all serve the economically and politically structured relationships of domination and sub-ordination.[1]

There is, therefore, no universal theory. Fundamental changes in social structure will cause corresponding changes even in the 'instinctual' response. Today, nothing is clearer than the fact that the obsolescence of the old capitalist way of life is bringing about new mental attitudes. We only have to consider the changes in our 'instinctual' attitudes to sex over the past half-century to see the proof of this. We are no longer horrified by homosexuality. We do not object to a man marrying his wife's sister, a practice which the English law still considered incestuous in the nineteenth century. Even our attitudes to brother–sister incest are changing – once even the idea was more than horrible, it was impossible.

Freud's incursions into anthropology were marred by his ethnocentricity: he saw everything through the 'universal' eyes of a cultured member of a Jewish middle-class family in Vienna. Malinowski soon showed that Freud's universal oedipus complex was not universal at all. Freud had tried to show that all mental and cultural life had its roots in infantile sexuality which is later repressed in children by paternal authority and patriarchal family life. The premise was that in all societies, not only in Vienna, there was a rigid conception of the individual family and marriage, with the father as a strict patriarch and the mother the affectionate, kind parent. Malinowski[2] showed that in other societies where there is no patriarchy none of the conditions required for the fulfilment of the oedipus complex exists. In matrilineal societies such as that of the Trobriands, it is the mother's brother who is the head of the legal family and is the severe arbiter within the family, while the father is the affectionate helper of his children who has to 'win' their friendship as they grow up. He frequently becomes their ally against the authoritarian principles represented by the matriarchal mother's brother.

We must therefore accept a correlation between the form of society and its prevalent cultural manifestations. Among the Trobrianders myths have a notable absence of 'father-killing' or parricidal *motifs*, and the most important type of sexual mythology is not oedipal but centres round stories of brother–sister incest – in matrilineal societies the closest sociological links are between brother and sister (see p. 169).

One of the merits of social anthropology has been to show up this element of blind ethnocentricity in our prophets. We are not struck in a universal biological mould. Writers on aggression, such as Robert Ardrey, can also be faulted for writing from a specific cultural viewpoint. Ardrey is a wholehearted participant in his own American competitive culture, the contented inheritor of the whole ethos of Western capitalism, a way of living and a system of values which has reached and passed its peak. For this reason none of his theories of innate aggression and territoriality can be considered universally applicable, either in a Pacific island or in that society of the 1970s which has succeeded in rejecting capitalism. Ardrey's idealized American businessman or farmer may be comparable to a destructive, aggressive, territory-defending ape; but in comparing the whole human race – past, present, and future – with this kind of capitalist animal he is doing a disservice to man's capacity to change his cultural and even his instinctive behaviour. Both Freud and Ardrey should be read as historical phenomena, representatives of a special kind of culture which is dying – a culture based on individual aggression, the market, classes, and the sovereign state.

But we still think that blood pacts, joking partnerships, and androgynous twins may be all very well for primitive society, which does not know the splendours and comforts of real love – that is, romantic love. One of civilization's great achievements, you may think, is the combination in romantic love of loving friendship, sexual passion, *and* marriage between a husband and wife who are also lovers, thus satisfying the whole gamut of man's emotional needs. Romantic love, based on marriage, is our major source of psychological reassurance and affection as well as sexual satisfaction. The theory is that as society grows more and more complex, urban, and impersonal, romantic love becomes progressively more important and has evolved towards the modern ideal of a fusion of spirituality and sex, friendship, and a home life shared between a husband and wife who no longer work together as a producing unit.

Again, in theory we do not need psychological comfort outside the family, but should find total satisfaction in our spouse and children. A man's wife, for example, is his beloved companion, his mistress, his adviser, his comforter, his frail protegée, his playmate, the mother of his children – and an important mother-figure to him. A wife needs her husband to be her lover, her tender friend, supporter, and defender, her constant companion, the father of her children, a baby in need of cosseting – and a father-figure. This is why the perfect marriage may become nauseatingly self-sufficient, shunning outside friends, even close kin of either partner. And the wonderful concept which has inspired these sentiments is this all-purpose and highly functional – but possibly moribund – notion, romantic love.

Not that romantic love as such is an invention of democratic capitalism. The romantic love story is a continuous thread running from Sappho and her girls ('for whenever I see you but for a moment, my voice will not come, my tongue is palsied. A subtle fire runs through my flesh, my eyes are blinded, my ears ring, sweat pours down from me. I tremble all over and am little short of dying'), through Hero and Leander, Dido and Aeneas, Romeo and Juliet, Paolo and Francesca, Lancelot and Guinevere, and the heroes and heroines of the majority of modern novels, plays, and films. Romantic love in the past and the present comes in many guises, not merely as a neat prelude to marriage. Schoolgirls fall in love with their teachers and each other. Plato was apparently romantically in love with Dion. We fall in love with the girl next door, the unattainable mayor's daughter, a distant film star – the modern Princess Faraway. Some people are romantically in love with their country or with their cat. All of these experiences have the magic touch of what we like to call 'real' love, the romantic passion of Western poem, painting, and film – 'civilized' love, born in Greece, elaborated in the middle ages, and insanely exploding in the twentieth century.

So far we have granted primitives the capacity for forming cooperative friendships and even credit them with enjoying those friendships for their own sake; but can they share our enjoyment of this spiritual–sexual loving? Do romantic bards in Tahiti sigh in vain for chaste princesses? Does the lesbian passion of Sappho or Mrs Nicolson and Mrs Trefusis find a parallel in the Mato Grosso? Do pygmy homosexuals fall madly in love like Los Angeles faggots and bind themselves in some kind of union based on heterosexual marriage?

The epithets 'romantic', 'passionate', 'falling in love' have been used quite freely by anthropologists describing courting couples throughout the world. Books on sex in Polynesia, almost pornographic in their detail, amount to quite an industry, while there is no shortage of ethnographic material describing adolescents in love, extra-marital love affairs, and the emotional and sexual attitudes of husband and wife.

In Bangwa, seemingly against all odds, romantic affairs between young men and girls are frequent. 'Against all the odds', because all girls are traditionally married at birth so that sexual escapades are automatically adulterous and the sanctions are horrible – a beating, pepper up the vagina, several days forced labour for the girl; banishment and, formerly, death for the boy. The temptations are also great, since a doddering chief may have a dozen or so nubile young wives in his compound; lovers dodge both the wary eye of his retainers and the medicines and fetishes which are scattered around compound and palace to wreak supernatural sanctions on adulterers. I have already mentioned an institutionalized 'lover' relationship whereby a rich old man would allow his young fiancée to have a boyfriend who was allowed a certain amount of sexual freedom. Married men talked to me nostalgically of the delights experienced as bachelors with their young mistresses. Such limited licence is essential in a society where girls marry soon after puberty and a man may reach his mid-thirties – middle-age in an African society – and still be single. Nevertheless if the girl lost her virginity her lover was treated as an adulterer and punished accordingly.

In other societies youths and girls are given much more liberty. Among the Kuma of New Guinea, girls are allowed a period of complete sexual freedom before marriage. Even a formal betrothal does not interrupt it: the girl avoids her future husband and associates with her lovers until after the marriage is finalized. The only right a man has at this stage is that of eventually claiming her as his wife and almost until the last minute, girls take lovers in wild abandon, from different villages and clans, safe in the certainty that their 'husbands' can say nothing.

In Africa, the Mandari of the Sudan have always used the institution of courtship for entertainment, love-making, and as a preparation for marriage.[3] Special houses of quite elaborate construction are built for a group of girls in a village, usually between five or six of them, where they receive visits from suitors and established boyfriends. Mandari parents no more interfere in the goings-on in these huts than American parents do when their children go dating. Mostly the love affairs are seen as passing fancies and not taken too seriously; such courting helps the girls to behave properly in society, talk entertainingly, and make love with finesse. Young men are prepared to walk long distances to court girls they have seen and fancied at markets or during visits to their village, and after dark the woodland paths are busy with the coming and going of parties of youths, all elaborately adorned or armed.

The procedure of courting among the Mandari is ritualized: a visitor always stands outside the door, for example, and asks for the girl he wants by name, never entering the courting-house unless told to do so. Once accepted, the pair chat and play, with a lot of affectionate petting although sexual intercourse should not take place. The public nature of the place and the presence of sisters and cousins make it almost impossible and if the couple want to make love they must do it outside the courting-huts. At night the girl sleeps with her lover, lying with her head on his shoulder in a prescribed position. This petting and courting among the Mandari is obviously a preparation for marriage, but although fights arise from jealousy a man does not acquire any exclusive rights to a girl merely by visiting her.

It does not seem that Mandari courting gives rise to romantic passion. Nevertheless, the courting patterns have an immediate resemblance to another ethnic institution, the dating of American suburban teenagers. In both societies premarital affairs are permitted, petting is the rule, and the pattern of courting is rigidly ceremonialized. Among both the Mandari and the Americans the institution is a preparation for marriage – the language and gestures of dating are a developing process towards adult sexuality. Despite the ritual the activity is felt to be enjoyable and rewarding for its own sake. Americans, however, emphasize dating in order to enhance an individual's self-esteem and self-assurance which differentiates it from the calm sexual relationship between Mandari boys and girls. Geoffrey Gorer[4] denies American dating the healthy role of Mandari love-making, maintaining that it is either an ecstatic success or results in humiliation, frustration, and failure. This would seem, to my mind, to be due to the fact that the American approach to love and sexuality has been tainted by ideas about romantic passion acquired from novels and films.

Strangely enough, facts about the most talked-about 'primitive lovers', the Polynesians, are few and unreliable, despite the countless books, popular, pornographic, and anthropological, which have been written about them. Even a social scientist who studied the Marquesan Islanders[5] had to rely on traditional lore and legend to present the sparse facts about their delight in sexual adventures, even with strangers; the minimal importance given to the loss of virginity; and their interest in what we should call pornography. Ever since Captain Cook's reports, we have known that sex in the Pacific is a culturally sanctioned, national sport. However, in all this material we have no indication that 'loving' was ever given the longing and pining which we associate with romantic passion. On another island (Mangaia) the author of an anthropo-sexual book insists that when a local man says he loves a girl he means only that he wants her sexually.[6] Passion, according to him, never goes further than a profound knowledge of sexual technique and a pride in male sexual prowess.

In Samoa, Margaret Mead[7] was no less interested in these aspects of love. She describes the premarital and extramarital romances of the Samoans, and stresses the fact that passion was always controlled – it was never allowed to disrupt stable unions, sexual relations established between married couples, or a boy or girl's peace of mind. Romantic frenzy is repudiated and no praise or sympathy is ever offered to anyone who is 'love-sick' or who prefers one man or woman to a more socially acceptable mate. Sex, as far as Margaret Mead saw it, was a delightful experience for the Samoans, expertly engaged in, but it was never allowed to engross the partners enough to threaten the social order – and it is precisely this which romantic love does in our culture. Nevertheless romance, love-making, and tender emotions are all found in Samoan society. A Samoan boy declares passionately that he will die if a girl refuses him her favours; but they laugh at stories of romantic love, scoff at fidelity to a long-absent wife or mistress, and quite happily believe that a new love affair is the best cure for an unhappy old one. This is a far cry from romantic love as we know it and the Samoans, told the story of Romeo and Juliet, reacted with incredulous contempt. The sharing of one's love among several mistresses is never considered out of harmony with declarations of undying love for each one of them. The Samoan lover composes ardent love songs and fashions long and flowery missives, invoking the moon and the stars and the sea. This gives Samoan love-making a resemblance to love-making in other parts of the world, but is very different from Western concepts of romantic love which are bound up with marriage and monogamy, exclusiveness, jealousy, and the undeviating fidelity of both partners. Romantic love to us is not just sex and sighing over a pretty girl by a sleepy lagoon.

In the vast ethnography on the Trobrianders,[8] we have abundant material on the facts of physical and romantic love to test any number of theories and challenge our prejudices. Sex plays a large part in the active, thinking, and dreaming world of the Trobrianders. They joke about it and meditate about it. And like the abode of the gods of the Ancient Greeks, the Trobriand paradise is a sexier, more hedonistic version of day-to-day life on the islands, where everyone is beautiful and indulges in a constant orgy of sex, with an accompaniment of personal display and luxury, good food, and aesthetic surroundings. Divine women are passionate to a degree unknown on earth; they crowd round new arrivals in the land of the dead, caressing them and introducing them to a never-ending series of sexual delights.

Love on earth for the Trobriander is a natural and common pursuit. It begins early on in childhood, small boys and girls indulging in sexual games in a frank manner – there is no actual taboo even on intercourse. More passionate affairs begin when adolescents have passed puberty. 'What was heretofore an un-

stable relation culminating in an exchange of erotic manipulation or an immature sexual act became a matter of keen en-
deavour.' Young men spend most of their free time pursuing
girls, working purposefully towards possessing them, and
through magical and other means they soon achieve their end; if
they don't, they change course and seek another partner. Ill-
success in love makes them miserable and should be avoided as
much as possible.

Trobriander 'passion' is felt not in the heart, but in the intestines, in the skin of the belly. Romance plays a part in their
affairs, especially when fired by the influence of a certain atmosphere, the excitement of night feasts, of music, or an elegant
seductive dress. This kind of stimulus transforms plain sex into
romance and plays an important part in all love affairs, as it does
all over the world. Sex and love for the Trobriander provide an
escape from the monotony of everyday life, particularly at
periods of permitted licence.

Adolescent lovers stay together for a period but on the whole
most want to enjoy their freedom. Courting-houses are built for
bachelors, who receive their mistresses on their own couches.
There are usually two, three, or four couples in these temporary
communities. Lovers stay together because of a personal
attraction and the enjoyment they get from each other. Marriage, however, is a different affair; it is not embarked on for love
or fun, but to have an economic partner, to have children, and
to acquire a full adult status through this important passage
rite. Formerly happy-go-lucky lovers, sleeping together in the
bachelors' house and going on amorous expeditions, once married become 'reasonable partners' in a social relationship which
involves distance, respect, and a division of labour. There are
even positive restraints on any gesture revealing a loving relationship between husband and wife: the relationship is friendly
but never passionate.

The fun of loving is reserved, therefore, to adolescents. Sex is
a pastime for the young, particularly during ceremonial periods
of licence. These feasts celebrate changes in the seasons or other
aspects of village life and are frequently the scene of short
passionate affairs between boys and girls. Music, moonlight, the
close contact of dancing, all lead to a relaxation of normal

restraints which ends in light-hearted sex under the trees. Harvest time, a period of display and mutual admiration, is a period when boys and girls from the villages go out with gifts of food, wearing sweet-smelling leaves in their armbands and flowers in their hair – the girls in new grass skirts and the boys with new pubic leaves.

Apart from the Trobrianders' frank approach to sex, these events have something in common with a country dance in England. More specifically Melanesian, however, is the annual feast known as the *milamila* which is associated with the return of the ancestor spirits to the village. It begins at full moon and is followed by a period of dancing which reaches its climax at the next full moon. There are lavish preparations for honouring the ancestors and there are elaborate dances, social promenades, tugs-of-war, and ceremonies between gaily dressed boys and girls which go on far into the night. Interestingly, love, like the kula, is seen as a reciprocal affair and this festival reflects this feeling. The milamila ceremony coincides with the blossoming of a certain tree, the flowers of which are collected in the jungle and made into wreaths and garlands and exchanged like kula valuables with the blowing of conch shells. 'We make kula with the wreaths,' they explain. The person who starts the exchange says, as he offers the wreath, 'Your valuable present,' and a small return gift of food and betel nut is given with the ritual kula phrase, 'Your first return gift.' A counterpart of the first present is then returned to the donor with the words, 'Your return gift.' The exact terminology of the kula is followed in these love affairs and symbolizes the relationship of complementarity and reciprocity in the love relationship, however temporary. Love magic, like that used for the kula, is also made; men become beautiful and sweet dreams are carried magically to the girl portraying their lover as eminently desirable. This kind of magic can also turn a girl's affections away from her lover to a new suitor.

At these festivals the equality between the sexes is shown by the fact that even girls are allowed their own form of wooing. While the boys, in their gala clothes, walk around the dancing green, singing, the girls come and tease them, begin to tickle and scratch them on the back, finally attacking them with mussel shells and bamboo knives. When the women have finished their erotic slashing and cutting, couples retire to the bushes to make love. This of course takes place during a specific period of ritual licence; sex is then even allowed within sight of a man's sisters or a woman's brothers, which in normal times would have been strongly taboo. Women also have other opportunities for taking the amorous initiative when they go on expeditions to other villages to seduce local boys. These semi-orgiastic festivities are mostly past splendours in the Trobriand Islands; the first missionaries to the islands asked the colonial administration for a special regulation to put down this 'abominable abuse' – a step towards preparing the Trobrianders to learn to accept our attitudes to Christianity and romantic love.

This last sentence might lead one to suppose that restrictions on sexual freedom between courting couples is the first step towards the frustrated agony associated with romantic love. It has been suggested that societies which permit adolescent courtship without sex may know romantic love – defined as the adoration of the unattainable. However, although most Melanesian societies permit a continuing and frank sexual development, the Trobrianders' neighbours and kula partners, the Dobu, insist on a long courtship, with no sexual consummation, and a relatively late marriage; but there is no corresponding glorification of chastity and no sign of romantic love.

What about Africa, for examples of the ideally chaste devotion of an individual to a single beloved? An American anthropologist has written an essay called 'Romantic Love among the Turu of Tanzania', but this unfortunately turns out to be an unabashed account of a people's adulterous affairs.[9] It is interesting that *mbuya*, the word used by the Turu to describe love affairs between men and women, is also used for bond friendships between men based on gift exchange – the use of the same term indicates that sexual loving shares elements of the equality and reciprocity of friendship. Nevertheless, according to the anthropologist the Turu indulge in exactly the same kind of mooning and jealous behaviour we Westerners associate with romantic love, although the relationships can hardly be said to involve the 'frenzy' of grand passion and seem to me to be little more than the *quasi*-licit adultery which is found in most societies. Adultery among the Turu – rarely for Africa – is actually encouraged to the extent that young girls are spurred on by their women leaders to think of taking lovers after they marry and older women admonish them not to confine their affections to their husband or to a single lover. With lovers, women can be freer with their bodies than with their husbands – between a husband and a wife there is great social distance, the husband being a superior being who has to be obeyed. Turu women therefore find sexual freedom and affection with their lovers: they may quarrel, leave each other, 'enjoy' emotional upsets. Husbands and wives, on the other hand, should not quarrel. The situation in a way parallels the division of domesticity between Greek men, their wives, and their boyfriends.

It would be hazardous in the extreme to compare the love-making of the Turu with our ideas of romantic love – the worshipping of a single chaste being with a sublimated passion which may be consummated in marriage. The feeling of mystery, the desire to worship the one-and-only at a distance, the ecstatic joy of merely being admitted unseen into her presence, are feelings found in Hindu, Moslem, Far Eastern, and European literature. Perhaps we are wrong to seek for parallels in the real-life facts of ethnography but should rather go to the literature. Sure enough, it is not difficult to find an example, in the romantic poetry of the Somali, of the kind of courtly love recognized in medieval Europe and transferred to Africa. Verses are written to distant, unattainable women, some of whom the poet has never seen and has no hope of seeing. This theme of romantic, frustrated loving is shown in this example:

> Woman, lovely as lightning at dawn,
> Speak to me even once.
>
> I long for you, as one
> Whose dhow in summer winds,
>
> Is blown adrift and lost,
> Longs for land, and finds –
>
> A grey and empty sea.[10]

With this Somali poem we are closer to European concepts of romantic love, associated with the troubadours and their ladies of

Provence and inspired in part by ideas which filtered across the Pyrenees from Moorish Spain – the same ideas may also, of course, have reached the Islamicized Somali. The adoration of the beloved object by the Moors, however, seems to have had more of carnal love in it. Much of their poetry is concerned with the adored one's physical characteristics and originally carried few mystic overtones; but the themes of romantic love are there – the virtues of chastity, falling in love, love at first sight, separation, and death.[11] Arabic poets drew directly on oriental ideas of love. They sang of true love as the reunion of souls, separated at creation, a love which might be expressed physically but whose essence was spiritual.

In Provence, the adored woman was described as a distant, untouchable object, the lover rarely (in poetry at least) achieving union with his beloved; she was in any case usually somebody else's wife and although the imagery is very sexual, there is little actual gratification. Lovers – in poetry – even went so far as to strip their ladies naked and caress them boldly, providing only that the act which kills love did not take place. Romantic loving in feudal times became a kind of sexual conspicuous consumption in so far as the violent passions of the lovers were rarely consummated; they paralleled those strange and interesting medieval displays in which, as at Limousin, there were competitions in extravagance: one knight ploughed up a plot of ground and sowed it with silver pieces; another burnt thirty fine horses alive; another cooked a feast on wax church candles. Romantic love is quite clearly a kind of conspicuous consumption, a mode of loving adopted by a society with plenty of leisure for love-making.

Over the centuries our notions of romantic loving have changed somewhat, although the themes of chastity, frustrated sexual desire, and adultery are rarely absent. Nor was romantic loving of this kind the sole ideology of those earlier times. Even the troubadours found time for sex, occupying themselves with pretty young girls and leaving their elegant verses to be sung aloud by junior members of the group. The chaste, aristocratic love of virgins gave way to the earthy poems of Jean de Meung, who put his 'dirty hands on the rose' – the rose being understood as a symbol of the vagina – and to that frank sexuality which culminated in the lusty antics of Aucassin and Nicolette. The eigtheenth century, too, was wanton rather than romantic; a new sexuality was given justification by those erotic practices from the South Seas which English and French explorers reported with delight. Diderot glorified the playful love-making of the Polynesians, who made love 'without quarrels, rivalry, jealousy or vengeance'.

Despite Diderot and de Meung, it was romantic passion without free love which became the common ideal in the nineteenth century, a romantic loving no longer restricted to the adulterous liaisons of troubadours or noble ladies and their *cavalieri serventi*. The frenzy and the madness of romantic passion became the expectation of everyone and it even became the rule that people who fell romantically in love should marry. Romantic love, instead of being an illness to be pitied, became a potentially desirable condition. Its cultural model was still the medieval period – Tristram and Isolt, and Lancelot and Guinevere, retold for modern ears by Wagner and Tennyson. Today its hold is still strong; not only middle-class women but even princesses and peasant girls are learning to demand the combined ecstasy of love at first sight, thwarted passion, and a final – though temporary – dreamy happiness, accompanied by the scent of orange blossom and with a climbing rose above the door of the cottage.

In my view, which is that of an anthropologist ill-versed in literature and history, the main feature of most epics of romantic love is not the frustration and the taboos on sex – Tristram and Isolt, Abelard and Heloise, certainly fornicated – but that the love between the hero and heroine in literature, opera, and life must be wrong in some way in order to be exciting. Whether consummated or not, romantic love was illicit love – adulterous in Western European myth, history, and literature, homosexual in Greece, incestuous elsewhere. Courtly love had nothing to do with marriage originally; the beloved, both in fact and in verse, was usually married or at least unmarriageable. The decision of the 'court of love' held by the Countess of Champagne declared that no love was possible between man and wife, and lovers might grant each other favours freely and from no legal necessity. Marriage was a humdrum practical affair and wives – in Europe until the eighteenth and nineteenth centuries, as in

Moslem countries and Ancient Greece – were humdrum and practical women. Andreas writes that 'everybody knows that love can have no place between husband and wife . . . For what is love but an inordinate desire to receive passionately a furtive and hidden embrace?'

If not illicit, the love was hopeless. Poets and priests and soldiers all loved feminine fantasms – a distant queen, someone else's wife, or a woman who was taboo (Isolt, for the interest of anthropologists, was the wife of Tristram's mother's brother). The idealized, chaste creatures died – Dante's Beatrice, Cino da Pistoia's beloved and Petrarch's Laura. In more recent times the hopelessness of passion has been a theme of novels and opera – death, madness, or banishment seem to be the only logical outcome of an idealized relationship of this kind. The other alternative climax to an impossibly romantic story is, of course, marriage. However, once the romance fades – not long after the final curtain and the mournful music – passion must be quickly replaced by something more enduring and practical.

Romantic love, to catch our fancy, is always off-beat, occurring outside the norms established by society. Isolt was married to a king. Abelard was a priest. The families of Romeo and Juliet were sworn enemies. Plato and Dion were men. In each case the dangerous power of the romantic frenzy is recognized, and to explain it the malice of the gods, or a love potion, is evoked.

Tristram and Isolt is the mythical model for modern concepts of adulterous, romantic love, a story of accursed lovers doomed by a magical potion. Although the themes are adultery, incest, and fornication, it became the archetype of the kind of passion glorified by nineteenth-century poets and musicians. I want to summarize the story in order to compare it with a myth which plays a similar role in Trobriand culture.

Tristram, a fine, young, and accomplished knight, a prince from north-western Britain, was kidnapped by pirates and carried to Cornwall where he found his way to the court of his mother's brother, King Mark, who accepted him as his sister's son and also as his heir. Wounded after killing the Irish giant Morholt who came to claim an annual tribute, Tristram was set adrift in a boat and carried to Ireland where he was cured by the queen. Years later Tristram returned to the same land to ask the hand of the Princess Isolt on behalf of his uncle and, having slain a dragon, succeeded in his quest. On the homeward journey they drank by accident the love potion which the queen had prepared for Isolt and King Mark, and so became bound by an imperishable love. Their love was adulterous, since Isolt became the wife of another; it was also incestuous, since King Mark was Tristram's close relative; and it was further taboo because Isolt was a king's wife.

In the myth, the love of Tristram and Isolt is relentless, risking all dangers, and plot follows counter-plot until Tristram and Isolt are found *in flagrante delicto* and Tristram flies to Brittany where he weds another Isolt, Isolt of the White Hand. She becomes his wife in name only and when he is wounded by a poisoned weapon he sends for Isolt to come and heal him. If she agrees to come, the ship she arrives in will bear a white sail; if not the sail is to be black. His wife discovers Tristram's secret and, furious with jealousy, tells him that the ship with Isolt aboard has a black sail. Tristram turns his face to the wall and dies. Isolt arrives too late and yields up her life in a final embrace.

This basic story has been altered and elaborated by writers of every century and language but the lurid legend has remained remorseless in its revelation of the hopelessness and morbidity of romantic love. (The lovers' final end, in Gottfried de Strasbourg's poem, is to go off to the Grotto of Love and, with its brass doors barred, to sit there side by side like two hermits, telling each other tales of those who had suffered or died for love.)

For my cursed anthropological purposes I must now find a myth in primitive society which celebrates a hopeless or illicit brand of passion, brought on by the action of a love potion, between two persons who cannot marry; if I can do this I might possibly find something in an exotic society which resembles romantic love, European style.

The Trobrianders at first sight seem the perfect example of the South Sea Islanders' untrammelled, even hedonistic approach to sex. As we have seen, they have no taboos on sex before marriage and adultery is a lightly punished misdemeanour. Our Christian culture, on the other hand, condemns adultery with great force:

Tristram and Isolt are punished by permanent damnation, while the fornication of Abelard is punished by castration. The Trobrianders have different taboos, mostly based on the fact that they have totemic kinship groups to which everyone belongs and members of these groups must not have sexual relations between groups or intermarry. Clan exogamy is the rule and there are strong taboos on sexual intercourse between close kin; incestuous relations in the Trobriands are supernaturally punished – by death. Incest is most serious if it occurs between uterine relatives – persons related through women, the social structure being a matrilineal, not a patrilineal one (see chart on p. 170). In one case described by Malinowski, a sixteen-year-old youth, Kima'i, was having an affair with his mother's sister's daughter, a cousin, but in Trobriand terms a very close clan sister. Under the rules of strict clan exogamy this was incest. The affair became known and was gossiped about in the village but no action was taken until an ex-lover of the girl, jealous of Kima'i, threatened him with sorcery. Kima'i laughed at him mockingly and forgot the matter. The sorcery was put into practice but it did not work and Kima'i remained hale and healthy. One evening, when all the villagers were gathered round, his enemy accused Kima'i of incest with his cousin, insulting him 'with certain expressions intolerable to a native'. The next morning Kima'i dressed up in his best clothes, climbed a tall coconut palm, and delivered his swan song, placing the onus of his death directly on the man who had exposed him. Then with the customary wailing he leapt to his death.

The interest in this pathetic story lies in the fact that the greater sexual sin for the Trobrianders is incest, not adultery, and that it is condoned in general practice but should not be publicly talked about. Brother–sister incest is the most reprehensible form of this taboo act, but it is extended to any woman of the same clan. Brother–sister incest is found only in Trobriand myths and I shall compare one of these with our adulterous Tristram and Isolt myth later in this chapter. Dreams about sisters are common, apparently, occurring frequently and haunting the dreamer because of their sinfulness. Between clan brothers and sisters, cousins and second cousins, however, sex is possible and is even smart and desirable, owing to the piquant difficulties in carrying it out. Incest is a temptation to the Trobrianders. Yet there are supernatural sanctions which include a terrible eruption of boils: the Trobriand lover makes counter-magic to deal with this. The moral shame is small and as with other rules of official morality throughout the world, he who breaks it is a 'gay dog', a Don Juan (the Trobrianders call it *suvasova yoku*).

Adultery in European culture since medieval times is also a kind of 'pretence' rule, with a great gap between the ideal form of faithfulness in marriage and the facts of social behaviour. We commit adultery with impunity despite the threats of the Church and even the law. Adultery in the Trobriands was not dangerous, being considered a light misdemeanour. It would seem that in both cultures it is the sexual sin which is the more heinous which is committed with the greater delight. 'From the point of view of the native libertine *suvasova* (incest) is indeed a specially interesting and spicey form of erotic experience.' A comparable situation in Europe was that of the Italian *cavaliere servente* which involved a triangular relationship between a husband, a wife, and her lover. This was a smooth and decorous arrangement and was never talked about in public. The husband, as soon as jealousy had gone the way of passion, politely resigned his romantic functions to some acceptable lover, on the strict understanding that the lover maintained his dignity and did nothing to lower his or his wife's credit in their social world. The lover submitted to a kind of voluntary servitude – for a short period or a lifetime – carrying his mistress's fan, calling her carriage, and embellishing her opera box, in return for the adulterous privileges tacitly handed over by her husband. Byron was a *cavaliere servente* to the young wife of a sixty-year-old landowner who was prepared for his wife's infidelity. Nevertheless, the husband in this situation remained complaisant so long as the situation remained discreet. At the first breath of scandal, he attempted to put an end to the adulterous liaison. In European culture, from the world of the Provençal troubadours to the ambience of Oscar Wilde, this situation of the complaisant cuckold has been a common one.

Incestuous liaisons, on the other hand, provide rarer themes in our culture, at least until recently. The story of Kima'i and his cousin has to become that of Anna Karenina and Vronsky to grip our attention. In the Trobriands the tragic romance of Kima'i and his 'sister' has an even more tragic parallel in a story of the passionate love of a brother and sister, which has interesting similarities with the Tristram and Isolt myth.

This time, the lovers are true brother and sister, which provides an intensification of the incestuous situation and could hardly happen in real life: any more, perhaps, than the infidelities of Isolt would have been tolerated at the court of a British king. Again, a love potion plays a central role. The Trobrianders have a method of brewing certain aromatic herbs in coconut oil and muttering spells over them – as we saw in the *kula* and during romantic harvest festivals – thereby giving them powerful dream-inducing properties. If the magic-maker can persuade the aroma from his brew to enter the nostrils of his beloved, she will be sure to dream of him, have sexual visions, and undergo romantic experiences which she herself will inevitably attempt to translate into actuality. A great potency is attributed to this magic and it is sold dear. One of the famous centres for making this love-magic is the eastern shore of the main island of the Trobriands where a fine beach of clean coral sand overlooks the open sea towards the west; beyond the reefs, two distant coral rocks may be seen on a clear day. One of these is the island of Iwa, the second centre of love-magic. On the main island the beach has become a kind of sacred shrine of love to the Trobrianders and here, in the white limestone beyond the fringe of luxuriant vegetation, is the grotto where the tragic myth of the lovers who were brother and sister was enacted. One of the manifest aims of the tale in the eyes of the Trobrianders is to account for the invention of love magic.

The story is a simple one. There lived in the village of Kumilabwaga a woman of the Malasi clan, who had a son and daughter. One day, while the mother was making her grass skirt, her son was making some magic from a pile of herbs in the hope of gaining the love of a certain girl. He placed some of the pungent leaves into clarified coconut oil and boiled them, reciting a spell over the brew as it bubbled. Then he poured it into a receptacle made of toughened banana leaves and placed it in the thatch of his hut. While he was away sea-bathing, his sister decided to go to the water-hole to fill coconut jars with water and as she passed under the spot where her brother had placed the infusion she brushed against the hut and some of the oil dropped down over her. Wiping it off with her fingers, she sniffed it and then went to get the water.

When she came back she went up to her mother and said: 'Where is the man, where is my brother?' According to Trobriand morality this was a dreadful thing to do, for no girl should inquire about her brother directly or speak of him as a 'man'. The mother, therefore, at once guessed what had happened and fearfully said to herself, 'Alas, my children have gone out of their minds.' The sister ran after her brother, finding him on the beach where he was bathing without his leaf cover. She loosened her grass skirt and, naked, tried to approach him. Horrified at what to him was a dreadful sight, he ran away along the beach until his way was barred by a precipitous rock. He turned and ran back to the far end, where another rock blocked his way. Three times along the beach, under the shade of the big overhanging trees, they ran and ran until the boy became exhausted and fell down overcome. His sister caught hold of him and the two fell together into an embrace in the shallow water.

Later, ashamed and remorseful but with their passion still strong, they went to the grotto where they remained without food, drink, and sleep until they died, clasped in one another's arms. Through their linked bodies there grew the sweet-smelling plant of the native mint.

At the time these events occurred a man on the coral island of Iwa – opposite to the shore – dreamed the whole story as it was happening and went in his canoe to the beach where he found the mint growing out of the chests of the two lovers in the grotto. From their mother he learnt the magical formula and took it, with some of the mint, to his own island. This is how the magic was found and it is on this beach that it is performed: the successful results of the spell are magically foreseen if two small fish – symbols of the lovers – can be seen playing together in the shallow water along the beach.

Myths like the Trobriand and Tristram and Isolt stories teach, through symbolic means, truths and aspects of reality which defy any objective or rational expression. The imagery of the myth represents some human needs and their contradictions. The myths of the Greeks and of the Dogon express their own kind of truth about duality epitomized by androgyny and twinship. These myths say something about Trobriand and European sexuality and passion. In one case, a story of illicit adultery becomes the ideal and most beautiful expression of passionate love in our literature. In the other, a story of heinous incest becomes the most exciting expression of passionate love in the Trobrianders' oral tradition. Both Trobrianders and Europeans betray their fascination with the breaking of a taboo – the taboo on having sexual intercourse with a sister or somebody else's wife. In both cases the love is romantic – hopeless, tragic – and in both cases its irresistible power is attributed to magic and the gods. Love, at least passionate love, becomes an aberration caused by accident. Both passionate pairs reject normality and contentment and their love grows more hopelessly intense the more it refuses to be satisfied. Both legends bring out the dangerous, fatal element of romantic love – that it is inexorably linked with death and involves the destruction of anyone who yields to it with his whole being. The myths are possibly warnings.

Myths may have been more than cautionary tales, adding zest and excitement to a life which at times can become grey both in a garden suburb and a palm-lined village. George Steiner has suggested that 'romantic ideals of life, notably the stress on incest, dramatize the belief that sexual extremism, the cultivation of the pathological, can restore personal existence to a full pitch of reality and somehow negate the grey world of middle-class fact. It is permissible to see in the Byronic theme of damnation through forbidden love – in the Wagnerian *Liebestod* – surrogates for the lost dangers of revolutionary action.'[12]

With these ideas in mind, it may become slightly less astonishing that the themes of romantic love – martyrdom, despair, incest, fornication, death – became the basis for a 'belief' in romantic love in Europe which spread from aristocratic adulterer and incestuous brother and sister to the prudish middle classes of the nineteenth century, finally flourishing as a twentieth-century phenomenon accepted as normality by factory girls and film stars alike. The theme of the tragic myth has become popularized and sentimentalized; the eternal triangle of novelette and film has reduced the tragedy of Tristram and Isolt to proportions suitable for the television soap opera. The message, though, is still there: the magic potion which leads to the eternal bliss of everlasting adultery does not bring about real love between two beings but rather a magical kind of loving, a love of being in love, which must end in death if it is to survive.

Yet we have become bound by a tradition which demands romantic love as a prerequisite for happiness, for complete psychological satisfaction; it is no longer a pitiable condition to be avoided, a frenzy to be mocked. How can we explain this universalization in our culture of that which is a rare phenomenon in others?

Christianity must take much of the blame. Adulterous, romantic loving seems to have been the product of the Church's widening of a gap between the spiritual and the erotic. Christianity teaches 'an impossible loving', as Nietzsche sadly complained. While we are taught to love our neighbours as ourselves and turn the other cheek if an enemy strikes us, sex becomes debased and fornication outside marriage becomes a sin, sometimes a crime. Eros among the Greeks, the Samoans and the Slinging-Slongs is allowed complete fulfilment; Christianity, however, demands that God be given first place in the heart. For centuries we have been taught a Christian morality which considers marriage and the setting-up of the family as the only motivation for sex – the body is a temple not for erotic pleasure but for the adoration of the Lord. Virginity has become a state of excellence instead of misfortune, symbolized by the chastity of the mother of Christ.

The main message of St Paul in his passionate efforts to redeem humanity from concupiscence was 'Flee fornication!' and if this was not possible a lustful man had better marry – 'If they cannot contain, let them marry: for it is better to marry than to burn.' Jerome went even further and added guilt to the trials of the marriage bed: 'It is disgraceful to love one's wife too much ... He who too ardently loves his wife is an adulterer.' While few followed the saint's advice to the letter, sex and eroticism became irrevocably associated with shame and guilt. Sex as a natural force went underground in Europe for two thousand years, a fact which must help explain the growth of romantic love in the medieval and later periods, a love founded on the frustration of desire and the thrill of adultery. The exclusion of the pleasures of sex in all circumstances made it inevitable that a special sanctity should be invented for them – outside marriage and outside the Church.

Romantic love has become the expectation of all of us and without it few of us would agree to marry. Many people sacrifice a lifetime to the possible attainment of this exalted standard. Many pay high penalties – innumerable women live frustrated and alone because they have never been touched by the poisoned arrow of what they imagine to be romantic love. Even more married women suffer permanent frigidity caused by having married without first 'falling in love' properly. Quite clearly monogamous Christian marriage based on the fragile, mysterious cement of romantic love is a poor container for all our emotional and erotic needs, since romantic love is notoriously short-lived and could hardly be expected to support the weight of a family, the care of children, and the inevitable frictions between husband and wife.

Romantic love, despite its promises, is the end of the story, not the beginning. In fortunate cases, romantic love slips imperceptibly into settled domestic affection, the flash of passion that united husband and wife becoming an unreal memory. Mostly, however, the reality is a dreadful shock. This cynic's view of love and marriage is given a 'statistical' aspect by Arnold Bennett in *Mental Efficiency*:

Personally I should estimate that not in one per cent even of romantic marriages are the husband and wife capable of *passion* for each other after three years. So brief is the violence of love! In perhaps thirty-three per cent passion settles down into a tranquil affection – which is the ideal.

In fifty per cent it sinks into sheer indifference, and one becomes used to one's wife or one's husband as to one's other habits. And in the remaining sixteen per cent it develops into dislike or detestation.

What are the social and cultural factors that have led us – unique among the societies of the world – to marry for love? We have no marriage rules (apart from the basic exogamy of incest prohibitions), no dowries, no bridewealth, no financial settlements. We look down on people who marry to have a useful brother-in-law or to make a pecuniary or social alliance. We don't often marry in order to have children or to acquire an economic partner unless we are peasants with a smallholding or an anthropologist who needs an assistant in the field. Bachelors and spinsters are not the despised, incomplete beings they are in simple societies where access to high rank and certain associations is closed to them. In our case marriage, like friendship, is the result of free mutual choice. Perhaps without the passion of romantic loving or its simulation, along with the withholding of sexual access until after marriage, people might not marry at all. Nowadays, however, romantic love seems to be going through a crisis – the memory of a short-lived, marvellous passion is not considered enough to make a marriage survive. More and more often, romantic love ends not in acceptance and adaptation to the harsh realities of marriage, but in boredom, disillusion, and open infidelity – and the search for a new passion and a new bout of hopefulness. Romantic love is still alone in producing the wonderful sense of wellbeing, the ecstatic feelings which transfigure both lover and beloved, but we are finding that it disregards all the important realities when two people decide to live together in marriage for a lifetime.

Romantic loving as a prerequisite for marriage seems to have developed alongside the growth of the middle classes. It bloomed not as a result of nostalgia for the medieval tradition and the right of individuals to free choice, but because of new ideas about free enterprise and exclusive rights to private property, together with an exaggerated respect for individual independence. In many ways the values of romantic love are associated with an unrestricted quest for profit. A woman – and it is of course almost always the woman who is adored and the man who does the adoring – became a kind of glorified commodity which you 'possessed'. A Victorian merchant worshipped his wife as he worshipped money and the commodities money could buy. Love is 'consuming'; jealousy, romantic love's evil counterpart, illuminates the possessing, owning nature of this new kind of love in marriage. The rage against a third person of whom one is jealous is based on the premise that your beloved belongs to you, is your possession, for your own individual consumption, an object over which you have complete psychological and physiological control. The whole ideology of the middle classes, which has been passed on to many of us, stresses premarital chastity and absolute fidelity as it stresses the sacredness of property. Dr Johnson made the explicit connection between sex and property, arguing that a woman's chastity was 'of the utmost importance, as all property depends on it'. In the middle of the eighteenth century romantic love ceased to be a frenzy or a tragic condition and became a desirable state; it was a development which coincided with the rise of the middle classes and modern capitalism, and it became linked with marriage. Until much later (really until the twentieth century), aristocrats and peasants, both in their different ways tied to the soil, still pursued 'marriages of convenience'. The middle classes, however, were mobile and their children were free in the sense that they could earn their living without the aid of land. Marriages based on romantic love became at least feasible for the bourgeoisie and as the major audience for poets and novelists, operas and songs, they learned to share the ecstasies of romantic love. They began, too, to boast of the enormous superiority of marriages founded on it to marriages based on 'arrangement'.

Our culture glorifies the freedom of the individual to choose his own way, his own wife, his own necktie – it is the result of an economic system in which the market regulates all transactions and social relations. Neither cooperation nor interdependence are strong aspects of our system of values – a person is 'on his own', 'out for himself', 'on his own feet', 'making his own way'. Instead of communication through an institutionalized exchange of women, gifts, or ceremonial objects, we have imposed a system of private enterprise which regulates social action. The middle classes – a small group – also became the upholders and propagandists of romantic love as a prelude to marriage. Their attitudes are portrayed in the nineteenth-century novel; they contrast forcefully with the aristocracy's low estimate of matrimony and their contempt for women. The working classes, of course, did not read novels ,while peasants, still members of a closed society, looked to the Bible and folk tales for their cultural traditions. Nevertheless, the romantic tradition has seeped down through all classes. With the help of missionaries and white teachers, colonialism even took it to Africa, South America, and the Pacific. After the working classes, the Third World will be the receptacle for Europe's cast-off values and economic institutions, as well as for worn-out railway stock. Africans become fervent Christians while their brothers in the West are fleeing the Church; they are being introduced to old capitalist techniques while Europe is making steps towards a socialist economy. And they are falling romantically in love at a time when we have begun to reject this lunatic relic of medieval passions which once helped to prop up an industrial social structure.

In societies which have been newly urbanized and industrialized – whether in Sicily, Africa, or Brazil – the main element in the changing relations between the sexes is the introduction of the notion of romantic love and marriages based on it. A corollary of this is the rejection of traditional restrictions on the selection of a marriage partner. In Bangwa, the right of marriage lords (distant relatives, if related at all) to dispose of girls in marriage to men of high status has been challenged more and more successfully by a new generation of younger men who work on plantations and in coastal towns, amassing enough money to outbid chiefs and nobles for their betrothed wives. The rationale, provided by missionaries and read in books, is that these young women, who have been 'married' since birth to a friend of their father, should have the right to *choose* their husbands and not have them chosen by their marriage lords. Material factors still count, of course, despite such glib phrases as 'I'm marrying him because I love him'; the best and most beautiful girls are still going where the money is – to those Bangwa men who have secure jobs in the national economy or the administration.

While in Bangwa the 'romanticization of marriage' has hardly begun, in urban situations in Africa a romantic relationship with a wife-to-be is becoming more and more the rule. This is observable in the attitudes of educated Africans, in contemporary African fiction and in the contents of magazines produced for African townspeople. One study[13] deals specifically with the notion of 'romance' and investigates the contents of letters to an advice column of a West African newspaper. The change of values is reflected in the letters in a striking way, particularly in the themes which keep cropping up. An ever-recurring one is the objection made to marriages arranged by parents and relatives. One young man, complaining that his mother objected to the girl he was in love with, comments that the Creator could not have intended any such restriction and the emphasis in marriage should only be on 'love and understanding'. The writers of other letters merely want to know whether girl-friends and fiancées really 'love' them: 'Is this love really from Heaven?' These letters reflect the feeling that romantic love is alien to their writers' normal way of thinking, at least about marriage, and it is doubtful whether the new ideas about Western love have been accepted wholeheartedly, particularly as far as exclusiveness after marriage is concerned; many European girls married to African husbands have found to their cost that fidelity in marriage is not part of the African's romantic ideal.

Nevertheless, imported popular magazines and books, advice from missionaries, the themes of popular films, all combine to foster the notion that romantic love and not material interest is the new basis for marriage. A corollary of this in newly industrialized societies all over the world is the rejection of traditional restrictions on the selection of wives – as in Bangwa. Western influences give wide currency to the language of romantic love, although the understanding of this language may still remain limited by existing social values. There is the difficulty experienced by some young people in even *recognizing* the presence of the intense emotional bond they have read about and which they have been told is the essential prerequisite of a satisfactory personal relationship between husband and wife. Once a man is free to choose his wife – and, more rarely, a girl is free to choose her husband – the existence of such a choice may produce a state of uncertainty, a doubt about what they are really looking for. Some people, indeed, are not prepared to accept the alien idea of romantic love: in one area of Indian society, educated girls themselves reject the idea of individual freedom and prefer to remain within the structure of traditional marriage arrangements.

*

Many of us in Europe and America are rejecting romantic love as the sole motivation for marriage: it is bound up with perverted ideas linked with adultery, taboos on normal tenderness and body contact, and the fraudulent Christian rule (which was, until very recently, a law in some American states) that a person can physically love a person of the opposite sex only after permission has been obtained from the state or the Church. Romantic love is being seen for what it is – a delusion, what Stendhal, in *De l'Amour*, called a 'miraculous capacity to discover in the love-object virtues which the beloved does not possess'. Fewer people are committing murder or suicide because of it; fewer kings are abandoning their thrones for it; fewer novelists are writing about it.

Romantic love is a fraud, since middle-class morality is in fact completely opposed to the fornicatory, adulterous aspects of the Tristram myth translated to the novel and the opera. The nineteenth-century idealized sexual love, painted *quasi*-pornographic pictures, wrote turgid love poetry – yet dreaded the idea of a naked leg or a frank sexual experience. No praise was high enough for physical passion in the abstract or for the nude body in painting and sculpture, yet sex was a taboo subject, highly sentimentalized and never mentioned in polite conversation. Young men and women in Victorian times met formally in public, a marriage was arranged, they might or might not be romantically in love; whatever the case, their innocence on the wedding night frequently made it a traumatic experience. In our own times, we learn to regard marriage with respect yet at the same time we breathe in a romantic atmosphere in art as in literature; adulterous passion has become the supreme hope of many happily married men and women.

There is no doubt in my mind that romantic love is past its prime; it has served its grand design as the handmaiden of a now moribund capitalist culture and an equally dead Puritan ethic. It served as a sexual lure, the sexual taboos themselves endowing the girl-friend or the fiancée with some of the virtues of a chaste virgin and surrounding her with an aura of mysterious desirability. In most other societies and in our own past, romantic love was sought before or outside marriage – marriage was scarcely for a sexual partner but served to link groups, provide

mothers and fathers for children, or join two people in a complementary work unit. There was no need until recent times to put
a high price on sex and glorify one individual woman in order to
persuade people to marry.

Romantic love has defrauded women. They have become
'objects of love', 'enthralled' by love, yet for some reason romantic love is also said to have raised the status of women – allowing
them to come into their own as the subjects of that courtly poetry
addressed to them in the medieval period. 'The indirect influence of women is incalculable at present, but to it, as well as to
the refinement of the condition of life which is favourable to
women, may be traced the increasing feminine element in poets
and poetry.' On the other hand, romantic love and frustrated sex
depend on women being rarely seen and ordinarily not heard,
imagination building on a furtive glance or a passing emotion –
infatuation can hardly occur in a society where men and women
share daily tasks, have intellectual intercourse, and where there
is a normal amount of sexual liberty. Women become possessions,
the property of their lovers, and in order to remain the pure
creature desired of romantic love a woman must play the pure
virgin all her life. The Victorian wife and mother was ideally a
virgin, like the Lady of courtly love: even a mother of thirteen
children was looked on as an innocent, a 'metaphorical maid',
since sexuality was an exclusively male field. Women were
shaped by the swathings of their garments to be walking symbols
of bourgeois society – half angel and half cretin. Despite the
glorification of the wife, and as the home became a shrine with
woman as its goddess, she slithered downhill fast as a woman.
Love became a concession offered to a woman by her husband;
men were allowed the emotional manipulation of women, since
the circumstances of romantic love are the only ones in which
the female is excused sexuality.

The true nature of romantic love is slowly being uncovered
but it is taking an unconscionably long time a-dying. We still
rush out to buy its sado-masochistic pleasures – 'true love best
recognizes itself, and, so to speak, measures and calculates itself
by the pain and suffering of which it is capable', writes Ortega y
Gasset with some satisfaction. The despair of love is still associated with the greatest ecstatic happiness for many of us. And

having once been through the painful delusion of falling in love and marrying, we are ready to do it again. Some people manage to do it three or four times, while others wait hopelessly all their lives. The literature read by many young people today – at least by girls – is still the romantic, chaste, dreamy, wind-in-the-palm-tree kind of fiction, with the dream man merely changing his attitudes and features and clothes to suit the current fashion. The myth of Tristram and Isolt has been strangely debased. Tristram today – and the name is perfect for the hero of a popular love story – may be the dark stranger who sweeps the typist off her tiny feet, the quiet boy next door who can provide a home and a position in society, the friendly working-class footballer who marries the upper-class model. The only common element between the two Tristrams is the romance and the unreality. The middle-class fraud comes in here again – the dream is always based on the capitalist morals of the well-heeled inhabitants of Hampstead Garden Suburb, but they themselves are sitting on their velvet sofas reading ecology, the new unromantic novel, or, perhaps, hard porn.

12   All the Lonely People

As I glance back over the typescript of this book and begin to write the last chapter I am astonished at the diverse and contradictory messages which the ethnography suggests: that we should start seeking the original duality of man in our innate androgyny and abolish romantic love, the traditional uniter of souls; that friendship is always erotic in some ways but that sexual intercourse is incompatible with friendship; that equality is basic to friendship but that we should kiss the boss's foot and ask him to be our loving friend; that we should give our sisters to our bitterest enemies and sling muck and insults at our dearest friends; that we should wear cosmetics in the interests of commerce rather than those of love.

The delight of ethnography is its capacity to surprise. The worth of anthropology is that it tries to offer theories of society. Social life in the diverse cultures we have looked at in this book is sustained not only through marriage laws, supernatural sanctions, and economic exchanges but through informal and formal friendships and a more general reciprocity in the business of living. In this way love helps all our worlds go round – even if it amounts to little more than a chat with a neighbour building a goat fence, helping an old lady cross the road, giving a stranger a friendly glass of water. Behaviour can be interpreted not only in terms of man's rights and duties as a member of bonded social groups or of his material and social success, but also in terms of the social relationships set up between friends and acquaintances, the network of individuals which a person constructs for himself and with whom he cooperates.

This aspect of friendship recalls the network studies initiated by anthropologists who found that the interplay of lineages, families, classes, and castes had very little to do with the modern urban situation.[1] This is a field of social studies where the informal ties between individuals are of major significance. Relations are seen to be based on personal reciprocity and contracts between individuals are on the whole informal, implicit, and lacking ritual or legal validation. These studies contrast with those of the structuralist–functionalist school of anthropology where behaviour is interpreted largely in terms of membership of bonded groups and involvement in social institutions.[2] The network approach was originally found suitable in the study of 'complex', 'open' societies in both Africa and Europe, but it has also been found to fill in gaps in structural studies, such as those of the Nuer and Tallensi segmentary systems where the lineage had always been seen as providing a comprehensive and systematic framework into which *all* daily activities could be fitted. Structuralist interpretations generalize about people according to their status and the roles they play. In a way this book has combined both approaches; it has attempted to interpret the behaviour of individuals in structured and unstructured situations – the 'in-between' structures of alliances and contracts.

Networks obviously depend on an ideology of friendship, not kinship. Between a man and his immediate community of friends and acquaintances the links and alliances are based on personal choice, the needs of his professional life or the formal roles of in-laws, namesakes, co-godparents, or blood brothers. In modern urban situations in Africa, migrant labourers have to become dependent on close friends and useful acquaintances. The new elites even make friendship into an ideology,[3] a means of expressing their new and special status; friendships between members of rising, economically superior, classes are critical in differentiating these members from lower strata. Friendship networks with people of the same status are the main means of confirming this status.

Friendship in both modern and primitive societies helps to maintain community structures as well as providing personal emotional satisfactions. Friendship is not just an 'extra', to be indulged in in order to make life a little more enjoyable. The word 'network' itself was originally intended to indicate an undifferentiated field of friendship and acquaintance playing an important role in all levels of society. In Turner's Morgan Lectures,[4] he suggested that the word 'community' could be applied to these aspects of social life, where the personal relations of men and women as individuals receive the main emphasis. In the context of 'community', our roles and status as individuals are ambiguous, disorganized, and lacking in controlled hierarchy. However, while friendship and amity as part of community relations provide important sociological data, they are extremely difficult for the sociologist to tackle and, like myself, he usually concentrates on those dyadic relations, such as joking partnerships, blood pacts, bond friendship, and compadrazgo, which are given structural form. But we should not forget that the values of friendship and cooperation operate in all satisfactory social relationships. There may be few specified roles but rather an intermeshing of attitudes and actions which are the expression of an attitude of mind, a willingness to cooperate and make the structure work.

Which are the 'open' and which are the 'closed' societies? It could be argued that small-scale societies give even more opportunities for the individual, despite much publicized institutions such as exogamy, pollution, taboos, and other religious and social restrictions. The theory has been that primitive man is persuaded to behave in a certain way by precept, moral law, and religion. Civilized man, on the other hand, has the promise of freedom, but in a sense we are objects manipulated by mysterious and unseen powers. Although in an 'open' society we are supposed to relate to each other on a person-to-person level, in fact for most of our daily needs we relate to faceless bureaucrats, machinery, and anonymous purveyors of food and goods. For the majority of us there is no free choice – we are there to be tricked and coerced in an industrial society where profits are maximized by a deaf, dumb, and blind labour force on behalf of a small, unseen minority. We live as free individuals, we are constantly told, but in fact we are crushed by the impersonality of the capitalist juggernaut which has invented its own religion, its own laws, its own kind of loving in its own interests, which are not ours. In primitive society, not particularly noted for lip-service to democracy and equality, there is at least cooperation, a basic desire to give and take, to create goodwill and promote human intercourse.

Freedom of choice of friends and the right to cast them aside at will are part of our Western ideas. We might pause and consider whether the free choice to make and break friendships is necessarily an improvement on obligatory relations. We imagine, with our stress on 'feeling' and 'free will', that we can make love, marry, and form friendships because we want to, because we have found the only girl in the world, the best cobber this side of the Ringarooma black stump. However, even in our society of unique, independent individuals spinning around in splendid isolation, prearranged marriages and preordained friendships might offer a more satisfying pattern in life which we are all seeking. Is it not odd to trust feelings which come and go, or to wait for the magical moment when the 'true friend' or the 'one and only' appears on the scene? I think myself that we have constructed our own myth, of a world full of hope, opportunity, and personal initiative, and that we are at a loss to know how to take advantage of it.

It seems false to establish friendships through 'empty' ritual and protect them by supernatural sanctions. We imagine that we have reached a superior level of culture because we have abandoned ascribed husbands and wives, and friends chosen for us. We can marry and go to bed with whom we like. But can we? Most of us find it enormously difficult to find a friend, or find a mate. Some of us never do. The choice is so wide that we live in permanent, often romantic, confusion. Moreover, we have added our own personal taboos and restrictions. Some of us cannot bear red-heads, people with snub noses, wide-apart eyes, Anglicans, or bowler-hats. And most people, while reading of the glamorous heroes and heroines who meet in the railway-station waiting-room and whisk each other off to permanent bliss in a Mayfair flat, still marry the girl next door or up the road. In describing relations of love and friendship, based on pragmatic or formal situations – between in-laws, spouses who marry because the law says so, between mothers' brothers and sisters' sons, twins and blood brothers – I am making a plea for a new look at friendship, through an appreciation of how other people organize their emotional lives and their practical alliances. Possibly the most important thing is to make the connection. 'One may arrive at the position that love is exclusively an act of will and commitment and fundamentally it does not matter who the two persons are.'[5]

Are we losing, in fact, the capacity to make friends? Our society is the furthest extension of the 'open' society in so far as most of us no longer belong to permanent, lifelong personal communities, where groups of intimates and inmates are linked to everyone else by a continuous tradition of reciprocity. We must all construct our own personal networks, since few statuses and roles, few friendships, marriages or business partnerships are determined by birth or any other kind of ascription. These personal networks may have to be constructed more than once in a lifetime. In modern situations it is possible to be surrounded by 'friends' one day and deserted the next, due to our much prized mobility. Friendship is a basic need but in our swift turnover of jobs, homes, and even marriages we are constantly starting off to look for a new 'community' of friends. Unfortunately we also know that the personal community you have to leave will survive very well without you.

In most societies described in this book the situation is not like this. There is permanency and continuity in many relationships outside the family. Our society, in going beyond the orderly, interpersonal exchanges of the Trobrianders in the kula, or West Africans in their joking relations, has become a conglomerate of unstable, self-centred individuals caught in shifting networks of a few friends, acquaintances, and relatives. The enforced mobility of work groups and the resultant discontinuity in personal relations – sometimes even the wife won't go with you – perhaps explains the unwillingness of modern individuals to embark on intense friendships. What is the point of having a 'best friend' or a 'blood brother' if you are constantly changing jobs and flats? While friendships formed in childhood may be maintained in the most adverse circumstances for long periods, in many cases distant friends are hardly better than no friends at all, since these relationships need contact and constant renewal. Friendships are maintained through interaction, reciprocity, by the expectation of a return in a not-too-distant future. Today the ephemeral nature of friendship is typified by the absolute immediacy of most exchanges between mates – far from the passionate delayed gift-giving of the kula partners: 'No! Have a pint with me now. You might be off tomorrow.'

Love as an intense reciprocal relationship between two halves of a whole is rare outside marriage. Yet on one level we go around loving everyone furiously or sweetly – with the constant 'Hello!' or 'Hi!', the bright plastic smile, the permanent WELCOME on the mat. This kind of behaviour seems to be nothing more than an expression of self-containment – 'I'm all right, don't worry! And I'm not going to do anything aggressive.' There is an all-pervasive feeling of loving and democratic cheer in the office, the pub, and the grandstand – yet so many people feel so intolerably alone. We are friends with everyone and yet have no friends. Associated with this terrible amorphous friendliness is the modern trend to diffuse formerly restricted roles of 'father', 'sister', and 'priest' and treat each other not as role-players but as 'whole persons'. This may sound good in theory but it often leads to confusion in practice. 'Call me David' gives me personally a feeling of dread, if it is someone I would rather call Professor or Uncle or Milkman. A teacher ceases to become a teacher but becomes the student's best friend. Your father, instead of being a superior transmitter of moral ideas mixed with a small dose of affection, begins to demand friendship. In this way statuses which once required a certain formality in behaviour have been diffused into general, and potentially demanding, friendly roles. Friendship, instead of providing sane links between groups or deep emotional satisfactions, has been converted into a general, undifferentiated friendly feeling.

In America in particular, this diffused extension of friendship is founded on convenience rather than any need for permanent emotional outlet – people are as superficially generous with their love as they are with their cookies and bourbon. This emotional promiscuity means that all relationships bear some resemblance to love and friendship. Even Uncle Sam is your friend, and the dustman next door. After being immersed in various friendship situations in many different societies, to me this hardly seems to be the kind of loving which will help solve individual personal problems, although it undoubtedly contributes to the smooth running of neighbourly relations. Behind the bright smile and the slap on the back there is distance and indifference; when it comes down to it we are still just individual atoms in a vast society, selfishly motivated – a *poussière d'individus*.

I suspect that the reasons for this and the results are very serious. Although it is not yet a common credo, it is becoming more and more obvious that on a certain practical level individuals survive better on their own. We have become so efficient at ordering our external needs that we no longer find that permanent friendships and sentimental attachments have anything 'in it for us'. While the home, the family, and marriage are institutions which are being attacked from all sides – by faculties of sociology, pop singers, and trendy priests – we are failing to form any other kind of emotional bond which might make the world a less grim place to live in. Dehumanization, isolation, the 'freedom' of the individual to do what he will, are accepted as part of our way of life. The result is apparent in the streets of terraced houses divided into single flats for single people; the vast hospital silences, where human beings are numbers and doctors have no time to talk to lonely patients and patients no longer expect it; whole days when a busy person may come into no real contact with any real person. There seems to be an insidious campaign to make us withdraw into ourselves, to set up a kind of spiritual – and indeed sexual – hermaphroditism, whereby we may become self-sufficient, narcissistic atoms in a cold-hearted world.

Friendship may even become politically dangerous. Two people in a bed-sitter are potential revolutionaries, sitting around talking and asking questions, not even needing the comfort of the media. Two people in two bed-sitters, however, are a different thing; they watch two television sets and placidly absorb government propaganda and capitalist-inspired entertainment: non-thinking individualists whose best friends are their television sets!

To me, it is the strangest thing that in Western Christian society, founded on the love of God and the fellowship of mankind, loneliness has become one of the hallmarks. We are the only people who have had drummed into them from childhood the impossible commandment to love our neighbours like ourselves and yet so many of us eke out an existence as loveless and unloved atoms – free individuals in an open society, condemned to form part of the great, grey sub-culture of the lonely. In other societies people are rarely lonely; they are also hardly ever alone, but are surrounded by kinsfolk, chattering neighbours, visiting friends. Even strangers are never completely ostracized but are drawn into the local network of interpersonal relations. And this loneliness is not a question of mobility, new housing estates without pubs, or snobbery. It is an attitude of mind; we have persuaded ourselves that being alone is good, that we need privacy for our peace of mind – 'privacy' is an English concept and an English word which has been taken over literally in other European languages. We even convince ourselves that the hideous life of a single person in a single room with his 'independence' and 'freedom' constitutes the best of all possible worlds.

Any serious consideration of the problems of contemporary society must include the acceptance of the growth of an intense and shocking loneliness: not only among old age pensioners and widows, but among divorced people and young people. Our culture has deprived us of any possible guidelines in making friends, apart from the casual accident of getting to know someone. In other societies these guidelines are many, as I have tried to show – from a simple statement such as 'I want to be your friend' to complex divinatory techniques. Until recently, people stayed lonely and liked it, but lately acute loneliness has driven the most reserved people to look for soul-mates through special agencies or advertisements. Some of the first large-scale organizations for the friendless were aimed at the previously married – those 'parents without partners', people who had experienced living with another person and, despite failure, were ready to try it again. Along with 'singles bars' and clubs, these organizations provide bleak cocktail parties or competitive dances where you pay for the privilege of accosting anyone you fancy. In the best of them there is an atmosphere of forced jollity and pathetic hope; in the worst there is a market place atmosphere where the odd pick-up becomes the norm and the dance or party is merely a cheap way to buy exemption from middle-class morality.

Thousands of small groups exist throughout the United States and England, started by unattached people, charity workers, and even unscrupulous business men. They may become national organizations, or international ones like Gay Lib. Along with friendship clubs and single interest groups there are the marriage bureaux and dating agencies run by computers. These organizations approached the problem of loneliness with bald efficiency. They employed sociologists to discover that, statistically, broken marriages are more common among couples with dissimilar economic, personal, and social backgrounds. Holes in punch cards are made to indicate age, education, race, religion, marital status, hobbies, even favourite colours. Cards of people of opposite sex are then run through the computer and if a perfect match is found, they are introduced. Cupid has been replaced by an electronic computer and a conveyor belt; love has been translated into matching holes in slips of cardboard.

Roughly a quarter of the people introduced in this way (for the payment of quite a large sum) eventually marry. Unfortunately, sociologists are unable to say whether these methods bring happiness. This ruthless matching of people, this celebration of humdrum sameness rather than complementarity and reciprocity presents a horrific picture of machine-made marriage. Real love does not grow up between people because they do the same things or belong to a specific class, hold the same opinions, talk alike, and look alike. Friendship agencies nevertheless thrive on the widespread concept that people have to be the same before they commune – two green peas in one green pod. 'You are a pretty unique individual,' advertises one such agency, 'but somewhere among our sixty thousand members there is a person who thinks and feels exactly like you.' This is a terrible vision of group conformity, with people being poured into a mould in order to find the uninspired happiness of mass-produced friendship.

Interestingly, however, the agencies and organizers of 'singles' activities do not stress community enjoyment; even the Swiss winter holidays and the Greek archaeological tours emphasize the 'single' aspect of their clientele in order to persuade the interested person to buy. Some people want an introduction to an individual, not a happy group. Others are content with joining a group of people who share common interests. In the columns of the weekly and daily papers there are countless advertisements encouraging 'socialist teachers', 'conservative gardeners', even 'gay Jews' to get together. Membership of such groups undoubtedly satisfies both emotional and practical needs on a certain level but it would be wrong to suggest that it can approximate the kind of satisfactions found by two people bound in devoted friendship. Even communes have stumbled against this block. Communes are supposed to aim at communities of fulfilled, happy human beings through particular and exclusive ties between individuals. Children have as many mothers as there are adult women in the group, in imitation, perhaps of the wide system of 'mothering' found in societies studied by anthropologists. In extreme cases, the 'womb mother' waives her maternal rights and gives her children only the same degree of affection as she shows to others. Lovers, friends, and fathers are also shared in the interests of the group. Privacy and private property, as well as private wives and private friends, are banned. Yet how many of these communes, which insist so adamantly on the theory, break down due to jealousy and envy? I believe that many commune theorists have misread anthropology and history in some aspects. The exclusive love between husband and wife, or between two friends, does not constitute an abnormal condition of a rejected capitalist society. Close, loving contacts between two individuals are basic needs, as basic as any need to belong to a group.

Nor is a sane, relaxed attitude to sex sufficient as a means for making satisfying friends. Despite the splendid achievements of the permissive society, sexuality cannot prevent loneliness and cannot provide the emotional bonds supplied by friendship. Many people use their bodies as a temporary anaesthetic against the real pain of being alone, but this sexual activity without emotional involvement may even be eroding our capacity for platonic loving.

Is the answer, then, some kind of union – like marriage – between a loving friendly couple, who also enjoy a complete physical compatibility? Unfortunately I do not believe that the needs of a man and a woman for love and friendship can be satisfied by one single partnership. There has been an attempt by a certain kind of couple to make marriage a Siamese-twin unit in which all emotional needs are satisfied. The woman throws off her sexual thraldom and immolates herself and her husband in an *egoisme à deux* which aims at satisfying all her husband's needs.

A Feiffer cartoon illustrates this situation perfectly (*Observer Magazine*, 9 December 1973):

This sums up the problem already presented by Charles Lamb in an earlier quotation (see p. 47). We need expressive emotional relations with all kinds of people – our wife, our male and female friends, our lover. The man who drinks with his friends every night often loves them as much as he loves his wife – in a different way. And his wife loves her friend next door, who comes in and watches television with her every afternoon. Yet how many married couples do we know who freely allow each other individual friends outside marriage, rather than the 'double' friend they both know and like? Togetherness carried to extremes devours the personality of both partners and they eventually become stranded in a dual solitude. Any attempt to establish a separate identity outside marriage becomes such a struggle and makes us so unpopular with our partner that it is usually abandoned.

Human relationships are being furiously shaken up by changes in the demographic, economic, and sexual spheres. Old hierarchies are breaking down and the relations between sex and age groups are becoming reoriented. Husbands and wives, the old and the young, the rich and the poor are moving out of clear-cut zones and safe roles. Men and women are exchanging functions, psychologically and practically, an exchange symbolized by uni-sex clothes, the wearing of wigs and make-up by men, the ferocity of the Women's Lib movement. The effect of these changes is to bring about a real reshaping of sexual and social *mores*. Kinsfolk, spouses, parents and children, lovers and friends will have different expectations. Along with this, there is a feeling of formlessness, a dread of the breaking-down of old values, which can only be counteracted by the values of personal friendship. For this reason there may be something a little attractive in the bizarre expressions of friendship found in other societies. Men must be allowed to seek different things from their mistresses, their mates, and their wives. Emotional relationships between members of the same sex should be encouraged. If a man wants to marry a man, and a woman live a confident life with another woman as 'husband and wife', let them; the important thing is the relationship. Today there is a growing emphasis on loving friendship which explains these anomalous marriages – and others between male and female homosexuals who marry for companionship, and heterosexuals who do the same thing and keep sex and romantic love outside the home.

Friendship must be taken as seriously as sex, aggression, and marriage. We come into the world programmed to need love – but not to marry. And since the need for love between two persons – rather than passion – is as real and basic as the need to satisfy our bodily wants, the whole sub-culture of the lonely should be seen as a deprived group, and something done about it. The lack of loving is a key to the new but almost universal problem of anxiety. We have become estranged from the simple human tendency to cling together, which is taken for granted in other cultures. We don't feed our children when they cry but at regular hours. Some mothers think the children will become perverted if they are cuddled too much. Comforting frightened children is bad for them and they must learn to be independent and manly. I spent the first year of my life gazing up at blue skies and gum trees, for fear that too much contact with human beings would spoil my brain. We must be quiet and not disturb our neighbours. The grotesque silence of a modern concert-hall is another expression of this inhumanity; the 'real' music lover has his opera at home on a studio-made recording where the performance is not spoiled by a flat note or a cough from the audience.

For long we have turned a blind eye to friendship needs, to the pain of loneliness and separation, and the psychological damage it can cause; being alone is *not* 'good for you'. Complete self-reliance makes for sterile pride and isolation and hence it is universally held that it is good to make friends, sharing interests and common experiences. Psychologists have found that friends are needed to concretize a man's world, to discover his complete human personality. That is why the dialogue of the confessional or the psychotherapist's couch sometimes provide the only outlets for friendless and lonely people. We must learn to forget the way personal relations worked – or did not work – fifty, or ten, years ago. As human beings we are capable of myriad variations in mood, belief, and social practice; in the fields of friendship and love, changes may be expected as the stale fabric of our old society is worn away.

I have no qualms, therefore, in elevating friendship into an imperative. Through reciprocity and trust separate interests are converted into harmonious ones. In most societies friendship is enjoined through a tradition of cultural interdependence between persons and groups, which are either real or 'invented' for the sake of the alliance. Ceremonial gift-exchange, the elaboration of a cosmology based on twin-friends, wife-exchange, these are all techniques for people to form pairs or paired groups rather than from any absolute necessity to exchange ornaments, women, or yams. Once alliances are achieved by external factors, ritual, ceremonial, legal, and moral sanctions support them and convert them into friendship. There is a demonstrable foregoing of self-interest on each side and a renunciation of hostile intent or indifference in favour of cooperation and friendliness.

Reference Notes

Introduction

1 HOGBIN, H. IAN, *Native Land Tenure in New Guinea*, Oceania, 1939.
2 WOLLSTONECRAFT, MARY, *A Vindication of the Rights of Woman:* with *Strictures on Political and Moral Subjects*, London, 1972.
3 RUSSELL, BERTRAND, *The Conquest of Happiness*, Allen & Unwin, 1930.
  FROMM, ERICH, *The Art of Loving*, Allen & Unwin, 1956.
4 BOHANNAN, PAUL, *Social Anthropology*, London, 1963.
5 HOMANS, G. C., and SCHNEIDER, D. M., *Marriage, Authority and Final Causes*, Free Press, New York, 1955.
6 FIRTH, RAYMOND and DJAMOUR, J., *Two Studies of Kinship in London*, Athlone Press, 1956.
7 SCHNEIDER, DAVID M., *American Kinship: A Cultural Account*, Prentice Hall, 1968.
8 FROMM, ERICH, *The Art of Loving*, Allen & Unwin, 1956.
9 LÉVI-STRAUSS, CLAUDE, *Tristes Tropiques*, Paris, 1955 and London, 1973.
10 SPENCER, ROBERT F., *The North Alaskan Eskimo: A Study in Ecology and Society*, Washington, 1959.
11 LORENZ, KONRAD Z., *On Aggression*, Trans. M. Latzke, Methuen, 1966.
12 ARDREY, ROBERT, *African Genesis: A Personal Investigation Into the Animal Origins and Nature of Man*, Collins, 1961; *The Territorial Imperative*, Collins, 1967.
13 LEWIS, JOHN and TOWERS, BERNARD, *Naked Ape or Homo Sapiens?*, Garnstone Press, 1969.
14 TIGER, LIONEL, *Men In Groups*, Nelson, 1969.
15 EIBL-EIBESFELDT, IRANAUS, *Love and Hate: On the Natural History of Basic Behaviour Patterns*, Trans. G. Strachan, Methuen, 1971.
16 OPIE, IONA and PETER, *The Lore and Language of School Children*, Oxford University Press, 1959.

Chapter 1

1 COOPER, ALFRED DUFF, *David*, Cape, 1943.
2 SAYERS, DOROTHY L. (trans.), *The Song of Roland*, Penguin, 1939.
3 Chapman's translation of Homer.
4 BRAIN, ROBERT, *Man In Africa*, Tavistock, 1969.
5 FINNEGAN, RUTH H., *Oral Literature In Africa*, Oxford University Press, 1970.

6 DUNDAS, ALAN, *The Structural Analysis of Oral Tradition*, Philadelphia Univ. Pennsylvania Press, 1971.

7 SAYERS, DOROTHY L. (trans.), *The Song of Roland*, Penguin, 1939.

8 MALINOWSKI, BRONISLAW C., *The Sexual Life of Savages in North-Western Melanesia*, Routledge & Kegan Paul, 1929.

9 MEAD, MARGARET, *Coming of Age in Samoa: A Psychological Study of Primitive Youth*, Penguin, 1943.

10 FIRTH, RAYMOND W., *Tikopia Ritual and Belief*, Allen & Unwin, 1967.

11 REINA, RUBEN, *The Law of the Saints: A Pokoman Pueblo and Its Community Culture*, Bobbs Merril, Indianapolis, 1966.

12 PITT-RIVERS, JULIAN A., *The People of the Sierra*, Weidenfeld & Nicolson, 1954; *Transactions of the New York Academy of Science*, 1954.

13 CAMPBELL, JOHN K., *Mediterranean Countrymen*, Mouton, Paris, The Hague, 1963; *Honour, Family and Patronage: A Study of Institutions and Moral Values In a Greek Mountain Community*, Oxford University Press, 1964.

14 CURLE, RICHARD H. P., *Women: An Analytical Study*, Watts, 1947.

15 LAMB, CHARLES, *The Complete Works of Charles Lamb in Prose and Verse*, Chatto & Windus, 1892.

16 TIGER, LIONEL, *Men In Groups*, Nelson, 1969.

17 GREER, GERMAINE, *The Female Eunuch*, Paladin, 1970.

18 SANTAYANA, GEORGE, *Little Essays*, London, 1920.

19 SIGNORINI, ITALO, *Rassegna Italiana di Sociologica Anno Dodicesimo*, 3, 1971.

Chapter 2

1 NICOLSON, NIGEL, *Portrait of a Marriage*, Weidenfeld & Nicolson, 1973.

2 NADEL, SIEGRIED F., *The Nuba: An Anthropological Study of the Hill Tribes of Kordofan*, Oxford University Press, 1947.

3 SIGNORINI, ITALO, *Rassegna Italiana di Sociologica Anno Dodicesimo*, 3, 1971.

4 BELL, CLIVE, *Civilization: An Essay*, Chatto & Windus, 1928.

5 MOORE, I. T., *Social Patterns in Australian Literature*, Angus & Robertson, Sydney, 1971.

6 LORENZ, KONRAD Z., *On Aggression*, Trans. M. Latzke, Methuen, 1966.

Chapter 3

1 LAWRENCE, D. H., *David: A Play*, Secker & Warburg, 1926.

2 LAWRENCE, D. H., *Women in Love*, Secker & Warburg, 1921.

3 TEGNAEUS, HARRY, *Blood-brothers: An Ethno-sociological Study of the Institutions of Blood Brotherhood with Special Reference to Africa*, Stockholm Ethnogr. Mus (NS), 1952.

4 ZINTGRAFF, EUGEN, *Nord-Kamerun*, Verlag von Gebrüder Paetel, Berlin, 1895.

5 SOUSBERGHE, LEON DE, *Pactes de sang et pactes d'union dans la mort chez quelques peuplades du Kwango*, 1960.

6 SELIGMAN, C. G. and B. Z., *Pagan Tribes of the Nilotic Sudan*, Routledge & Kegan Paul, 1932.

7 EVANS-PRITCHARD, EDWARD E., *Africa*, 1933; *Witchcraft, Oracles and Magic Among the Azande*, Oxford University Press, 1937.
8 ROBERTSON SMITH, WILLIAM, *Lectures on the Religion of the Semites*, A. C. Black, 1894.
9 WESTERMARCK, EDWARD A., *Marriage*, Benn, 1929.
10 MAIR, LUCY P., *An African People in the Twentieth Century*, Routledge & Kegan Paul, 1934.
11 FORTES, MEYER, *The Dynamics of Clanship Among the Tallensi*, Oxford University Press, 1945.
12 PAULME, DENISE, *Africa*, 1939; *French Perspectives in African Studies*, Oxford University Press, 1973.

Chapter 4

1 MINTZ, J. W. and WOLF, E. R., *An Analysis of Ritual Co-godparenthood*, 1950.
2 ANDERSON, GALLATIN, *The Italian Godparenthood Complex*, 1957.
3 HAMMEL, E. A., *Alternative Social Structures and Ritual Relations in the Balkans*, Prentice Hall, 1968.
4 LEACH, EDMUND R., *Rethinking Anthropology*, Athlone Press, 1961.
5 GILLIN, JOHN P., *Moche: A Peruvian Coastal Community*, Washington, 1945.
6 KOSVEN, M. O., *Sovetskaya Etnografiya*, 1963.

Chapter 5

1 PITT-RIVERS, JULIAN A., *Transactions of the New York Academy of Science*, 1954; *The International Encyclopedia of the Social Sciences*, Macmillan, New York, 1968.
2 KUPER, HILDA, *An African Aristocracy: Rank among the Swazi of Bechuanaland*, Oxford University Press, 1947.
3 MAQUET, J., *The Premise of Inequality in Ruanda*, Oxford University Press, 1961.
4 LEACH, EDMUND R., *Aspects of Caste in South India, Ceylon and North-West Pakistan*, Cambridge University Press, 1960.
5 MAYER, ADRIAN C., *Caste and Kinship in Central India: A Village and Its Region*, Routledge & Kegan Paul, 1960.
6 DUMONT, LOUIS, *Homo Hierarchicus: The Caste System and Its Implications*, Paladin, 1972.

Chapter 6

1 *Larousse Encyclopedia of Mythology*, Batchworth, 1959.
2 BEIDELMANN, T. O., *Africa*, 1963.
3 KINGSLEY, MARY, *Travels in West Africa, Congo Français, Corisco and Cameroons*, Macmillan, 1897.
4 MITTLER, PETER J., *The Study of Twins*, Penguin, 1972.
5 *Man, Twins, Birds and Vegetables* Vol. 1, Correspondence, 1966/7.
6 SOUSBERGHE, LEON DE, *Pactes de sang et pactes d'union dans la mort chez quelques peuplades du Kwango*, 1960.

7 GRIAULE, MARCEL, *Dieu d'eau entretiens avec Ogotemmêli*, Paris, 1948.
GRIAULE, MARCEL and DIETERLIN, GERMAINE, *African Worlds*, Oxford University Press, 1954.

8 GRIAULE, MARCEL, *Dieu d'eau entretiens avec Ogotemmêli*, Paris, 1948.
GRIAULE, MARCEL and DIETERLIN, GERMAINE, *African Worlds*, Oxford University Press, 1954.

9 DIETERLIN, GERMAINE, *French Perspectives in African Studies*, Oxford University Press, 1973.

10 PAULME, DENISE, *Africa*, 1939.

11 GRIAULE, MARCEL, *Dieu d'eau entretiens avec Ogotemmêli*, Paris, 1948.

12 GRIAULE, MARCEL, *Dieu d'eau entretiens avec Ogotemmêli*, Paris, 1948.

13 PAULME, DENISE, *Africa*, 1939.

14 MITTLER, PETER J., *The Study of Twins*, Penguin, 1972.

15 *Larousse Encyclopedia of Mythology*, Batchworth, 1959.

Chapter 7

1 CARNEGIE, DALE, *How to Win Friends and Influence People*, Kingston Press, 1953.

2 SPENCER, ROBERT F., *The North Alaskan Eskimo: A Study in Ecology and Society*, Washington, 1959.

3 THOMAS, ELIZABETH MARSHALL, *The Harmless People*, Penguin, 1969.

4 SPENCER, ROBERT F., *The North Alaskan Eskimo: A Study in Ecology and Society*, Washington, 1959.

5 MACCARTHY, F. D., *Oceania*, 1939.

6 MORRIS, TERENCE and MORRIS, PAULINE, *Pentonville: A Sociological Study of an English Prison*, Routledge & Kegan Paul, 1963.

7 MALINOWSKI, BRONISLAW C., *Argonauts of the Western Pacific: An Account of Native Enterprise and Adventure in the Archipelagoes of Melanesian New Guinea*, Routledge & Kegan Paul, 1922.

8 UBEROI, J. P. S., *The Politics of the Kula Ring: An Analysis of the Findings of Bronislaw Malinowski*, Manchester University Press, 1962.

Chapter 8

1 FLEMING, PATRICIA, *Current Anthropology*, 1973.

2 LÉVI-STRAUSS, CLAUDE, *Totemism*, Trans. R. Needham, Beacon Press, Boston, 1963.

3 REAY, MARIE, *The Kuma: Freedom and Conformity in the New Guinea Highlands*, Melbourne University Press, 1959.

4 BRAIN, ROBERT, *Bangwa Kinship and Marriage*, Cambridge University Press, 1972.

5 GOODY, JACK, *The Social Organization of the LoWiili*, Oxford University Press, 1967.

6 GRIAULE, MARCEL, *French Perspectives in African Studies*, Oxford University Press, 1973.

7 DOUGLAS, MARY, *Man* (NS), 1968.

8 PEDLER, F. J., *Africa*, 13, 1940.

9 RIGBY, PETER, *Cattle and Kinship among the Gogo*, Cornell University Press, Ithaca, 1969.

10 LABOURET, HENRI, *Le Cameroun*, Paris, 1937.
11 TURNER, BARRY, *Exploring the Industrial Sub-Culture*, Macmillan, 1972.

Chapter 9

1 LORENZ, KONRAD Z., *On Aggression*, Trans. M. Latzke, Methuen, 1966.
2 ARDREY, ROBERT, *African Genesis: A Personal Investigation Into the Animal Origins and Nature of Man*, Collins, 1961.
3 LAWRENCE, D. H., *Kangaroo*, Secker & Warburg, 1923.
4 TIGER, LIONEL, *Men In Groups*, Nelson, 1969.
5 FARIS, JAMES C., *Cat Harbor: A Newfoundland Fishing Settlement*, St Johns: Inst. Soc. & Econ. Research, 1966.
6 MORRIS, TERENCE, and MORRIS, PAULINE, *Pentonville: A Sociological Study of an English Prison*, Routledge & Kegan Paul, 1963.
7 TUNSTALL, JEREMY, *The Fishermen*, MacGibbon & Kee, 1962.
8 AUBERT, VILHELM and ARNER ODDVAR, *Acta Sociologica*, 1959.
9 LANTZ, HERMANN R., *People of Coaltown*, Southern Illinois Press, 1971.
10 TIGER, LIONEL, *Men In Groups*, Nelson, 1969.
11 LORENZ, KONRAD Z., *On Aggression*, Trans. M. Latzke, Methuen, 1966.
12 WALKER, NIGEL D., *Crime and Punishment in Britain*, Edinburgh University Press, 1968.
13 ARDREY, ROBERT, *African Genesis: A Personal Investigation Into the Animal Origins and Nature of Man*, Collins, 1961.
14 DENNIS, NORMAN, HENRIQUES, FERNANDO, and SLAUGHTER, CLIFFORD, *Coal Is Our Life: An Analysis of a Yorkshire Mining Community*, Eyre & Spottiswoode, 1956.
15 ARDENER, SHIRLEY G., *Man* (Sexual Insult and Female Militancy), 1973.
16 LEVI, CARLO, *Christ Stopped at Eboli*, Trans. F. Frenaye, Cassells, 1948.
17 LÉVI-STRAUSS, CLAUDE, *Totemism*, Trans. R. Needham, Beacon Press, Boston, 1963.
18 DOUGLAS, MARY, *Purity and Danger: An Analysis of Concepts of Pollution and Taboo*, Routledge & Kegan Paul, 1966; *Proceedings of the R. Anthrop. Inst.*, 1972.
19 DRIBERG, J. H., *Man* (The 'Best Friend' Among the Didinga), 1935.

Chapter 10

1 FREUD, SIGMUND, *Civilization and Its Discontents*, L. & V. Woolf, 1930.
2 EIBL-EIBESFELDT, IRANÄUS, *Love and Hate: On the Natural History of Basic Behaviour Patterns*, Trans. G. Strachan, Methuen, 1971.
3 SUTTIE, IAN D., *The Origins of Love and Hate*, Routledge & Kegan Paul, 1935.
4 RUSSELL, BERTRAND, *The Conquest of Happiness*, Allen & Unwin, 1930.
5 GOODALL, JANE, *In the Shadows of Man*, Collins, 1971.
6 UCHENDU, VICTOR C., *The Igbo of Southeast Nigeria*, Holt, Rinehart & Winston, New York, 1965.
7 GARDNER, ROBERT B., *Gardens of War: Life and Death in the New Guinea Stone Age*, Deutsch, 1969.
8 STRATHERN, ANDREW J., *The Rope of Moka*, Cambridge University Press, 1971.

9 SMITH, ADAM, *The Theory of Moral Sentiments: To Which is Added a Dissertation on the Origin of Languages*, London, 1774.

Chapter 11

1 FROMM, ERICH, *The Art of Loving*, Allen & Unwin, 1956.
2 MALINOWSKI, BRONISLAW C., *Sex, Culture and Myth*, Rupert Hart-Davis, 1963.
3 BUXTON, JEAN, *Man* (Girl's Courting Huts in Western Mandari), 1963.
4 GORER, GEOFFREY, *The Americans: A Study in National Character*, Cresset Press, 1948.
5 SUGGS, ROBERT C., *Marquesan Sexual Behaviour*, Constable, 1966.
6 MARSHALL, DONALD S., *Island of Passion: Ra'ivavae*, Allen & Unwin, 1962.
7 MEAD, MARGARET, *Coming of Age in Samoa: A Psychological Study of Primitive Youth*, Penguin, 1943.
8 MALINOWSKI, BRONISLAW C., *The Sexual Life of Savages in North-Western Melanesia*, Routledge & Kegan Paul, 1929.
9 SCHNEIDER, HAROLD, *Human Sexual Behaviour*, Basic Books, New York, 1971.
10 FINNEGAN, RUTH H., *Oral Literature in Africa*, Oxford University Press, 1970.
11 ROUGEMONT, DENIS DE, *Passion and Society*, Trans. M. Belgion, Faber, 1940.
12 STEINER, GEORGE, *In Bluebeard's Castle: Some Notes Toward a Redefinition of Culture*, Yale University Press, 1971.
13 JAHODA, GUSTAV, *Africa* (Love, Marriage and Social Change: Letters to the Advice Columns of a West African Newspaper), 1959.

Chapter 12

1 MITCHELL, JAMES CLYDE, *Social Networks in Urban Situations*, Manchester University Press, 1969.
2 DOUGLAS, MARY, *Natural Symbols: Explorations in Cosmology*, Barrie & Rockliffe, 1970.
3 BARNES, JOHN A., *Local Level Politics*, Aldine, Chicago, 1969.
4 TURNER, VICTOR W., *The Ritual Process: Structure and Anti-structure*, Routledge & Kegan Paul, 1969.
5 FROMM, ERICH, *The Art of Loving*, Allen & Unwin, 1956.

Bibliography

ALEXANDRE, PIERRE (ed.), *French Perspectives in African Studies*, Oxford University Press, 1973.

ANDERSON, GALLATIN, 'Il Comparaggio: the Italian godparenthood complex', *S. West. J. Anthrop.*, 13, 1957, pp. 32–53.

ARDENER, SHIRLEY G., 'Sexual insult and female militancy', *Man* (NS), 8, 1973, pp. 422–40.

ARDREY, ROBERT, *African Genesis: a personal investigation into the animal origins and nature of man*, Collins, 1961; *The Territorial Imperative*, Collins, 1967.

AUBERT, VILHELM, and ODDVAR, ARNER, 'On the social structure of the ship', *Acta Sociologica*, 3, 1959, pp. 200–219.

BACON, FRANCIS, 'Of friendship', *Bacon's Essays*, J. M. McNeill (ed.), Scholars Library, 1959.

BARNES, JOHN A., 'Networks and political processes', *Local Level Politics*, Marc J. Swartz (ed.), Aldine, Chicago, 1969.

BEIDELMANN, T. O., 'The blood covenant and the concept of blood in Ukaguru', *Africa*, 33, 1963, pp. 321–42.

BELL, CLIVE, *Civilization: An Essay*, Chatto & Windus, 1928.

BOHANNAN, PAUL, *Social Anthropology*, London, 1963.

BRAIN, ROBERT, 'Friends and twins in Bangwa', *Man in Africa*, Mary Douglas and Phyllis Kaberry (eds.), Tavistock, 1969; *Bangwa Kinship and Marriage*, Cambridge Univ. Press, 1972.

BUXTON, JEAN, 'Girls' courting huts in western Mandari', *Man*, 63, art. 56, 1963, pp. 49–51.

CAMPBELL, JOHN K., 'The kindred in a Greek mountain community', *Mediterranean countrymen*, J. Pitt-Rivers (ed.), Mouton, Paris and The Hague, 1963; *Honour, Family and Patronage: a study of institutions and moral values in a Greek mountain community*, Oxford Univ. Press, 1964.

CARNEGIE, DALE, *How to Win Friends and Influence People*, Kingston Press, 1953.

COOPER, ALFRED DUFF, *David*, Cape, 1943.

CURLE, RICHARD H. P., *Women: An Analytical Study*, Watts, 1947.

DENNIS, NORMAN, HENRIQUES, FERNANDO and SLAUGHTER, CLIFFORD, *Coal Is Our Life: an analysis of a Yorkshire mining community*, Eyre & Spottiswoode, 1956.

DIETERLIN, GERMAINE, 'A contribution to the study of blacksmiths in West Africa', *French Perspectives in African Studies*, P. Alexandre (ed.), Oxford Univ. Press, 1973.

Friends and Lovers

DOUGLAS, MARY, *Purity and Danger: an analysis of concepts of pollution and taboo*, Routledge & Kegan Paul, 1966; 'The social control of cognition: some factors in joke perception', *Man* (NS), 3, 1968, pp. 361–76; *Natural Symbols: Explorations in Cosmology*, Barrie & Rockliffe, 1970; 'Self evidence' (Henry Myres Lecture), *Proceedings of the R. Anthrop. Inst.*, 1972, pp. 27–43.

DRIBERG, J. H., 'The "best friend" among the Didinga', *Man*, 35, art. 110, 1935, pp. 101–2.

DUMONT, LOUIS, *Homo Heirarchicus, essai sur le système des castes*, Gallimard, Paris, trans. as *Homo Heirarchicus: the caste system and its implications*, Paladin, 1972.

DUNDAS, ALAN, 'The making and breaking of friendship', *The Structural Analysis of Oral Tradition*, Pierre and Elli Köngäs Maranda (eds.), Univ. Pennsylvania Press, Philadelphia, 1971.

EIBL-EIBESFELDT, IRANÄUS, *Love and Hate: on the natural history of basic behaviour patterns*, trans. G. Strachan, Methuen, 1971.

EVANS-PRITCHARD, EDWARD E., 'Zande blood brotherhood', *Africa*, 6, 1933, pp. 369–401, reprinted in Evans-Pritchard, E. E., *Essays in Social Anthropology*, Faber, 1962; *Witchcraft, Oracles and Magic Among the Azande*, Oxford Univ. Press, 1937.

FARIS, JAMES C., *Cat Harbor: a Newfoundland Fishing Settlement*, Inst. Soc. & Econ. Research, St Johns, 1966.

FINNEGAN, RUTH H., *Oral Literature in Africa*, Oxford Univ. Press, 1970.

FIRTH, RAYMOND, W., 'Twins, birds and vegetables: problems of identification in primitive thought', *Man* (NS), 1, 1966, pp. 1–17; 'Bond friendship in Tikopia', *Tikopia Ritual and Belief*, Allen & Unwin, 1967.

FIRTH, RAYMOND W., and DJAMOUR, J., 'Kinship in a South Borough', *Two Studies of Kinship in London*, R. Firth (ed.), Athlone Press (LSE Mongr. soc. anthrop, 15), 1956.

FLEMING, PATRICIA, 'The politics of marriage among non-Catholic European royalty', *Current Anthropology*, 14, 1973, pp. 231–49.

FORDE, DARYLL (with DOUGLAS, M.), 'Primitive economics', *Man, Culture and Society*, H. L. Shapiro (ed.), Oxford Univ. Press, New York, 1960.

FORTES, MEYER, *The Dynamics of Clanship among the Tallensi*, Oxford Univ. Press, 1945.

FOSTER, GEORGE, 'Confradia and compadrazgo in Spain and Spanish America', *S. West. J. Anthrop.*, 9, 1953, pp. 1–28.

FREUD, SIGMUND, *Civilization and Its Discontents*, L. & V. Woolf, 1930.

FROMM, ERICH, *The Art of Loving*, Allen & Unwin, 1956.

GARDNER, ROBERT B., *Gardens of War: life and death in the New Guinea stone age*, Deutsch, 1969.

GILLIN, JOHN P., *Moche: A Peruvian Coastal Community*, Smithsonian Inst. of soc. anthrop., Publ. 3, Washington, 1945.

GOODALL, JANE, *In the Shadows of Man*, Collins, 1971.

GOODY, JACK, *The Social Organisation of the LoWiili*, Oxford Univ. Press, 1967.

GORER, GEOFFREY, *The Americans: a study in national character*, Cresset Press, 1948.

GREER, GERMAINE, *The Female Eunuch*, Paladin, 1970.

GRIAULE, MARCEL, *Dieu d'eau entretiens avec Ogotemmêli*, Paris, 1948, trans. as *Conversations with Ogotemmeli: An Introduction to Dogon Religious Ideas*, Oxford Univ. Press, 1965; 'The mother's brother in the Western Sudan', *French Perspectives in African Studies*, Pierre Alexandre (ed.), Oxford Univ. Press, 1973.

GRIAULE, MARCEL, and DIETERLIN, GERMAINE, 'The Dogon', *African Worlds*, Daryll Forde (ed.), Oxford Univ. Press, 1954.

HAMMEL, E. A., *Alternative Social Structures and Ritual Relations in the Balkans*, Prentice Hall, Englewood Cliffs, 1968.

HEILBRUN, CAROLYN G., *Towards Adrogyny: aspects of male and female in literature*, Gollancz, 1973.

HOGBIN, H. IAN, 'Native land tenure in New Guinea', *Oceania*, 10, 1939, pp. 113-65; *Transformation Scene: the changing culture of a New Guinea village*, Routledge & Kegan Paul, 1951.

HOMANS, G. C., and SCHNEIDER, D. M., *Marriage, Authority and Final Causes*, Free Press, New York, 1955.

JACOBSON, DAVID, 'Friendship and mobility in the development of an urban elite African social system', *S. West. J. Anthrop.*, 24, 1968, pp. 123-38.

JAHODA, GUSTAV, 'Love, marriage and social change: letters to the advice columns of a West African newspaper', *Africa*, 29, 1959, pp. 177-90.

KINGSLEY, MARY, *Travels in West Africa, Congo Français, Corisco and Cameroons*, Macmillan, 1897.

KOSVEN, M. O., 'Kto takoiy krestniyi otets? (Qui'est ce "le parrain"?)', *Sovetskaya Etnografiya*, 3, 1963, pp. 95-107.

KUPER, HILDA, *An African Aristocracy: rank among the Swazi of Bechuanaland*, Oxford Univ. Press, 1947.

LABOURET, HENRI, *Le Cameroun*, Centre d'Etudes de Politique Etrangère, Paris, 1937.

LAMB, CHARLES, 'A bachelor's complaint of the behaviour of married people', *The Complete Works of Charles Lamb in Prose and Verse*, Chatto & Windus, 1892.

LANTZ, HERMANN R., *People of Coaltown*, Southern Illinois Press, 1971.

Larousse Encyclopedia of Mythology, Batchworth, 1959.

LAWRENCE, D. H., *Women in Love*, Secker, 1921; *Kangaroo*, Secker, 1923; *David: A Play*, Secker, 1926.

LEACH, EDMUND R. (ed.), *Aspects of Caste in South India, Ceylon and Northwest Pakistan*, Cambridge Univ. Press (Cambr. Pap. soc. anthrop., 2), 1960; *Rethinking Anthropology*, Athlone Press (LSE Mongr. soc. anthrop., 22), 1961.

LEVI, CARLO, *Christ Stopped at Eboli*, trans. F. Frenaye, Cassells, 1948.

LÉVI-STRAUSS, CLAUDE, *Tristes Tropiques*, Plon, Paris, 1955, trans. J. and D. Weightman, Cape, 1973; *Totemism*, trans. R. Needham, Beacon Press, Boston, 1963.

LEWIS, JOHN, and TOWERS, BERNARD, *Naked Ape or Homo Sapiens?*, Garnstone Press, 1969.

LORENZ, KONRAD Z., *On Aggression*, trans. M. Latzke, Methuen, 1966.

MACBEATH, ALEXANDER, *Experiments in Living: a study of the nature and foundations of ethics and morals in the light of recent work in social anthropology*, Macmillan, 1952.

MACARTHY, F. D., ' "Trade" in aboriginal Australia, and "Trade" relationships with Torres Strait, New Guinea and Malaya', *Oceania*, 9, 1939, pp. 405-38; 10, pp. 80-104, 171-95.

MAIR, LUCY P., *An African People in the Twentieth Century*, Routledge & Kegan Paul, 1934.

MALINOWSKI, BRONISLAW C., *Argonauts of the Western Pacific : an account of native enterprise and adventure in the Archipelagoes of Melanesian New Guinea*, Routledge & Kegan Paul, 1922; *The Sexual Life of Savages in North-western Melanesia*, Routledge & Kegan Paul, 1929; *Sex, Culture and Myth*, Rupert Hart-Davis, 1963.

Man, 1966/7, 'Correspondence: Twins, birds and vegetables', vol. 1, E. E. Evans-Pritchard and R. W. Firth, pp. 398-9; E. R. Leach, pp. 557-8; vol. 2, R. W. Firth and E. R. Leach, pp. 129-30.

MAQUET, J., *The Premise of Inequality in Ruanda*, Oxford Univ. Press, 1961.

MARSHALL, DONALD S., *Island of passion : Ra'ivavae*, Allen & Unwin, 1962.

MAUSS, MARCEL, *The Gift*, trans. I. Cunnison, Cohen & West, 1954.

MAYER, ADRIAN C., *Caste and Kinship in Central India : a village and its region*, Routledge & Kegan Paul, 1960.

MEAD, MARGARET, *Coming of Age in Samoa : a psychological study of primitive youth*, Penguin, 1943.

MINTZ, J. W., and WOLF, E. R., 'An analysis of ritual co-godparenthood (compadrazgo)', *S. West. J. Anthrop.*, 6, 1950, pp. 341-68.

MITCHELL, JAMES CLYDE (ed.), *Social Networks in Urban Situations*, Manchester Univ. Press, 1969.

MITTLER, PETER J., *The Study of Twins*, Penguin, 1972.

MONTAGU, M. F. ASHLEY (ed.), *Man and Aggression*, Oxford Univ. Press, New York, 1968.

MOORE, I. T., *Social Patterns in Australian Literature*, Angus & Robertson, Sydney, 1971.

MORRIS, TERENCE and PAULINE, *Pentonville : a sociological study of an English prison*, Routledge & Kegan Paul, 1963.

NADEL, SIEGFRIED F., *The Nuba: an anthropological study of the hill tribes of Kordofan*, Oxford Univ. Press, 1947.

NICOLSON, NIGEL, *Portrait of a Marriage*, Weidenfeld & Nicolson, 1973.

NUMELIN, RAGNAR, J., *The Beginnings of Diplomacy : a study of intertribal and international relations*, Oxford Univ. Press, 1950.

OPIE, IONA and PETER, *The Lore and Language of School Children*, Oxford Univ. Press, 1959.

PAULME, DENISE, 'Parenté à Plaisanteries et Alliance par le Sang en Afrique Occidentale', *Africa*, 12, 1939, pp. 433-44; 'Blood pacts, age classes and castes in Black Africa', *French Perspectives in African Studies*, P. Alexandre (ed.), Oxford Univ. Press, 1973.

PEDLER, F. J., 'Joking relationship in East Africa', *Africa*, 13, 1940, pp. 170-73.

PIKE, STEPHAN, 'Friendship to death in rural Thai society', *Human Organization*, 27, 1968.

PITT-RIVERS, JULIAN A., *The People of the Sierra*, Weidenfeld & Nicolson, 1954; 'Ritual kinship in Spain'; *Transactions of the New York Academy*

Bibliography

of Science, 2nd ser., 20, No. 5, 1954, pp. 424–31; 'Kinship: pseudo-kinship', *The International Encyclopedia of the Social Sciences*, vol. 8, Macmillan, New York, 1968.

REAY, MARIE, *The Kuma : freedom and conformity in the New Guinea Highlands*, Melbourne Univ. Press, 1959.

REINA, RUBEN, *The Law of the Saints: a Pokoman pueblo and its community culture*, Bobbs Merril, Indianopolis, 1966.

RIGBY, PETER, *Cattle and Kinship among the Gogo*, Cornell Univ. Press, Ithaca, 1969.

ROBERTSON SMITH, WILLIAM, *Lectures on the Religion of the Semites*, A. & C. Black, 1894.

ROUGEMONT, DENIS DE, *Passion and Society*, trans. M. Belgion, Faber, 1940.

RUSSELL, BERTRAND, *The Conquest of Happiness*, Allen & Unwin, 1930.

SANTAYANA, GEORGE, *Little Essays*, L. P. Smith (ed.), London, 1920.

SAYERS, DOROTHY L. (trans.), *The Song of Roland*, Penguin, 1939.

SCHNEIDER, DAVID M., *American Kinship: a cultural account*, Prentice Hall, Englewood Cliffs, 1968.

SCHNEIDER, HAROLD, 'Romantic love among the Turu of Tanzania', *Human Sexual Behaviour*, D. S. Marshall and R. C. Suggs (eds.), Basic Books, New York, 1971.

SELIGMAN, C. G., and B. Z., *Pagan Tribes of the Nilotic Sudan*, Routledge & Kegan Paul, 1932.

SIGNORINI, ITALO, 'Angonwole agyale: il matrimonio tra individui dello stesso sesso . . .', *Rassegna Italiana di Sociologica Anno dodicesimo*, 3, 1971.

SIMMEL, GEORG, *Conflict*, trans. K. H. Wolff, Free Press, New York, 1964.

SMITH, ADAM, *The Theory of Moral Sentiments . . . to Which is Added a Dissertation on the Origin of Languages*, London, 1774.

SOUSBERGHE, LEON DE, *Pactes de sang et pactes d'union dans la mort chez quelques peuplades du Kwango*, Academie Royale des Sciences d'Outre-Mer C – Classe de Sciences Morales et Politiques, *Mémoires*, (NS) 22, No. 2, 1960.

SPENCER, ROBERT F., *The North Alaskan Eskimo : a study in ecology and society*, Smithsonian Inst. Bureau of Am. ethnol., No. 171, Washington, 1959.

STEFANISZYN, B., 'Funeral friendship in central Africa', *Africa*, 20, 1950, pp. 290–306.

STEINER, GEORGE, *In Bluebeard's Castle : Some Notes Toward a Redefinition of Culture*, Yale Univ. Press, 1971.

STRATHERN, ANDREW J., *The Rope of Moka*, Cambridge Univ. Press, 1971.

SUGGS, ROBERT C., *Marquesan Sexual Behaviour*, Constable, 1966.

SUTTIE, IAN D., *The Origins of Love and Hate*, Routledge & Kegan Paul, 1935.

TEGNAEUS, HARRY, *Blood-brothers : an ethno-sociological study of the institutions of blood brotherhood with special reference to Africa*, Stockholm, Ethnogr. Mus. (NS), 10, 1952.

THOMAS, ELIZABETH MARSHALL, *The Harmless People*, Penguin, 1969.

TIGER, LIONEL, *Men In Groups*, Nelson, 1969.

TUNSTALL, JEREMY, *The Fishermen*, McGibbon & Kee, 1962.

TURNER, BARRY, *Exploring the Industrial Sub-culture*, Macmillan, 1972.

TURNER, VICTOR W., *The Ritual Process : structure and anti-structure*, Routledge & Kegan Paul, 1969.

UBEROI, J. P. S., *The Politics of the Kula Ring: an analysis of the findings of Bronislaw Malinowski*, Manchester Univ. Press, 1962.

UCHENDU, VICTOR C., *The Igbo of Southeast Nigeria*, Holt, Rinehart & Winston, New York, 1965.

WALKER, NIGEL D., *Crime and Punishment in Britain*, Edinburgh Univ. Press, 1968.

WESTERMARCK, EDWARD A., *Marriage*, Benn, 1929.

WOLLSTONECRAFT, MARY, *A Vindication of the Rights of Woman: with strictures on political and moral subjects*, London, 1792.

ZINTGRAFF, EUGEN, *Nord-Kamerun*, Verlag von Gebrüder Paetel, Berlin, 1895.

Index

Index

feudalism, 92
'companionship', 30, 34-5, 91
Firth, R., 16, 133
fish, coral, 21, 211
fishermen, 122, 194, 195-6, 197
Fobessong, Chief, 79-80
France
    compadrazgo in, 92
    philosophy in, 135
Freud, Sigmund, 12, 181, 207-9, 211, 222-4, 225
friendship
    diffused, 258
    formalization of, 9, 18-19, 20, 75-6, 105-7, 118, 206
    ideology of, 254
Fromm, Erich, 12, 223
Fulani, the, 220
    blood pacts, 88
    exchange by, 150
funerals, 18, 81-2, 103, 180-81, 182
    Alcalá, 44, 181
    Azande, 85
    Bangwa, 33-4, 38, 49, 181
    Chinautleco, 101-2, 181
    Dogon, 180
    dropsy, 81
    godparents at, 94, 101-2, 181
    joking at, 180, 181, 182, 184, 185
    New Guinea, 81-2

Galega, Fon of Bali, 80
Ganda, blood friends among, 85, 86
ganders, friendship among, 72-4, 193
gangs, 96, 189-93
George V, King, marriage of, 166
German
    brotherhoods, 75, 194
    colonization, 78-9, 106, 218
Germanic people, rulers of, 92, 124
Germany, 204, 212
    fascist, 204
    in 1940s, 212
Gesta Romanorum, 76
Ghana, 169
    joking relations in, 178
    male marriage in, 10, 11
gifts, 9, 20-21, 145, 147, 166-7, 265
    between enemies, moka, 217
    kula, 38, 158-64, 232
    in love affairs, 232
    of women, 156, 164, 167-9, 172, 175, 176, 184, 265
godparents, see compadrazgo

Gogo, of Tanzania, 183-4, 219
Goldsmith, Oliver, 17
Goodall, Jane, 212
Gorer, Geoffrey, 229
Greece
    ancient, 65-8, 69, 213
        women of, 66-8, 237
    mythology of, 125-6, 141-2
    see also Saraktsani shepherds
Greek Orthodox church, 94
Greer, Germaine, 48, 199-200, 201, 202
Griaule, Marcel, 134, 135, 138, 179
group membership, 187-206
    and aggression, 188-93
    animal, 187-8, 192, 193, 209
    vs. danger, 194-7
    national, 203-5
    sexually exclusive, 189, 192-3, 194, 197-8, 199-200
    women and, 198, 201-2
groups, organized, 260-62
    alliance by marriage, 97, 167-9, 175
    amity between, 213-21
Guatemala, see Chinautleco

Hagen, the, of New Guinea, 217
haircut, a child's first, 95, 103-4
Hawaii, 215-16
Heaven, concepts of, 124, 230
Hebrews, the ancient, 15, 65, 148, 149, 204-5
Hermaphrodite, 141
Herodotus, 76, 149
Hindu
    castes, 118-19
    marriage, 18
    mythology, 142
Homer, 30, 34, 65
homoeroticism, 42, 193, 200
homosexuality, 14, 24, 62, 63, 64-5, 67, 143, 262
    in Australia, 68, 71, 72
    in Brazil, 20
    church for, 60-61
    female, 14, 58-60, 226-7
    and friendship, 40-42
    in ancient Greece, 65-7
    and marriage, 60-62, 264
    platonic, 143
hospitality, 125-6, 213-14, 215, 218
Howthon, John, marriage of, 92
hunters, 193, 197, 214-15
    in myth, 88